RAPID REVIEW
OF ENGLISH GRAMMAR

RAPID REVIEW
OF ENGLISH GRAMMAR SECOND EDITION
A TEXT FOR STUDENTS OF ENGLISH AS A SECOND LANGUAGE

JEAN PRANINSKAS

PRENTICE-HALL, INC., ENGLEWOOD CLIFFS, NEW JERSEY

Library of Congress Cataloging in Publication Data

PRANINSKAS, JEAN.
    Rapid review of English grammar.

    1. English language—Text-books for foreigners.
I. Title.
PE1128.P67 1975   428′.2′4   74–23239
ISBN 0–13–753145–1

Printed in the United States of America

10

Prentice-Hall International, Inc., London
Prentice-Hall of Australia, Pty. Ltd., Sydney
Prentice-Hall of Canada, Ltd., Toronto
Prentice-Hall of India Private Limited, New Delhi
Prentice-Hall of Japan, Inc., Tokyo

CONTENTS

This is not in any sense a new book. It is, I truly believe, a very much improved edition of *Rapid Review of English Grammar*. The original was written in 1957, specifically to meet the needs of students who were having difficulty reconciling their traditional language training in their home countries with the structural approach to language teaching as it was then being practiced in the United States. The many enthusiastic letters I have received from teachers and students testify that this aim was successfully accomplished.

The preface to the first edition stated unequivocally where and with whom the book could be used and how it must be taught and studied. In the intervening years I have observed it being taught in a dozen different countries under widely differing circumstances and for different purposes. I have come to understand that a textbook is not the controlling factor in a classroom, nor should it aim to be. It must be sufficiently substantive and flexible to allow for selection and interpretation. My original intention to the contrary, *Rapid Review* seems to have this quality. Perhaps all that need be mentioned here, then, is the scope and arrangement of material and the new features of this edition.

Each of the twenty lessons consists of four parts: model paragraphs, explanations of grammatical patterns, exercises, and assignments. The model paragraphs serve two purposes. They illustrate the natural use of the patterns in simple, colloquial prose, and they provide an easily understood context for the practice exercises. The grammatical explanations are brief, ad hoc descriptions of surface structure phenomena. They make no pretense of being the God's Truth Algorithm which produces all of the grammatical and none of the ungrammatical sentences of English. They are provided for those persons—of whom there seem to be many—whose previous education has conditioned them to approach language learning as an intellectual pursuit rather than as the development of a skill. Any teacher who disagrees with a particular explanation should feel free to substitute his or her own. There is nothing sacred about the grammatical descriptions.

The exercises have been carefully devised to give focused oral practice in the use of items and arrangements presented in each lesson, and in contrasting these with the patterns that have been presented before. They are all contextualized in accordance with the model paragraphs or with a real life situation within the milieu of the students, so that at no time is a student required or expected to produce a sentence without some truth value. Of course, much more engaging exercises can be devised for any particular class based on the lives and fortunes of the participants. Those teachers who have several hours to prepare for each class will want to try their hands at producing some. To them, let me offer a caveat: Knowing what to put into an item is only a small part of the project; it's knowing what to leave out that is of greatest importance in maintaining the focus of a lesson.

The assignments are designed to give practice in the conventions of writing clearly stated sentences. The word *paragraph* is used very loosely to refer to any string of sentences about the same topic. The formal development of a paragraph is nowhere dealt with explicitly, as I consider that beyond the scope of this work. It has been demonstrated, however, that students who work through the assignments in *Rapid Review* are well prepared to benefit from a course in composition.

Those who have used the book before will find a number of minor changes many of which were suggested by helpful colleagues. Most obvious, perhaps, is that the order of lessons has been revised; e.g., the perfect tenses now come much earlier in the course than they did before, and causatives are no longer juxtaposed with cause/result clauses. Of more consequence, in my opinion, is the rearrangement of the material within each lesson. Whereas previously the sentence pattern frames were displayed after the presentation of the items that constitute them, they now appear at the beginning of each lesson, thus placing the emphasis on the whole sentence rather than on its parts. Many of the exercises have been reconstructed to provide a greater ratio of student to teacher speaking time. Unworkable items have been replaced by workable ones, directions for administering the exercises have been spelled out in greater detail, and sample responses are included. Finally, the review drills, formerly in an appendix, are now distributed throughout the book, between the lessons.

People I wish especially to thank for help with this revision are Marion Lanson, June McKay, Mary Hussey, Ralph Walker, Amal Nasr, and Abdul Karim.

RAPID REVIEW
OF ENGLISH GRAMMAR

VERB *BE*: FORMS, PATTERNS, USES
ARTICLES, DEMONSTRATIVES,
PRONOUNS, CONTRACTIONS

This is a book. It's a big green book. It's about English grammar. The first lesson is short and easy, but the other lessons are long and hard. The model paragraphs are not always interesting, but they are very helpful.

The paragraphs are about Professor and Mrs. Allen and their friends. The practice exercises are about those people too. Here they are.

This is Professor Allen.
He's bald.

This is Betty.
She's the Allens' niece.

This is Mrs. Allen.
She's very attractive.

This is Bill Brown.
He is serious.

This is Professor Baker.
He is forgetful.

This is Jack Jones.
He's carefree.

This is Mrs. Baker.
She's a good cook.

This is Jane.
She is frivolous.
Her hair is red.

This is George.
He's Greek.

This is Mr. Miller.
He's the new economics
professor.

Sue Liu isn't here now.
She's away.

The explanations are simple. The instructions are clear. The work is abundant. Results are guaranteed. Are you ready?

Sentence patterns. The basic unit of any language is the sentence. To speak and write correctly we must know how to put words together in the proper order to make statements and questions. In each lesson we will look at some patterns of English sentences. If you follow the patterns carefully, your sentences will be correct.

2 **Statements with verb** *be*

SUBJECT	VERB	COMPLEMENT				
Noun/Pronoun or Demonstrative	Be (not)	Article	Adjective	Noun	Place	Time
This	is	a	big	book.		
It	is		green.			
Mr. Allen	is	an	English	professor.		
He	isn't				here	now.
He	is				away.	
His students	aren't		American.			
They	are		foreign	students.		

3 **Yes/no questions with verb** *be*

a.

VERB	SUBJECT	COMPLEMENT					RESPONSE
Be (not)	Noun/pronoun or demonstrative	Art	Adj	Noun	Place	Time	
Is	Mr. Allen				here	now?	No, he isn't.
Isn't	he				away?		Yes, he is.
Are	his students		young?				Not very young.
Aren't	they			freshmen?			No, they're not.
Is	George	a	foreign	student?			Yes, he is.
Isn't	that			George	there?		Yes, it is.

b. Responses

1. Note particularly the response to the fourth question. Both parts are negative. That is the only way the statement can be made in English.
2. Note the response to the last question. The speaker is referring to George but he uses the pronoun *it*. When the subject of the question is *this* or *that*, the answer is *it* even when a person is indicated (see Lesson VIII, § 6a).

4 Information questions with verb *be*

a.

QW	VERB	SUBJECT			COMPLEMENT	
	Be	Art	Adj	Noun	Place	Time
What	is	a	foreign	student?		
Who	is			George?		
Where	is			he		now?
When	was			he	here?	
Who	is				here	now?

b. Singular question–plural answer. Note particularly the last question in the box above. The verb form is singular, but the answer may be plural: *Who is here? Jack and Bill.* The verb in the question is always singular unless the subject contains a plural word, as in *Who are those girls?*

5 Forms of *be*

a. Present

PERSON	SINGULAR	PLURAL
1	am	
2	← are →	
3	is	

b. Past

PERSON	SINGULAR	PLURAL
1	was	
2	← were →	
3	was	

Pronouns used with *be*

a. Forms

PERSON	SINGULAR	PLURAL
1	I	we
2	← you →	
3	he she it	they

b. Use

Repeat the pronoun each time when making several statements about the same person or thing.

c. Non-use

Never use a third person pronoun without first mentioning the person or thing to which it refers.

George is away. He isn't here.

7 **Contractions of *be*.** In speech and in all writing except the most formal we usually shorten the present forms of *be* and combine them with other words. We call the resulting forms *contractions*.

a. With pronouns

PERSON	SINGULAR	PLURAL
1	I'm	we're
2	←——— you're ———→	
3	he's she's it's	they're

b. With other words

1.	DEMONSTRATIVES:	that's
2.	QUESTION WORDS:	who's, what's, where's
3.	PLACE WORDS:	here's, there's

c. These contractions are never used as the last word of a sentence.

8 **Negation and contractions of *not*.** Both present and past forms of *be* are joined with *not*, excepting *am*. The *not* is shortened.[1] These are the usual forms.

isn't	wasn't	aren't	weren't

[1] See Pronunciation helps (§ 16).

5

9 **Demonstratives**

SINGULAR	PLURAL
----this that	these those

a. *This* and *these* refer to people or things close to the speaker.

b. *That* and *those* refer to people or things which are some distance from the speaker.

c. Demonstratives may be used alone in noun position [2] or before nouns in adjective positions.[3] They are used to point out, to indicate, to show.

10 **Place words** [4]

a. *Here* is where the speaker is.

b. *There* is any other place which can be pointed to, or another place previously mentioned.

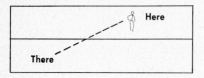

11 **Question words** [5]

a. *Who* asks about a person or persons.

b. *What* asks about a thing or things.

c. *Where* asks about a place or places.

d. *When* asks about a time.

---

[2] Sometimes called demonstrative pronouns
[3] Sometimes called demonstrative adjectives
[4] Adverbs of place
[5] Also called interrogatives

12 **Uses of verb be.** In English, *be* is used to express some situations which are expressed by different verbs—or by no verb at all—in other languages. Use *be* to tell about the following situations.

a. Profession, trade, occupation

Mr. Allen is a professor.
Betty is a student.

b. Nationality

Bill is American.
George is Greek.

c. Age

George is twenty.
This book is old.

d. Characteristics

Bill is serious.
Jack is carefree.

e. Condition

Mrs. Allen is ill.
This page is torn.

f. Size and shape

Mr. Allen is tall.
This book is big.

g. Color

This book is green.
The print is black.

h. Place

Professor Allen is here.
Sue Liu is away.

Articles

a. *A/an* [6] are two forms of the same word. It means *one*. Most singular nouns are preceded by *a* or *an*. *One* is used before a noun only to suggest a contrast with two or more: *I have three cigarettes but only one match.* The choice of *a* or *an* depends on a phonetic rule.

RULE	EXAMPLES	
Use *a* before a word which begins with a consonant sound.[7]	a professor	a house
	a student	a university
Use *an* before a word which begins with a vowel sound.[7]	an author	an honor
	an instructor	an undergraduate

b. *The* is a problem word for many students of English. We won't try to learn all about it at once. In this lesson we will practice only one way it is used. Use *the* when there is only one of something.

the sun	the president of this university
the moon	the captain of our football team
the universe	the teacher of this class

[6] The indefinite article
[7] For definitions of *consonant* and *vowel* see Pronunciation helps (§ 16).

Names and titles

TITLE	GIVEN NAME	FAMILY NAME	USAGE
Mr.	William	Allen	a. No title is used before a given name when the family name is not mentioned.
Mr.	——	Allen	
——	William	——	b. Sometimes a man is called simply by his family name.
——	——	Allen	
Mrs.	William	Allen	c. In social situations a woman uses her husband's given name.[8]
Mrs.	Ruth	Allen	
Mrs.	——	Allen	d. On legal documents she uses her given name.
——	Ruth	——	
Miss	Betty	Allen	e. *Miss* is the title for a woman who has never been married.
Miss	——	Allen	
——	Betty	——	
Ms.[9]	Sue	Smith	f. *Ms.* is a new title used by modern women who do not wish to be identified as married or unmarried.

15 **Adjective forms for nationalities**

N-ENDING	SIBILANT [10] ENDING	MISCELLANEOUS
American	Danish	Czech
Belgian	English	
Colombian	Turkish	
German		
Hungarian	Dutch	Greek
Iranian	French	
Korean		
Lithuanian	Japanese	Iraqi
Norwegian		
Russian	Swiss	Eskimo

[8] This practice may be changing as a result of the Women's Liberation Movement.
[9] See Pronunciation helps.
[10] See Pronunciation helps.

Pronunciation helps

a. Vowel sounds. You have probably learned that the vowels are *a, e, i, o, u,* and sometimes *y.* These are the letters which usually represent vowel sounds, but there are many more than six vowel sounds in English. Vowel sounds are the sounds produced when the vocal cords vibrate and the air escapes from the mouth without being stopped (as for *p* or *k*) or squeezed (as for *f* or *s*). Here are examples of vowel sounds:

> The sound represented by *a* in *am*
> The sound represented by *e* in *be*
> The sound represented by *i* in *it*

b. Consonant sounds. All the sounds which are not called vowel sounds are called consonant sounds. Here are examples of consonant sounds:

> The sound represented by *l* in *lesson*
> The sound represented by *m* in *man*
> The sound represented by *s* in *see*

c. Sibilant sounds. Sibilant sounds are consonant sounds which are characterized by a noise which is called hissing. There are six sibilant sounds in English. They are:

> The first sound in *sing*
> The first sound in *zoo*
> The first sound in *shirt*
> The middle consonant sound in *measure*
> The first and last sounds in *church*
> The first and last sounds in *judge*

d. A/an. The usual pronunciation of *a* when it precedes a noun is a central vowel sound which phoneticians write [ə]. Listen to your instructor's pronunciation and imitate it. *An* is pronounced with the same vowel sound.

e. The. Many speakers of English pronounce *the* in two different ways, depending upon what follows it. *The* rhymes with *a* [ə] when it is followed by a word beginning with a consonant sound. *The* rhymes with *be* when it is followed by a word beginning with a vowel sound.

f. *Ms.* is pronounced like *miz*. It rhymes with *his*.

g. Names followed by *is*. Although we write contractions *he's* and *she's*, we don't usually write contractions with names. However, we often omit the vowel sound of *is* when it follows a name.

> *Mr. Allen is . . .*   sounds like *Mr. Allenz.*
> *Jack is . . .*   sounds like *Jacks.*

h. Names and question words followed by *are*. *Are* is usually pronounced like *her* without the *h* when it follows names and question words. It is not usually stressed.

> Mr. and Mrs. Allen are here.   Mr. and Mrs. Allen-er here.
> Who are they?   Who-er they?
> What are they here for?   What-er they here for?
> Where are they from?   Where-er they from?

i. *Isn't*. Although we remove a vowel when we make a contraction from *is not*, we add a vowel sound when we pronounce it, but in a different place.

> *isn't* sounds like *izint*

j. This and *these*. These two words differ from each other in two ways. Their vowel sounds are different and their final sibilant sounds are different. Be sure to make both of these differences in your pronunciation. Your instructor will help you hear them.

k. They're/there. *They're* and *there* are pronounced in the same way. When they occur together in a sentence, however, they don't sound exactly alike because one is stressed and the other isn't, and stress changes the pronunciation of words somewhat. Your instructor will help you hear the difference.

17 **Punctuation.** Notice the boldface capital letters and marks of punctuation in the following sentences.

> **Mr**⊙ **William A**llen is a professor⊙
> **Is Mrs**⊙ **A**llen a professor⑦
> **No**⸴ she isn⊘t⊙
> **Is Miss B**rown an instructor⑦
> **No**⸴ she⊘s a student⊙
> **T**his is an **E**nglish class⊙
> **T**he teacher is **P**rofessor **A**llen⊙

a. Capitals

The first word of every sentence begins with a capital letter.
All titles begin with capital letters.
All names begin with capital letters.
Adjective forms derived from the names of nations begin with capital letters.

b. Apostrophes

Every contraction contains an apostrophe (') in the place where one or more letters have been left out.

c. Periods

Every statement is followed by a period (.).
Most abbreviations are followed by periods (Mr., Mrs., Dr.).[11]

d. Commas

A comma (,) follows *yes* or *no* in a short or long response.

e. Question marks

Every question is followed (not preceded) by a question mark (?).

f. Indentation

A paragraph is a sequence of sentences about one topic. One way to indicate a paragraph is to indent the first sentence. To indent means to start writing a few spaces to the right of the left-hand margin. There are three paragraphs on page one of this lesson. This is also a paragraph. It is a sequence of six sentences about the topic of paragraphing, and the first sentence is indented.

[11] An abbreviation is a short way of writing something. Abbreviations are standard forms; you cannot invent them. These periods are not used in Britain.

Questions students sometimes ask

a. Is it really correct to use contractions? Are they good English?

Yes, they are very good English and they are much more generally used than the long forms.

b. Is it better to say *he's not* or *he isn't?*

It doesn't make any difference which you use because they both mean exactly the same thing. Some people use *he's not* when they want to emphasize the *not* and *he isn't* at all other times.

c. Why is *professor* sometimes written with a capital initial and sometimes with a small one?

When the word *professor* stands before a name it is a title, as in *Professor Allen.* In all other positions it is an ordinary common noun and is not capitalized.

19 **Exercises** are designed to give you practice in speaking quickly and correctly. Questions are based on the information in the model paragraphs and in the explanations, to provide meaning and continuity to your statements. Students who become familiar with the characters and think about their responses will derive the most benefit. Exercises should be done with books closed.

a. Tell some things about yourself. Tell your nationality, your age, your occupation, and some of your personality traits. Try to use different adjectives (cheerful, generous, kind, nervous, . . .). Follow the patterns in Lesson I (§§ 2, 12, 15).

> I am American. I am thirty-two. I am a teacher.
> I am quiet and studious.[12]

b. The instructor will tell you about some of the characters in the book. Ask your neighbor a yes/no question about the same information (§ 3).

> Instructor: Mr. Allen is tall.
> Student 1: Is Mr. Allen short?
> Student 2: No, he isn't.
> Student 3: Is he tall?
> Student 4: Yes, he is.

1. Mrs. Allen is a librarian.
2. She is slim and attractive.
3. She is pleasant and sociable.
4. Mr. Baker is a chemistry professor.
5. He is rather elderly.
6. He is very kind.
7. Mrs. Baker is a housewife.
8. She is rather heavy.
9. She is a good cook.
10. Jack is carefree.
11. Bill is studious.
12. Jane is frivolous.
13. Betty is serious.
14. George is very bright.
15. Sue Liu is charming.

c. Make negative statements to oppose the following affirmative ones about the past (§§ 5b, 8).

> Instructor: Sue was sad.
> Student: She wasn't happy.

1. Bill's room was large.
2. It was light.
3. It was comfortable.
4. George was poor.
5. His clothes were old.
6. His suitcase was light.

[12] Instructor: Describe yourself.

7. Sue was rich.
8. Her clothes were beautiful.
9. Her suitcase was heavy.

10. Mrs. Allen was sick.
11. She was weak.
12. She was unhappy.

13. The lesson was short.
14. The items were easy.
15. They were useful.

d. Make information questions from the following statements and answer them. Substitute a question word for the word the instructor is saying when he raises his hand [13] (§§ 4, 11).

Instructor: *Mr. Baker* is a chemist.
Student 1: Who is a chemist?
Student 2: Mr. Baker.
Instructor: Mr. Allen is *away.*
Student 1: Where is Mr. Allen?
Student 2: He's away.

1. *Sue Liu* is Chinese.
2. *Her room* is large.
3. It is *near the library.*
4. *Bill Brown* is a good student.
5. He's *in the library* now.

6. This is a *practice exercise.*
7. *These* are questions.
8. Those are *answers.*
9. The questions are *here.*
10. *The answers* are there.

11. *Mr. and Mrs. Allen* are here.
12. *Their friends* are outside.
13. The lunch is *in the car.*
14. The picnic is *at noon.*
15. *We* are very happy.

e. The instructor will mention something in this room. Repeat the word your instructor says, preceding it with *a/an* or *the,* whichever is appropriate (§ 13).

1. teacher
2. student
3. book
4. desk
5. chair
6. window
7. door
8. ceiling
9. floor
10. radiator
11. blackboard
12. eraser
13. pen
14. pencil
15. briefcase

[13] Instructor: Raise your hand while saying the italicized words.

f. Tell how you would address a letter to each of the following (§ 14).

1. A man named Sam Smith
2. His wife, whose name is June
3. His daughter Sue, who is not married
4. His daughter Ella, who is married to Dr. Robert Rice
5. Her husband
6. Mr. William Allen, who is your professor
7. Your friend's professor, Bruce Baker
8. Bill Brown's mother, Bertha, who is a widow
9. The lady next door, Carey Clark, who is divorced
10. Lilly Lewis, whose marital status you don't know

20 **Assignments** are for writing. They may be done in class, if there is time, or as homework. The purpose of the assignments is to practice the patterns of the lesson, not to show your teacher what else you know. Some of them are very simple. Try to do them perfectly.

a. Write a paragraph about a friend of yours. Try to use only the statement patterns in Lesson I. Be sure to indent your paragraph and to punctuate it carefully.

b. Draw a very simple sketch of some object which you see every day, such as a textbook, a slide rule, or a pen. Write a paragraph about it. Practice the sentence patterns in Lesson I.

c. Write five yes/no questions to ask your classmates using the different forms of the verb *be*.

d. Write five information questions to ask your classmates. Use the question words *who*, *what*, *where*, and *when* and the forms of the verb *be*.

REVIEW I

a. Answer the following questions in accordance with the text. Use contractions wherever they are appropriate.

1. Who is George?
2. Where is Sue Liu?
3. Is Jane studious?
4. Who is Professor Miller?
5. Is Mrs. Allen ill?

6. What is this? *
7. What color is it?
8. Is it very small?
9. Are the lessons hard?
10. Are the sentences long?

11. Who is Mr. Allen's niece?
12. Whose hair is red?
13. Who is forgetful?
14. Who is the new economics professor?
15. Who is a foreign student?

b. Phrase a question about each of the following.

1. the textbook
2. the model paragraphs
3. the exercises
4. the assignments
5. the explanations

6. Professor Allen
7. Mrs. Allen
8. Professor Baker
9. Mrs. Baker
10. Professor Miller

11. Jack Jones
12. Bill Brown
13. Betty Allen
14. Jane Johnson
15. George and Sue

c. Write the following paragraph on the blackboard from dictation. Be sure to indent.

    This is an English class. It's about English grammar. The professor is an American man. He's a good teacher. The students aren't American. They're foreign. They are interesting and serious students.

* Hold up a textbook.

SIMPLE PRESENT: S-FORMS, AUXILIARY *DO*
COMPOUND SENTENCES: *AND, BUT, ;*

Jack lives in a dormitory. He gets up at seven o'clock in the morning. He eats breakfast at seven thirty. He goes to class at eight o'clock. He studies in the library in the afternoon. He does homework assignments and watches TV in the evening. He goes downtown on Saturdays, and he goes to the movies on Saturday nights. He goes to church on Sundays.

Bill doesn't live in a dormitory; he has a room in a private home. He doesn't have classes in the morning on Tuesdays and Thursdays. On those days he sleeps until nine o'clock. He doesn't like movies but he likes concerts. He listens to music on the radio at night.

Jack doesn't know Bill but he sees him every day. They are in the same chemistry class. Betty Allen is in that class too. She knows them both and they know her. They work in the same laboratory. It is a large sunny laboratory and they like it very much.

1 **Simple present tense** is not a very descriptive name. It is not at all simple since it requires the use of *s*-FORMS (§ 8 below) as well as SIMPLE FORMS—the ones you find in a dictionary. It doesn't express present activity, either. For that we need another tense, the continuous present. Sentences with present tense verbs in them express repeated, customary, and habitual actions like those you read about in the model paragraphs. They also express general truths such as *water runs downhill.*

2 **Affirmative statement pattern**

SUBJECT	VERB	COMPLEMENT		
Noun/Pronoun	Simple/S-Form	Object	Place	Time
Jack	lives		in a dormitory.	
He	gets up			at seven o'clock.
He	eats	breakfast	in the dormitory	at seven thirty.
The Allens	have	breakfast	at home	at eight.

3 **Auxiliary *do*.** To make negative statements or questions we need the auxiliary *do*. The forms of *do* combine with *not* into contractions (cf. I, 8). These are the usual forms:

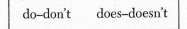

do–don't   does–doesn't

4 **Negative statement pattern**

SUBJECT	VERB		COMPLEMENT		
	Aux *Do* Simple / S-Form	Main Simple	Object	Place	Time
Bill	doesn't	live		in a dormitory.	
He	doesn't	have	classes		on Tuesdays.
Jack and Bill	don't	work		in the lab	on Saturdays.

5 **Yes/no question pattern**

AUX DO (NOT)	SUBJECT	VERB	COMPLEMENT			RESPONSE
Simple/S		Simple	Object	Place	Time	
Does	Jack	eat	breakfast	in the dorm	at seven thirty?	Yes, he does.
Doesn't	he	see	his friends		then?	Yes, he does.
Do	the Allens	get up			early?	No, they don't.
Don't	they	have	breakfast		at eight?	Yes, they do.

6 **Information question patterns**

a. Subject unknown

1. *Affirmative*

QW	VERB	COMPLEMENT			RESPONSE
	S-Form	Object	Place	Time	
Who	takes [1]	chemistry?			Jack and Betty and Bill.
Who	works		in the lab	on Saturdays?	Nobody.
What	amuses	Jack?			TV.
What	relaxes	Bill?			Good music.

2. *Negative*

QW	AUX DO + NOT	VERB SIMPLE	COMPLEMENT OBJECT	RESPONSE
Who	doesn't	take	chemistry?	George.
Who	doesn't	do	homework?	Jane.
What	doesn't	disturb	the Allens?	Parties.

b. Part of complement unknown

QW	AUX DO (NOT) SIMPLE/S	SUBJECT	VERB SIMPLE	COMPLEMENT (PARTS KNOWN)
Who [2]	does	Betty	see	in the lab?
What	doesn't	Bill	like?	
Where	do	the Allens	live?	
When	don't	they	entertain	guests?

c. Verb unknown

QW	AUX DO (NOT) SIMPLE/S	SUBJECT	PRO-VERB DO	COMPLEMENT
What	does	Jack	do	on Saturdays?
What	doesn't	Bill	do	on Tuesdays?
What	do	the Allens	do	for recreation?

[1] Note that the verb form is singular even though the response is plural.
[2] *Whom* is also correct in this position. Most people use *who*.

7 **Pro-verb *do*.** When the activity is unknown, we use the substitute verb *do,* as in the sentences in § 6c.

8 **S-Forms** are simply forms of verbs which end in *s.*

a. Spelling

RULES	EXAMPLES	
a. Most s-forms are made by adding s to the simple form of the verb.	get live buy	gets lives buys
b. When the simple form ends in o, or in a letter or combination of letters which represent a sibilant sound (I, 16c), es is added to the simple form.	go do miss watch	goes does misses watches
c. When the simple form ends in y preceded by a consonant, the y is changed to i and es is added.	study hurry dry	studies hurries dries
d. Be and have are irregular.	be have	is has

b. Distribution. S-forms are used after singular nouns and demonstratives and after the pronouns *he, she,* and *it.* Simple forms are used in all other cases.

9 Pronouns: object forms

a.

PERSON	SINGULAR	PLURAL
1	me	us
2	←——— you ———→	
3	him her it	them

b. Use *it* for babies and animals when the sex is unknown.

c. Use *it* (not *she*) for ships and countries except in journalism, literature, propaganda.

d. Never use a third person pronoun without first mentioning the person or thing to which it refers.

Betty knows the boys.
She likes them.
She studies with them.

10 **Whom** is the object form of *who*. It is used in formal writing but seldom used in conversation except directly after a preposition, as in the question *With whom does Betty study?* A much more common and perfectly acceptable pattern is *Who does Betty study with?*

Compound sentences: *and, but,* **;**

When two simple sentences are grammatically parallel and closely related in context, they are usually combined into a single compound sentence.

a. *And* joins two affirmative statements.[3]

Jack goes downtown on Saturdays, and he goes to the movies on Saturday nights.

Do not join unrelated sentences like the following:

George is twenty. Mr. Allen is tall.

b. *But* joins contrastive patterns, affirmative and negative.

Bill doesn't like movies but he likes concerts.

c. **;** In writing, two simple statements are sometimes joined by a semicolon instead of by *and* or *but*. *Bill doesn't live in a dormitory; he has a private room.* The semicolon is a rather formal mark of punctuation; a period works just as well. Never use a comma in this way.

12 **Phrase** is a word used differently in different grammar books. In this one it means a group of words which work together as a unit to perform a single function, to fill one of the positions in a sentence pattern. Phrases are of many different types and patterns. A phrase does not have a subject and related verb.

[3] For a more complete statement see IX, 5, 6.

13 **Place phrases** are usually introduced by prepositions, and thus they are also called prepositional phrases.

a.

PLACE PHRASES			
Preposition	Article	Adjective	Noun
in	a		dormitory
in	the		library
in	a	sunny	laboratory
at	the		movies
at			home

b. Two or more place phrases may be used together: *on the table near the door; in the box on the shelf.*

14 **Place toward.** Verbs of motion such as *go, walk, run* are followed by place phrases beginning with *to.* Some of them include the definite article and some do not. *Home* and *downtown* are exceptions. Learn the expressions in the box.

SUBJECT	VERB	PLACE		
		To	The	Noun
We	go	——	——	home.
We	go	——	——	downtown.
We	go	to	——	class.
		to	——	school.
		to	——	church.
		to	——	bed.
We	go	to	the	library.
		to	the	movies.
		to	the	store.
		to	the	country[4]/city.

[4] *Country* alone means nation, but *the country,* as used here, means any rural area.

15 **Time phrases** are frequently of the same pattern. The noun names a time. The prepositions must be memorized, as they differ with different time expressions. The presence or absence of the article is also fixed.

a.

TIME PHRASES		
Prepo	(Art)	Noun
in	the	morning
in	the	afternoon
in	the	evening
at	——	noon
at	——	night
on	——	Saturdays

b. The *s* on the end of *Saturdays* indicates that the activity occurs regularly. We add *s* to days of the week and to other time words: *on weekdays, on holidays, on weekends, on Saturday nights.*

c. Time phrases with *every* are not introduced by a preposition: *every day, every week, every year.*

d. Time is often expressed by two or more consecutive phrases: *at seven thirty in the morning, at four in the afternoon.*

16 **Verbs with prepositions.** Many prepositions are determined by the verb which precedes them rather than by the noun which follows. In this lesson we have the example *listen to.* (See also III, 9; X, 12; XII, 13; XIII, 14.)

17 **Two-word verbs** are phrases consisting of a verb followed by a particle (preposition or adverb) which somehow changes the meaning of the verb. The two words together function as a single verb in a sentence pattern. The one in this lesson is *get up,* meaning to arise from bed.

Pronunciation helps

a. Voiced sounds are all of the sounds which are made while the vocal cords are vibrating. All of the vowels and more than half of the consonants represent voiced sounds.

b. Voiceless sounds are sounds made without vibrating the vocal cords. The sounds represented by the letters *f*, *p*, *t*, and *k* are examples of voiceless sounds.

c. Pronunciation of an *s-form* depends upon the final sound of the simple form of the verb from which it is formed.

RULES	EXAMPLES
When the simple form ends in a sibilant sound, the *s*-form has one more syllable than the simple form, and that syllable sounds like the verb *is*.	reaches misses dresses watches
When the simple form ends in a voiced sound which is not a sibilant, the final sound of the *s*-form is voiced. It sounds like the *z* in *zoo*.	lives does goes has
When the simple form ends in a voiceless sound which is not a sibilant, the final sound of the *s*-form is voiceless, like the *s* in *Sue*.	gets eats sleeps

Imitate your instructor's pronunciation of the examples. Be sure to pronounce the additional syllable after a sibilant sound.

d. *Do, does, don't.* Listen carefully to the pronunciation of these three forms of *do*. Notice that the vowel sound in each form is different from that of the others, although they are all represented by *o*.

e. *Them.* Be sure to hold your lips firmly together when pronouncing the last sound in this word. Unless you do, it will sound as though you are saying *then*, which is an entirely different word.

19 Punctuation

Jack gets up at seven o⊙clock in the morning⊙
He watches **TV** in the evening⊙
He goes downtown on **S**aturdays ⊙ and he goes to the movies on
    Saturday nights⊙

Bill doesn't live in a dormitory ⊙ he has a private room⊙
He doesn't have classes on **T**uesdays⊙

Jack and Bill are in the same **c**hemistry class⊙
They take **C**hemistry 212 from Professor Baker⊙
They don't have classes on **N**ew **Y**ear⊙s **D**ay⊙

a. Capitals

Names of specific courses are written with capital initials.
Names of areas of study are not written with capital initials.
Names of the days of the week are written with capital initials.
Names of holidays are written with capital initials.
TV, a common abbreviation of *television*, is always capitalized.

b. Apostrophes

Notice the apostrophe in the word *o'clock*.
The same mark is used in the expression *New Year's Day*.

c. Semicolons

This mark (;) may be used to make compound sentences without
connectives (§ 11), but it is not much used except in long or
formal sentences.

d. Commas

Long compound sentences require a comma before the connective, but
very short ones do not. There is no definition of long or short for this
rule. Every writer must decide for himself.

Questions students sometimes ask

a. The following sentence is in the model paragraph at the beginning of this lesson: *Bill doesn't have classes in the morning on Tuesdays and Thursdays.* Shouldn't it be *Bill hasn't classes . . . ?*

No. In American English the verb *have* [5] follows the same pattern as all other verbs except *be*. The British use *Bill hasn't classes* and *Hasn't Bill classes,* so, of course, they are quite acceptable, but the usual pattern in America is with *do.*

b. In § 10 there is the following sentence: *Who does Betty study with?* Isn't it wrong to end a sentence with a preposition?

No, it isn't wrong; it is a very common practice, particularly in conversation. You will find many more sentences which end with prepositions in the following lessons.

21 **Exercises**

a. Answer the following questions with short responses. State actual facts about yourself and answer the other questions in accordance with the text (§ 5).

1. Do you live in a dormitory?
2. Do you live in a private room?
3. Do you get up at seven o'clock in the morning?
4. Do you eat breakfast at home?
5. Do you study on Saturday nights?

6. Does Jack live in a private room?
7. Does he watch TV in the evening?
8. Does he study in his room in the afternoon?
9. Does he take chemistry?
10. Does he know Betty Allen?

11. Do Jack and Bill study chemistry?
12. Do you study chemistry?
13. Does Betty Allen study chemistry?
14. Do Mr. and Mrs. Allen study chemistry?
15. Does Professor Baker teach chemistry?

[5] *Have* is sometimes an auxiliary. In that case the pattern is different. (See XI, 2.)

b. Answer the following questions with short responses. Get your information from the model paragraphs (§§ 6, 7).

1. Who lives in a dormitory?
2. When does he get up?
3. When does he eat breakfast?
4. Where does he go at eight o'clock?
5. Where does he study in the afternoon?

6. When does he study in the library?
7. When does he do homework assignments?
8. When does he watch TV?
9. When does he go downtown?
10. When does he go to church?

11. Where does Bill live?
12. When doesn't he have classes?
13. What doesn't he like?
14. What does he like?
15. What does he do at night?

c. Answer the following questions about yourself. Answer in complete sentence patterns (§ 2).

1. What do you do at seven o'clock in the morning?
2. What do you do at ten o'clock in the morning?
3. What do you do at noon?
4. What do you do in the afternoon?
5. What do you do in the evening?

6. Where do you study?
7. Where do you sleep?
8. Where do you eat?
9. Where do you work?
10. Where do you go on Sundays?

11. When do you get up?
12. When do you attend classes?
13. When do you eat lunch?
14. When do you do your assignments?
15. When do you go to the movies?

d. Change the subject of each of the following sentences to Mr. Smith [6] (§ 18c).

1. We have *many books*.
2. *We* study hard.
3. We catch a *bus* every morning.
4. We go *to class* every day.
5. We arrive *on time*.

6. We write *on the blackboard*.
7. *We* use chalk.
8. *We ask questions*.
9. *We* do exercises.
10. We take *quizzes*.

11. We walk to *class*.
12. *We* talk to the teacher.
13. We watch *TV* in the lounge.
14. We eat lunch *at noon*.
15. We read *in the library* in the afternoon.

e. Change the statements of exercise d to yes/no questions and then answer them with negative statements. Vary the subject (§§ 4, 5).

> Instructor: We have many books.
> Student 1: Do we have many books?
> Student 2: No, we don't have many books.
> Student 3: Does Mr. Smith have many books?
> Student 4: No, Mr. Smith doesn't have many books.

f. Student 1: Ask the student nearest you a yes/no question about his daily activities.
Student 2: Answer the question with a short response (§ 5).

> Student 1: Do you study in the library?
> Student 2: No, I don't.

g. Make information questions from the items in exercise d. Substitute question words for the words your instructor says while he holds up his hand (the italicized words). Remember that verb forms will be singular (*s*-forms) even when the answers are plural (§§ 6, 7).

[6] Instructor: Ignore the italics when presenting exercise d. You will need to use them for exercise g.

h. Repeat the given sentence substituting a pronoun for the words your instructor says while he is holding up his hand (§ 9).

> Instructor: We need English and we study *English* every day.
> Student: We need English and we study it every day.

1. Betty knows Jack and she likes *Jack.*
2. She knows Bill too, and she works with *Bill* in the chemistry laboratory.
3. She sees *the boys* every day.
4. Betty asks Bill questions and he helps *Betty.*
5. They like chemistry and they get good grades in *chemistry.*
6. Bill never goes to movies; he doesn't like *movies.*
7. He likes music and he listens to *music* every night.
8. Jack has a sister and he visits *his sister* on holidays.
9. She cooks delicious dinners and he always enjoys *those dinners* very much.
10. Jack always thanks his sister for dinner after he eats *dinner.*
11. Our teacher helps *my classmates and me* with the English language.
12. He doesn't learn *the language* for us.
13. He teaches *my classmates and me* the patterns of English.
14. He gives *everyone in the class* opportunities for practice.
15. When we make mistakes he corrects *our mistakes.*

i. Student 1: Ask the student nearest you an information question about his daily activities (§§ 6c, 7).
Student 2: Answer the question with a short response (§ 2).

j. Student 1: Ask one of your classmates a question about a custom in his country.
Student 2: Answer the question with a short response (§ 6).

k. Change the pattern of the following sentence to the ones required by the different places of destination (§ 14). *We go to school every day.*

1.	home	6.	classes	11.	city
2.	library	7.	home	12.	church
3.	downtown	8.	store	13.	library
4.	church	9.	country	14.	school
5.	movies	10.	downtown	15.	bed (night)

22 Assignments

a. Write a paragraph about your daily activities. Use as many of the sentence patterns from Lessons I and II as you can. Be sure to include some sentence patterns joined by *and* and *but*.

b. Write a paragraph about a friend who has different daily activities from yours. Tell what he does on weekdays and on Sundays and holidays. Try to use only the patterns in Lessons I and II.

c. Write ten questions to ask your instructor about his customary activities. Be sure to include many different question patterns. Use the question words *who, what, where, when.*

REVIEW II

a. Change the following statements to yes/no questions and answer them. Include some negative answers. Use contractions where they are appropriate.*

   1. We're in *class*.
   2. *We* understand the lesson.
   3. Some students understand *everything*.
   4. *They're* lucky.
   5. *They* get good grades.

   6. *George* is lucky.
   7. He *works hard*.
   8. He gets *good grades*.
   9. *He* has three brothers.
10. They *work hard too*.

11. This is *an English class*.
12. *The classroom* is small (large).
13. It has *blackboards* on the walls.
14. The students write *on the blackboards*.
15. George *erases the blackboards* after class.

b. Make information questions from the statements in drill a and answer them. Substitute question words for the italicized words.

c. Read the following sentences aloud, substituting a pronoun or a place word for the italicized words.

   1. We have classes *in this room* three times a week.
   2. Mr. Allen is our teacher and *Mr. Allen* corrects our papers.
   3. We listen to *Mr. Allen*.
   4. Mr. Allen helps *the students in this class*.
   5. He invites the students to his house on Sundays and they go *to his house*.

* The italics apply to drill b only.

6. Mrs. Allen serves tea *at her house*.
7. The Chinese students like *tea*.
8. The Colombian students don't like tea; *the Colombian students* prefer coffee.
9. *Mrs. Allen* serves cookies with the tea.
10. All the students like *the cookies*.

11. The foreign students talk to Mrs. Allen and they tell *Mrs. Allen* about their countries.
12. When students tell her about Greece, she tells them that she was *in Greece*.
13. She asks the students if they are happy *in the United States*.
14. The students usually say that *the students* are.
15. They miss their familes, though, and their families miss *the students*.

d. Indent and punctuate the following paragraph.

frank fillmore is a young doctor he doesn't have an office he works in a hospital he goes to work at five oclock in the morning and he goes home at three thirty in the afternoon wednesday is dr fillmore's day off and he usually visits his former physiology teacher who is belgian they are going to spend the christmas holidays together

CONTINUOUS PRESENT: *ING*-FORMS, AUXILIARY *BE*
EXPLETIVE *THERE*

This is the reference room in the main library. There are many books on the shelves. There are many large tables in this room, and many students are working at the tables. One student is looking up a word in the big dictionary on the table near the door. A tall boy is asking the reference librarian a question. Several people are reading. A pretty blond girl is copying some information from an encyclopedia into her notebook.

This is the school cafeteria. There is a long line of people by the counter. Some people are standing and waiting. Some are choosing their food and putting it on their trays. A fat boy is ordering some ice cream. A thin lady is picking out a salad. The cashier is taking money and making change. Some people are already eating. Betty Allen is eating in the cafeteria this evening. She is finishing her dessert right now.

This is our classroom. We are sitting in our seats and we are paying attention to the instructor. We are listening carefully but we don't understand everything. We are looking at the blackboard and we see the sentence patterns there. We are thinking about prepositions but we don't remember them very well. We want to learn English well now because we need it.

1 **Activity in process** is expressed by a verb phrase made from a present form of the auxiliary *be* plus an *ing*-form. The resulting tense has many different names. We shall call it the *continuous present*.

2 **Auxiliary *be*** has the same forms and the same characteristics as verb *be* (Lesson I). It combines with pronouns and with *not* to form contractions. It changes place with the subject to make questions.

3 ***Ing*-forms** are simply forms of verbs which end in *ing*. They have many different uses in the grammar of English. In many grammar books they are called by different names when they do different jobs. Some of those names are *present participle, gerund, verbal, verbal noun, verbal adjective*. We shall simply call them *ing-forms*.

4 **Spelling of the *ing*-forms**

RULES	EXAMPLES	
a. When the simple form of a verb ends in a single e, the e is dropped before adding *ing*.[1]	have write choose	having writing choosing
b. When a one-syllable verb ends in a single consonant (excepting *w, x,* and *y*) preceded by one vowel, the consonant is doubled before adding *ing*.	sit stop run	sitting stopping running
A final consonant preceded by two vowels is not doubled.	look wear	looking wearing
c. When a verb of more than one syllable ends in a single consonant preceded by one vowel, the final consonant is doubled when the last syllable is stressed.	admít forgét prefér	admitting forgetting preferring
The final consonant is not doubled when the last syllable is unstressed.	lísten remémber	listening remembering
d. When the simple form of a verb ends in *ie*, the e is dropped and the *i* is changed to *y* before adding *ing*.	die tie lie	dying tying lying
e. In all other cases, *ing* is added to the simple form.	do see stand study	doing seeing standing studying

[1] Exception: *be–being*

5 **Statement pattern**

a.

SUBJECT	VERB PHRASE		COMPLEMENT	
	Aux Be (Not)	Ing	Object	Place
Many students	are	working		at the tables.
A pretty girl	is	copying	something	from an encyclopedia.
One student	is	looking up	a word	in the dictionary
				on the table
				near the door.
The cashier	isn't	eating.		
The fat boy	isn't	picking out	a salad.	
The customers	aren't	hurrying.		

b. **Time** is not mentioned in these sentences because the verb phrase tells us that the time is *now*.

c. **The continuous present** is also used to express actions or conditions during a period of time including the present: *Sue is working hard this semester.*

6 **Yes/no question pattern**

a.

AUX *BE* (NOT)	SUBJECT	VERB	COMPLEMENT	
		Ing-Form	Object	Place
Is	the tall boy	asking	a question?	
Are	many students	reading?		
Aren't	Jack and Bill	studying		in the library?
Isn't	the cashier	eating?		

b. Negative yes/no questions are almost always expressed with contractions as in the examples above. When the full form of *not* is used it is in a different position—just before the *ing*-form. The tone is rather formal: *Are you not being disrespectful?* The full form is not used before the subject.

7 Information question patterns

a. Subject unknown

QW	VERB PHRASE		COMPLEMENT		RESPONSE
	Aux Be (Not)	Ing	Object	Place	
Who	is	making	change?		The cashier.
Who	is	finishing	dessert?		Betty.
What	is	happening		at the counter?	People are waiting.
Who	isn't [2]	studying		in the library?	Jack and Bill.

b. Verb or part of complement unknown

QW	AUX BE (NOT)	SUBJECT	VERB Ing-Form	RESPONSE
What	is	the thin lady	picking out?	A salad.
What	is	Betty	eating?	Dessert.
Who	is	the tall boy	talking to?	The librarian.
Where	is	he	standing?	By the reference desk.
What	aren't	Jack and Bill	doing?	Studying.

8 **Non-action verbs** are not generally used in the continuous present. These are verbs which express mental states or conditions and the verbs of perception. Some of the more common ones, which are frequently misused by learners, are the following:

VERBS NOT USED IN CONTINUOUS PRESENT				
Mental State			Condition	Perception
believe	like	remember	belong	feel* (The floor feels cold.)
think*	love	forget	own	smell* (The fish smells spoiled.)
know	need		have*	taste* (The milk tastes sour.)
seem	prefer		owe	hear
understand	want		cost	see
	wish		mean	
			resemble	
* Only when it means believe			* Only when it means own	* Only when used intransitively, as illustrated.

[2] Review I, 4b

9 **Verbs with prepositions** (cf. II, 16) in this lesson are:

look at
think about
talk to

10 **Two-word verbs** (cf. II, 17) in this lesson are:

look up (information): search for in a reference book
pick out (something): choose

11 *There* is not always a place adverb (cf. I, 10). Sometimes it is an *expletive,* that is, a word which means nothing in particular but which calls attention to the existence of whatever is mentioned in the rest of the sentence. *Be* usually follows the expletive and it agrees in number, singular or plural, with the subject, which comes after it. Most simple statements beginning with the expletive *there* require a place expression to complete them.

Sentence patterns with expletive *there*

a. Statement

EXPLETIVE THERE	BE (NOT) AUX/VERB	SUBJECT	VERB ING	COMPLEMENT		
				Object	Place	Time
There	is	a long line			in the cafeteria	now.
There	are	many people	waiting		by the counter.	
There	isn't	anyone			by the fountain.	
There	aren't	enough people	serving	the hot food.		

b. Yes/no questions

BE (NOT) [3] AUX/VERB	EXPLETIVE THERE	SUBJECT	VERB ING	COMPLEMENT			RESPONSE
				Object	Place	Time	
Is	there	a long line			in the cafeteria	now?	Yes, there is.
Are	there	many people	waiting		by the counter?		Yes, there are.
Isn't	there	anyone			by the fountain?		No, there isn't.
Aren't	there	enough people	serving	the hot food?			No, there aren't.

c. Information questions

QW	BE (NOT) AUX/VERB	EXPLETIVE THERE	SUBJECT	VERB ING	COMPLEMENT		RESPONSE
					Object	Place	
Where	is	there	an encyclopedia?				On the shelf.
Where	are	there	students	working?			In the library.
When	isn't	there	a line			in the cafeteria?	At five o'clock.
When	aren't	there	many students	looking up	information	in the library?	On Saturdays.

---

[3] See 6b of this lesson. The generalization applies also to sentences with expletive *there*.

Possessive forms of pronouns are of two kinds: those used before nouns, as modifiers, and those used in place of nouns.

a. Before nouns [4]

PERSON	SINGULAR	PLURAL
1	my	our
2	← your →	
3	his her its [5]	their

b. Without nouns

PERSON	SINGULAR	PLURAL
1	mine	ours
2	← yours →	
3	his hers its	theirs

1. These forms are used with names of parts of the body:

   Wash your hands.   Close your eyes.

2. They are also used with nouns naming family or other personal relationships:

   Betty lives with her uncle.
   Jack and Bill are her classmates.

Possessives used without nouns must refer to something already mentioned or implied:

   That book is mine.   Where is yours?

14 **Whose** [6] is the possessive form of *who.* It is usually used before a noun: *Whose book is that? Whose uncle is Mr. Allen?* It can be used without a noun when the items possessed are in sight and are being indicated. *Whose is this? Whose are these notes?*

---

[4] In some books these are called possessive adjectives.
[5] Do not confuse *its* with *it's.* What is the difference? (See I, 7.)
[6] Do not confuse *whose* with *who's.* They sound the same.

15 **Pronunciation helps**

a. *Ng.* These two letters together represent a single, distinctive sound which is not like the sound represented by *n* nor the one represented by *g.* It is made by closing off the air at the back of the mouth by the velum and letting it escape through the nose. The *ng* sound is a *continuant;* i.e., you can continue to make it as long as you have air in your lungs. It is not a *stop* sound like the *g* in *go.*

b. *Studying* has three syllables, as do *hurrying, worrying, carrying, burying,* and similar words.

c. *There/their/they're* are all pronounced alike by many people. Be careful not to confuse them when writing.

16 **Common errors to avoid**

a. Students sometimes forget that it is necessary to use *be* with an *ing*-form. They say or write things like *I trying to understand* instead of *I'm trying to understand.* An *ing*-form alone never functions as a verb. It requires the auxiliary *be.*

b. Another common error is the use of expletive *there* without a place expression, as in the compound sentence *I like Miami; there are many nice beaches. There* in that sentence is an expletive and the sentence is incomplete. It lacks a place expression. To complete it we may add an adverb *there: I like Miami; there are many nice beaches there.*

17 **Exercises**

a. Answer the following questions about yourself right now. Make complete statements (§ 5).

1. Are you standing?
2. Are you looking at the ceiling?
3. Are you listening to music?
4. Are you writing a letter?
5. Are you thinking about home?

6. Are you sitting in a chair?
7. Are you looking at the blackboard?
8. Are you listening to your instructor?
9. Are you writing notes?
10. Are you thinking about your lesson?

11. Where are you sitting?
12. What are you looking at?
13. Who are you listening to?
14. What are you writing?
15. What are you thinking about?

b. Ask and answer yes/no questions about the model paragraphs of this lesson using the given verbs in the continuous present (§ 6).

> Instructor: stand
> Student 1: Is the librarian standing near the door?
> Student 2: No, she isn't. She's sitting by the reference desk.

1.	work	6.	stand	11.	pick out	16.	sit
2.	look up	7.	wait	12.	take (money)	17.	pay (attention)
3.	ask	8.	choose	13.	make (change)	18.	listen to
4.	read	9.	put	14.	eat	19.	look at
5.	copy	10.	order	15.	finish	20.	think about

c. Using the same verbs as in exercise b, ask and answer information questions. Base your answers on the information in the model paragraphs (§ 7).

> Instructor: look at
> Student 1: What are the students looking at?
> Student 2: The blackboard.

d. Compose a sequence of two sentences. In the first one mention a place. In the second use expletive *there* and place adverb *there* (§§ 12, 16b).

> **Student:** I buy my books in the Union Bookshop.
> **There are many bargains there.**

e. Make sentences beginning with the expletive *there* and including the given word and an appropriate place phrase (§§ 11, 12).

> **Instructor:** clouds
> **Student:** There are clouds in the sky.

1.	stars	6.	gasoline	11.	bread
2.	fish	7.	oil	12.	food
3.	trees	8.	water	13.	beer
4.	flowers	9.	a spare tire	14.	clothes
5.	birds	10.	tools	15.	money

f. Repeat the sentences read by your instructor, adding possessive pronouns in appropriate places [7] (§ 13a).

> **Instructor:** We do assignments in the evening.
> **Student:** We do our assignments in the evening.

1. I eat breakfast at seven o'clock.
2. You eat breakfast at eight o'clock.
3. George drinks coffee black.
4. Mr. and Mrs. Allen like cream in coffee.
5. Their pet cat drinks cream every morning.

6. We have English class at three o'clock.
7. John always brings a notebook to class.
8. The other students don't always bring notebooks.
9. They write notes in the textbooks.
10. I don't like to write notes in a textbook.

11. Betty is wearing a new dress today.
12. She is preparing a chemistry lesson in the library now.
13. Bill is listening to records.
14. Mr. Allen is smoking a pipe.
15. You are studying an English lesson.

---

[7] Items 7, 9, and 10 can be done two ways.

g. Student 1: Point to something in the room and ask whose it is. Choose something that belongs to someone in the room (§ 14).

Student 2: Answer the question by pointing to the owner and using the appropriate pronoun (§ 13b).

> Student 1: (pointing to an umbrella)
> Whose umbrella is that?
> Student 2: (pointing to the owner)
> It's his.

h. Your instructor will read two sentences. Repeat the first sentence, but change the second one so that the noun is not repeated. Make the necessary change in the pronoun form. Stress the pronoun in the second sentence (§ 13b).

> Instructor: This is my pen. Your pen is in your pocket.
> Student: This is my pen. Yours is in your pocket.

1. Your language is Spanish.
   My language is English.

2. John brings his notebook to class.
   George doesn't bring his notebook.

3. Bill does his homework in his room.
   Betty does her homework in the library.

4. The Bakers like their car.
   The Allens like their car too.

5. Jack and Bill have their chemistry class at three o'clock.
   We have our chemistry class in the morning.

6. Bill helps Betty with her problems.
   No one helps Bill with his problems.

7. Bill writes his English homework in ink.
   Jack writes his English homework in pencil.

8. Jack carries his calculator in his briefcase.
   Bill and Bob carry their calculators in their pockets.

9. Professor Allen has his classes in the morning.
   Professor Baker has his classes in the afternoon.

10. Some people eat their dinner at noon.
    I eat my dinner in the evening.

11. Betty is eating her dinner in the cafeteria.
    Mr. and Mrs. Allen are eating their dinner at home.

12. Mrs. Allen is eating her dinner.
    Mrs. Baker is preparing her dinner.

13. The reference librarian is doing her work.
    The cafeteria cashier is doing his work.

14. Some people do their assignments on time.
    Some people do their assignments late.

15. Jack receives his check every week.
    I receive my check once a month.

i. Point to a part of your body and tell what it is. Use the words *right* and *left* when appropriate (§ 13a).

Instructor: (pointing) This is my left foot.

j. Substitute each of the given words into the given sentences, changing the verb tense only when necessary (§ 8).

1. I am listening to the birds.

John	watch	own	look at	train
he	like	understand	see	admire
hear	raise	feed	count	enjoy

2. We are studying our lesson now.

need	do	read	study	discuss
write	listen to	like	forget	plan
understand	remember	know	prepare	understand

3. George is writing to his mother.

think about	father	help	need	speak to
love	resemble	support	read to	listen to
work for	believe	understand	assist	hear

Assignments

a. Go to a place where there are many people doing different things. Write a paragraph telling about the activities of the people around you. Do not change the time reference; write about now. Be careful to use the appropriate sentence patterns (§ 5).

b. Write five simple questions to ask your classmates about their countries. Use the expletive *there* in each question (§§ 11, 12, 16b).

c. Write the *s*-forms and the *ing*-forms of the following verbs. Be sure that each one is spelled correctly (II, 8; III, 4).

1.	make	6.	go	11.	blow	16.	answer	21.	save
2.	say	7.	die	12.	watch	17.	begin	22.	pay
3.	think	8.	have	13.	plan	18.	call	23.	run
4.	write	9.	employ	14.	mix	19.	cut	24.	start
5.	worry	10.	read	15.	contain	20.	hear	25.	happen

REVIEW III

a. Student 1: Ask your neighbor a question about one of his habits and then ask him a question about his present moment activity. Include the given words.

      Student 2: Give short responses to the questions.

> Instructor: smoke
> Student 1: Do you smoke?
> Student 2: Yes, I do.
> Student 1: Are you smoking?
> Student 2: No, I'm not.

1. eat candy	6. drink coffee	11. practice English
2. chew gum	7. play tennis	12. draw pictures *
3. play chess	8. wear ties *	13. write letters *
4. drive a car	9. swim	14. play baseball
5. read magazines *	10. discuss politics	15. think about home

b. Change the following statements to information questions. Substitute question words for the italicized words.

1. *A tall boy* is asking the librarian a question.
2. The librarian is listening to *the tall boy*.
3. The librarian is listening to *the tall boy's* question.
4. A blond girl is copying *information*.
5. *A big dictionary* is on the table near the door.
6. There is a big dictionary *on the table near the door*.
7. *Some students* are working at a large table.
8. One student is looking up *a word*.
9. There is a long line of people *by the counter in the cafeteria*.
10. Some people are *putting food on their trays*.
11. Some people are putting *food* on their trays.
12. The cashier is taking money from *the thin lady*.
13. The coffee boy is *serving coffee*.
14. *Betty Allen* is eating dessert.
15. She doesn't eat *in the cafeteria* on Sundays.

* Items 5, 8, 12, and 13 must be changed to the singular in the present continuous. Why?

c. Repeat the following sentences using contractions wherever they can be used. Remember that certain contractions are not used as the last word of a sentence (I, 7a; III, 5).

1. It is not Sunday; it is Monday.
2. I am tired and I know you are.
3. We do not smoke in class.
4. Jack lives in a dormitory but Bill does not.
5. George thinks English spelling is hard and it is.
6. There is a boy from Germany in this class.
7. Is there a boy from France? No, there is not.
8. Is there one from Mexico? Yes, there is.
9. We do not have many students from Canada.
10. The students think Mr. Allen is a good teacher and he is.
11. Richard is a senior but Jack and Bill are not.
12. There are fifteen students in this class.
13. Are there fifteen students in this class? Yes, there are.
14. We are all serious students.
15. Are we all serious students? Yes, we are.

FREQUENCY, TIME, PLACE
NUMBERS AND RELATED TOPICS

Bill doesn't have a private telephone; he uses the public phone in the drug store near his house. Sometimes he calls up his mother, long distance. He usually makes a person-to-person call. He picks up the receiver, drops a dime in the coin box, and dials the operator. He says, "I want to speak to Mrs. William Brown in Westview. The area code is 357 and the number is 408-3972." Bill often calls his mother after nine p.m. because the charge is always less at night. He calls her in the morning on the twenty-first of April. That's her birthday. He wishes her a happy birthday and asks her how she feels. After three minutes he says good-bye and hangs up.

1 **Frequency adverbs** are used to express approximately how many times a customary or habitual action or condition is repeated. They are not generally used with continuous tenses. Here are the common ones listed in order of declining frequency:

Affirmatives: always usually frequently often sometimes occasionally
Negatives: seldom rarely hardly ever never
Interrogative: ever?

2 **Position of frequency adverbs** in affirmative statements is determined by the verb. They immediately precede the verb in simple present statements (II, 2) unless the verb is *be* (I, 2), in which case they follow.

a.

SUBJECT	(FA)	VERB	(FA)	COMPLEMENT	
Bill	often	calls up		his mother	after nine p.m.
The charge		is	usually	less	at night.

b. Some of the affirmative frequency adverbs, particularly *sometimes,* also appear at the beginnings and ends of sentences. Not all frequency words fit this pattern, however.

Sometimes Bill calls up his mother in the morning.
Bill calls up his mother in the morning sometimes.

c. Negative statements of frequency are of two kinds: those negated by frequency adverbs, and those negated by *not*.

SUBJ	AUX + NOT	FA	VERB (OTHER)/BE	FA	COMPLEMENT Object	Place	Time
Bill	doesn't	often	call		his mother		in the morning.
Bill		seldom	calls		his mother		in the morning.
She			isn't	usually		at home	then.
She			is	hardly ever		at home	then.

d. Yes/no questions about frequency

VERB *BE* OR AUX *DO*	SUBJ	FA	VERB (NOT *BE*)	COMPLEMENT		
				Object	Place	Time
Does	Bill	ever	call	his mother		in the morning?
Is	she	frequently			at home	then?

e. Information questions

QW	AUX *DO*	SUBJECT	FA	VERB	COMPLEMENT			RESPONSE
					Object	Place	Time	
Who			sometimes	calls	his mother		in the morning?	Bill.
When	does	Bill	usually	call	his mother?			At night.
Where	does	Mrs. Brown	usually	go			in the morning?	To the store.
What	does	she	usually	do		there?		She buys food.

3 **Time at the beginning.** In the sentence patterns we have examined so far, all the time expressions are in the same position—at the end of the sentence. When a speaker wishes to emphasize time, or when he feels a need for variety in his sentence patterns, he puts the time expression at the beginning.

TIME	NORMAL WORD ORDER
On Saturday nights	Jack goes to the movies.
On Tuesdays	Bill doesn't get up early.
At noon	there is always a long line in the cafeteria.
Right now	the students are having an English lesson.
Today	they are studying prepositions.

4 **Place at the beginning.** A place expression may also come at the beginning of a sentence for emphasis or variety, though this is a less frequent pattern. It happens most often in the presence of expletive *there*.

a.

PLACE	NORMAL WORD ORDER
In the drug store	there is a public telephone.
In the reference room	there are many encyclopedias.
There	the students do their assignments.
There	Jack studies in the afternoon.

b. When *there* at the beginning refers to a place previously mentioned, the rest of the sentence pattern is normal, as in the illustrations above. However, when *there* refers to something being pointed to, the rest of the sentence is inverted. The same thing happens with *here*.

PLACE	INVERTED WORD ORDER	
	Verb	Subject
There	is	the bookstore.
Here	come	the Allens.
There	goes	the bus.

5 **Some facts about numbers.** There are two kinds of numbers: cardinal and ordinal. Cardinal numbers are used in counting and reckoning. Ordinal numbers indicate rank. There are some inconsistencies in the spelling and pronunciation of the numbers. Pay particular attention to the underlined forms.

a.

CARDINAL		ORDINAL	
1	one	1st	first
2	two	2nd	second
3	three	3rd	third
4	four	4th	fourth
5	five	5th	fifth
6	six	6th	sixth
7	seven	7th	seventh
8	eight	8th	eighth
9	nine	9th	ninth
10	ten	10th	tenth
11	eleven	11th	eleventh
12	twelve	12th	twelfth
13	thirteen	13th	thirteenth
14	fourteen	14th	fourteenth
15	fifteen	15th	fifteenth
16	sixteen	16th	sixteenth
17	seventeen	17th	seventeenth
18	eighteen	18th	eighteenth
19	nineteen	19th	nineteenth
20	twenty	20th	twentieth
21	twenty-one	21st	twenty-first
30	thirty	30th	thirtieth
40	forty	40th	fortieth
50	fifty	50th	fiftieth
60	sixty	60th	sixtieth
70	seventy	70th	seventieth
80	eighty	80th	eightieth
90	ninety	90th	ninetieth
100	one hundred	100th	one hundredth
1,000	one thousand	1,000th	one thousandth
1,000,000	one million	1,000,000th	one millionth

b. When a noun is modified by both an ordinal and a cardinal, the ordinal always comes first.

ORDINAL	CARDINAL	NOUN		
The first	five	exercises	are	easy.
The second	five	exercises	are	hard.

6 **More about time**

a. Hours and minutes are expressed in the following ways.

Hours of the day are not numbered beyond twelve. We use the abbreviations a.m. and p.m. instead. The hours before noon are designated a.m.; those after noon are designated p.m. You will also see these two terms written in capital letters: A.M., P.M. Either way is correct, but be consistent in your usage.

6:00   six
          six o'clock

6:10   six ten
          ten (minutes)[1] after six

6:15   six fifteen
          a quarter after six
          a quarter past six

6:30   six thirty
          half past six

6:45   six forty-five
          a quarter to seven
          a quarter of seven

6:55   six fifty-five
          five (minutes) to seven
          five (minutes) of seven

12:00 noon
          midnight

b. Days of the week are capitalized and should be spelled correctly, though some of them are difficult.

Sunday Monday Tuesday Wednesday Thursday Friday Saturday

---

[1] The word *minutes* may be omitted.

c. Months and seasons differ in different parts of the world. In the
United States they are roughly as follows:

Spring	**Summer**	**Fall**	**Winter**
March	June	September	December
April	July	October	January
May	August	November	February

When writing a date on a letter or assignment, write the complete name
of the month and be sure it is spelled correctly.

d. Dates are generally read as ordinal numbers (§ 5).
Years are expressed in groups of ten.

> January 1, 1975 = January first nineteen seventy-five
> July 4, 1776 = July fourth seventeen seventy-six

In the United States, abbreviated dates are written with the month first.
This is just opposite to the practice in most parts of the world, including
Britain. It sometimes causes confusion for people who are not aware
of the difference.

> 3/4/72   means March 4, 1972.
> 6/9/60   means June 9, 1960.

e. Prepositions used with times and dates (cf. II, 15).

RULES	EXAMPLES		

1. *in* before months
  years
  seasons
  special expressions
	in September in January
	in 1970 in 1776
	in summer in winter
	in the morning in the afternoon
			in June
			in 1492
			in spring
			in the evening

2. *on* before days of the week dates	on Tuesday on Friday on July 4th on the 25th of December		
3. *at* before the time of day special expressions	at seven thirty at 5:15 at noon at night		at half past six at midnight

When time, day, and date all occur in one sentence, the time precedes
the day and no preposition is used before the date: *The meeting is at
2 o'clock on Tuesday, August 15.*

More about place

a. Addresses are written with the number of the building first, followed by the street, city, state, and ZIP code. The ZIP [2] code is a five-digit number, and every address in the United States has one. It is important to include the ZIP code for speedy delivery of mail.

> 5629 South Wood Street
> Chicago, Illinois 60636

Numbers are read either as a series of cardinals (§ 5) or in sets of tens. Zero is pronounced as the letter *o*.

$$204 = \text{two-o-four}$$
$$914 = \text{nine fourteen}$$
$$5629 = \begin{cases} \text{five six two nine} \\ \text{or} \\ \text{fifty-six twenty-nine} \end{cases}$$

b. Prepositions used with places

RULES	EXAMPLES	
1. *in* before continents	in Europe	in South America
countries	in Brazil	in France
states	in California	in Texas
cities and towns	in Chicago	in New York
2. *on* before streets	on Main Street	on Broadway
3. *at* before numbers of buildings	at 5629 South Wood Street	

[2] The letters *ZIP*, always written in capitals, stand for zone improvement plan, but people pronounce them as one word rhyming with *ship*.

8 | **Telephone calls.**   Most telephone numbers are pronounced as a series of cardinals. In most cases *zero* is pronounced as the letter *o*: 407-8320 is four-o-seven, eight-three-two-o. When two or more zeroes come together, they are pronounced differently: 407-8300 is four-o-seven, eight-three hundred.

All *local calls* and *station-to-station long distance calls* may be dialed. Directions for long distance dialing differ from area to area. They will be found in the front pages of your local telephone directory. If you wish to make a *person-to-person* call, you must *dial "o"* for *operator*. The operator will ask you for the *area code* and for the name of the person you wish to speak to. You must be prepared to spell the name in the English pronunciation of the letters of the alphabet. The operator will also ask for the number of the phone from which you are calling. If you wish to have the charge for the call paid by the person you are calling, you may ask the operator to make the call *collect*.

Be sure that you understand all the italicized terms in the paragraph above and that you can spell them correctly.

9 | **Two-word verbs** used in connection with telephoning are:

call up [3] (someone): telephone
pick up (something): lift with the fingers
hang up: place the telephone receiver on its hook

10 | **Transitive versus intransitive.**   One of the two-word verbs we learned never takes an object. Some of the others must have an object to complete their meaning. Still others are used both ways. As we shall learn later, some transitive two-word verbs pattern in a peculiar way when their objects are pronouns—but let's leave that for another lesson.

TRANSITIVE (always has an object)	BOTH (may or may not have an object)	INTRANSITIVE (never has an object)
look up something pick out something pick up something	call up hang up	get up

[3] *Call* alone is also used in place of the verb *to telephone*.

11 | United States money

a penny = one cent	a quarter = twenty-five cents
a nickel = five cents	a half-dollar = fifty cents
a dime = ten cents	change = a collective term for coins
	(metal money)

When we write amounts of money in numbers, the cent sign follows the number, but the dollar sign precedes it.

5¢	$.05	$1.49	a dollar forty-nine	one forty-nine
10¢	$.10	$5.20	five dollars and twenty cents	five twenty
25¢	$.25	$59.95	fifty-nine ninety-five	

We frequently omit the words *dollars* and *cents* when we express quantities of money. Whether we mean dollars and cents or only dollars is known from the context.

Macy's sells sport shirts for five ninety-eight. ($5.98)
A new RCA TV costs five ninety-eight. ($598.)

12 | Simple mathematical terms

+	plus	=	equals
−	minus	¼	one fourth
÷	divided by	⅓	one third
×	{times	½	one half
	{multiplied by	4^2	four squared

13 **Pronunciation helps**

a. **Pause and intonation.** There are several places in the model paragraph of this lesson where a comma indicates a slight pause and a rise and fall of the voice. Almost every native speaker of American English uses the same patterns in those positions. Listen carefully while your instructor reads the paragraph and try to imitate his intonation. Pay particular attention to the fourth and fifth sentences.

b. **Teens and -ties.** It is often difficult to distinguish between a learner's pronunciation of *40* and his pronunciation of *14*, or of *30* and *13*. To be sure of being understood, stress the last syllable of the teens and the first syllable of the -ties.

thirteén	thírty	fifteén	fífty
fourteén	fórty	sixteén	síxty

c. **The ordinals.** The sounds represented by the letters *th* are often very difficult for students to pronounce because there are many languages in which these sounds do not occur. The voiceless *th* sound at the end of ordinal numbers seems particularly difficult when it follows another consonant sound. Practice the pronunciation of fifth, eighth, twentieth, etc., and make sure you can be understood.

d. **Telephone numbers.** When you give a telephone number to an operator, it is easier for her to hear it correctly if you pause and drop your voice in the places where she expects you to. If a number has seven digits, pause after the third; if it has ten, pause after the third and sixth.

357-0472	357 (pause) 0472
298-357-0472	298 (pause) 357 (pause) 0472

14 Punctuation

The meeting is at 2 o'clock on **T**uesday, **A**ugust 15th.

It's not in the **m**orning.

Bill calls up his mother after nine p ⊙ m ⊙

He calls her person-to-person, not station-to-station.

He picks up the receiver ⊙ drops a dime in the coin box ⊙ and dials the operator.

He says ⊙⁽ᵂ⁾ I want to speak to Mrs. William Brown in Westview. The area code is 357, and the number is 408-3972. ⁽ᵂ⁾

There are over 5 ⊙ 000 ⊙ 000 telephones in the United States.

twenty-one   5629 **S**outh **W**ood **S**treet
               Chicago, **I**llinois   60636

a. Capitals

Names of the days of the week are capitalized.
Names of the months are capitalized.
Words designating parts of the day are not capitalized.
Names of streets, cities, states, countries, and continents are capitalized.
The first quoted word of a speaker is capitalized.

b. Periods

Note the periods in a.m. and p.m. When one of these abbreviations comes at the end of a sentence, no additional sentence-closing period is required.

c. Hyphens

Note the hyphens in the expressions *person-to-person* and *station-to-station*.
Compound numerals such as twenty-one and thirty-six are hyphenated.

d. Commas

Note the commas after *receiver* and *box*. The sentence in which they occur has only one subject but it has three verbs with their objects. Commas are used to separate three or more grammatically equal sentence parts in a series.

Note the comma after *says*. In direct quotation a comma separates the introductory statement from the actual words of the speaker.

When English-speaking people write large numbers, they use commas, not periods, to separate the digits into groups of thousands.

Note that in the address there is no comma between the number and the street. There is a comma between the city and the state, but no comma between the state and the ZIP code.

e. Quotation marks (" ")

Quotation marks are placed before the first word and after the last word of a quoted utterance. Both marks are above the words, not below them. In handwriting, quotation marks should be made to curve toward the words they enclose, although on a typewriter they are straight, for an obvious reason.[4] Even when a quotation includes more than one sentence, it is enclosed by only one set of marks.

15 **Common errors to avoid**

Students whose languages do not employ punctuation as we know it often place marks in what seem to be very peculiar places. The following examples of incorrect placement of punctuation are taken from student papers.

WRONG	RIGHT	REASON
While I was waiting for the reaction to take place , I wrote up yesterday's report.	While I was waiting for the reaction to take place, I wrote up yesterday's report.	Commas, semicolons, and periods always go on the line with the words that precede them.
My teacher always says, " Be sure you understand the assignment before you try to do it."	My teacher always says, "Be sure you understand the assignment before you try to do it."	Quotation marks go on the line with the words they enclose.

[4] What is it?

16 **Exercises**

a. Change each of the following sentences to ones with approximately the same meaning which include adverbs of frequency. You should find a sentence for each of the different words (§§ 1, 2).

> Example: John is late to class every day.
> Response: John is always late to class.

1. Betty eats in the school cafeteria about once a week.
2. Bill calls up his mother in the morning once a year.
3. Professor Allen doesn't ever smoke cigarettes.
4. Jack has eight o'clock classes every semester.
5. Does Bill go to the movies at any time?
6. George gets to class early on most days.
7. He isn't ever absent.
8. Mrs. Allen entertains friends about once a week.
9. On those occasions she eats potatoes.
10. She eats dessert about once or twice a year.
11. She doesn't eat candy at all.
12. Betty studies with Bill some days.
13. There are people in the reference room all the time.
14. Are foreign students homesick at any time?
15. Do they think about home some days?

b. Change the word order of the following sentences to another acceptable word order (§§ 3, 4).

> Example: We don't have class on Saturdays.
> Response: On Saturdays we don't have class.

1. Jack goes downtown every Saturday.
2. He watches TV in the evening.
3. He studies in the library in the afternoon.
4. He sees many other students in the library.
5. He goes home at five o'clock.

6. Bill doesn't have classes on Tuesdays and Thursdays.
7. He sleeps late on those days.
8. There is a hot plate in his room.
9. There he often makes coffee.
10. He often goes home on weekends.

11. At noon George eats dinner.
12. After dinner he takes a nap.
13. Everyone takes a nap after dinner in George's country.
14. It is very hot there in summer.
15. George often thinks about his country on holidays.

c. Give a cardinal number for an ordinal, an ordinal for a cardinal (§ 5).

1.	2nd	6.	83rd	11.	81st
2.	12th	7.	16th	12.	5
3.	3	8.	61	13.	101
4.	72	9.	40	14.	44
5.	57	10.	9th	15.	75th

d. Write on the blackboard from dictation (§ 5).

1.	6,700	6.	824	11.	976
2.	15,021	7.	342,076	12.	12,000,000
3.	3,000,002	8.	3,017	13.	83,706
4.	14,000	9.	8,647,000	14.	9,017
5.	2,010	10.	21,042	15.	611

e. Express these times in another way (§ 6).

1.	4:35	6.	6:20	11.	10:40
2.	7:45	7.	2:30	12.	12:30
3.	8:15	8.	5:10	13.	1:15
4.	12:00	9.	9:25	14.	3:55
5.	1:05	10.	11:50	15.	6:45

f. Repeat the following sentence, adding one hour and one day each time (§ 6).

> Instructor: I get up at 5 o'clock in the morning on Mondays.
> Student: I get up at 6 o'clock in the morning on Tuesdays.

Change to noon and afternoon when necessary.

g. Repeat exercise f with the following sentence (§ 6).

> I go to bed at 7 o'clock in the evening on Mondays.

h. In response to the cue word, tell the class when you were born. Pay particular attention to the preposition you use (§ 6e).

> Instructor: season → Student: I was born in summer.
> Instructor: month → Student: I was born in July.
> Instructor: date → Student: I was born on the 22nd of July.

1. month	6. date	11. season
2. date	7. season	12. date
3. month	8. month	13. month
4. month	9. season	14. month
5. season	10. date	15. date

i. Tell the class where your home is and where you are living now. Be specific about your present address (§ 7).

> Response: My home is in Iran but I am living at 45 Main Street in College Town now.

j. Read the telephone numbers your instructor writes on the blackboard. Express them in the way an operator would expect to hear them (§§ 5, 8).

1. 286-8537	6. 627-9432	11. 321-5549
2. 314-4763	7. 091-3059	12. 327-9999
3. 590-5420	8. 213-2549	13. 435-6900
4. 380-2617	9. 840-8761	14. 436-2000
5. 317-3209	10. 999-0077	15. 326-5359

k. Spell your family name. Be especially careful of the pronunciation of the names of the vowels.

l. Student 1: Ask your neighbor his telephone number.
Student 2: Answer the question with a short response, not a complete sentence. If you don't have a telephone, give someone else's number (§ 8).

m. What do the following abbreviated dates signify in the United States (§ 6d)?

1. 6/9/72	6. 2/29/56	11. 4/7/73
2. 8/4/65	7. 1/1/87	12. 9/8/54
3. 12/2/67	8. 5/3/21	13. 7/22/16
4. 3/5/98	9. 7/6/74	14. 3/18/45
5. 11/11/18	10. 10/12/10	15. 6/17/58

n. Do the following problems orally. Tell what each equals (§ 12).

1. $5 + 2$	6. $\frac{1}{2} \times 4$	11. 6×3
2. 5×6	7. $\frac{1}{4} \times 12$	12. $9 \div 2$
3. $6 - 3$	8. $9 - 5$	13. 5^2
4. $27 \div 9$	9. 4^2	14. $7 - 7$
5. $8 - 3$	10. $8 + 7$	15. $9 \div 0$

o. Answer the following questions as well as you can. Give short responses (§§ 8, 11).

1. What costs a penny?
2. What costs a nickel?
3. What costs a dime?
4. What costs a quarter?
5. What costs a dollar?

6. How many quarters are there in a dollar?
7. How many cents are there in a quarter?
8. I have a nickel and six pennies. How many coins do I have?
9. I have ten dimes. How much do I have in change?
10. I have a quarter, a dime, and a nickel. How much do I have in change?
11. You want to make a telephone call from a public telephone. You have only a one-dollar bill. What do you need?
12. You want to call up someone but you don't have enough money. What kind of call do you make?
13. You want to make a local call. What must you do?
14. You want to make a long distance call. What must you know besides the number?
15. What kind of long distance calls can be dialed?

Assignments

a. Write a paragraph about the usual activities of a member of your family. Include several of the adverbs of frequency in both affirmative and negative patterns. Include time and place expressions in different positions in the sentence.

b. Write five information questions based on the model paragraph. Use the question words *what, when, where, who, whose.*

c. Write out the words for the following numbers: 14, 8th, 20th, 40, 3rd, 9th, 12th, 50, 90, 32.

d. Following is a list of some of the verbs we have been using in the exercises. Sort them into three groups: (1) those which always have objects, (2) those which never have objects, and (3) those which are used both ways. Give your lists appropriate titles (§ 10).

ask	like	read	sit	study
eat	live	say	sleep	use
go	make	see	stand	work

REVIEW IV

a. Repeat the following sentence and then make all the changes that are necessary to accommodate each given word. Don't try to remember the original sentence. Listen carefully to your neighbor and make your sentence from his.

Jack has dinner in the dormitory in the evening.

lunch	dinner	I	my friends
Miss Liu	the school cafeteria	a snack	hotel
breakfast	breakfast	restaurant	home
many students	drugstore	dinner	every day

b. Start with the given sentence and change it to accommodate each word in the list below.

Dr. Jones buys a new car every year.

1.	Mrs.	6.	month	11.	understand
2.	coat	7.	now	12.	Mr.
3.	winter	8.	a	13.	not
4.	two	9.	read	14.	like
5.	books	10.	the	15.	discuss

c. Follow the same procedure with the sentence below.

Bill is calling up his mother.

1.	brother	6.	pick up	11.	study
2.	every week	7.	dial	12.	isn't
3.	every day	8.	a number	13.	eat
4.	Betty	9.	123-4567	14.	read
5.	now	10.	every evening	15.	(is) sleep

d. Indent and punctuate the following paragraph.

tom tucker makes a lot of long distance telephone calls he made twenty three in february thirty two in march and forty one in april most of them were station to station but a few were person to person and they were very expensive he always says my telephone bills are much too high i must stop making so many long distance calls

LESSON

V

UNCOUNTABLES AND PLURAL FORMS QUANTITIES AND NUMBER AGREEMENT

This is a conversation between Jack and Betty.

Jack: What do you do here in summer?

Betty: I take one course in summer school and I play a lot of tennis. Sometimes I go on picnics with my friends. We have lots of fun.

Jack: Where do you go on picnics?

Betty: There aren't many good places near here. We usually go to Lake-of-the-Woods.

Jack: What do you take with you?

Betty: We always take a lot of food: bread, meat, tomatoes, potato chips, pickles, fruit, cake, and coffee. We buy a little ice cream and a few cold drinks at the lake. There's a refreshment stand there.

Jack: Are there any boats at the lake?

Betty: Yes, there are some, but we don't use them. None of my friends like to go boating. A few of us play the guitar and we all sing. Sometimes we take off our shoes and go wading. On very hot days we put on our swimming suits and go swimming.

Jack: Is there a charge for swimming?

Betty: Yes, there is, but it's not very much.

Jack: Is there any entertainment at the lake in the evening?

Betty: No, there isn't any entertainment; we entertain ourselves. We always have a good time at Lake-of-the-Woods. My aunt and uncle go with us sometimes and they always enjoy themselves too.

George frequently consults his adviser. This is a conversation between them.

Adviser: Do you need a little help again?

George: Yes, I do. I need some information and some advice.

Adviser: Are you having any trouble?

George: Yes, I'm taking economics with Professor Miller, but I'm not making out[1] very well. I have very little knowledge of mathematics. What do you advise?

Adviser: I advise hard work. Economics is a difficult subject but it doesn't require much knowledge of mathematics.

---

[1] *Make out is a two-word verb which means to succeed.*

1 **Uncountables.** Some things by their very nature are uncountable. Thus the words that name them are also uncountable; they have no plural forms, and they are not preceded by *a/an*.

2 **Categories of uncountables.** The idea of countableness is not the same in all languages, so it is not safe to translate. Particularly words for concrete things made up of small particles, such as hair, grass, and rice, may be countable in your language but they are uncountable in English. The kinds of words which are generally treated as uncountable in English can be roughly classified into four groups. There are examples of each in the model paragraphs.

ABSTRACT	MATERIAL	GENERIC [2]	NON-PLURALS WITH FINAL S
advice	meat	fruit	economics
help	rice		mathematics
information	bread	apparatus	physics
knowledge	cake	equipment	civics
	coffee	machinery	
trouble	ice cream	furniture	mumps [3]
work			measles [3]
	water	mail	
enjoyment	oil	luggage	news
fun		jewelry	
recreation	grass	clothing	tennis
relaxation	hair	money	(and other games)

3 **Quantity terms used only with uncountables**

a. *A little* is used before uncountables in affirmative statements and in questions.

> George needs a little information.
> Does he need a little help?
> Doesn't he want a little advice?

b. *Much* is used mainly in negative statements and in questions.

> We don't have much money but we have a lot of fun.
> Do you have much homework?

---

[2] Generics are wholes composed of dissimilar units.
[3] The diseases are not quite like the other words in these lists but we do say, "There's a lot of mumps going around."

4 **Number agreement.** Verbs used with uncountables are always singular forms. Pronouns used to substitute for uncountable nouns are singular forms.

> Advice *is* cheap but experience *is* dear.
> Opportunity *knocks* but once.
> Virtue *is its* own reward.

> My furniture *is* worn out.
> I need to replace *it*.

5 **Double duty words.** Many words, of course, are either countable or uncountable depending upon how they are used. Very often the meaning of a countable form is quite different from the meaning of the uncountable. Here are a few examples.

UNCOUNTABLE	WORD	COUNTABLE
commerce in general	business	a store or factory
visitors	company	a business enterprise
metal money, coins	change	an alteration
the transparent material	glass	a drinking receptacle
		(pl.) spectacles
the metal	iron	a household appliance for
		smoothing clothing
the material	paper	a newspaper
		a written composition
		(pl.) official identification
space	room	a partitioned area
the beverage	tea	a late afternoon party
exertion, labor	work	an artistic composition: graphic,
		literary, musical
the quality of being young	youth	a young person

6 **Countables** must be preceded by *a/an* to indicate a single instance. For more than one a plural form is used. Most plural nouns regularly end in *s*.

7 **Regular plural forms**

a. Spelling

RULES	EXAMPLES	
1. When the simple form ends in *s, z, ch, sh,* or *x,* add *es.*	box wish	boxes wishes
2. When the simple form ends in *o* preceded by a consonant, add *es.*	tomato mosquito	tomatoes mosquitoes
3. When the simple form ends in *f* or *fe,* change the *f* or *fe* to *v* and add *es.*	leaf wife self	leaves wives selves
4. When the simple form ends in *y* preceded by a consonant, change the *y* to *i* and add *es.*	party library	parties libraries
5. In all other cases add *s* to the simple form.	friend studio day	friends studios days

b. Exceptions—add *s* only

1. When *ch* is pronounced like *k.*	epochs, stomachs
2. When the *-o* word has to do with music—and some other cases.	pianos, sopranos
3. These three *-f* words only. Some others have two plural forms.	chiefs, roofs, handkerchiefs

8 **Irregular plural forms** are few. The ones you are likely to need are the following:

foot	feet	mouse	mice	woman	women	ox	oxen
tooth	teeth	man	men	child	children		

Foreign plural forms

a. A few nouns of Greek or Latin origin retain their original plurals.

analysis	analyses	crisis	crises	phenomenon	phenomena
basis	bases	datum	data	stimulus	stimuli

b. Other common nouns from Latin have gained an English plural without losing the original. Both forms are used. The Latin is the more formal.

formula	formulae	formulas
medium	media	mediums
memorandum	memoranda	memorandums

 No special form for plural

a. *Deer, fish,* and *sheep* do not have special forms. We say *two deer, three fish, four sheep.*

b. *Series* and *means* look and sound like plural forms, but they are also used as singulars: *a series of operations; a means of transportation.*

 Plural-only words

a. Names of some things which are composed of two similar parts are always plural. Some of the most frequently used ones are:

scissors	trousers	glasses
tweezers	pants	spectacles
tongs	pajamas	binoculars

b. Two very ordinary words which have no singular forms are *clothes* and *people.*

12 **Quantity terms used only with plurals**

a. *A few* is used before plurals in affirmative statements and in questions.

> George has a few friends in College Town.
> Do you have a few minutes to spare?
> Don't they have a few boats at the lake?

b. *Many* is used before plurals in all sentence patterns.

> Betty has many friends.
> She doesn't have many relatives.
> Does Jane have many clothes?

13 *Of* follows *many, much, a few,* and *a little* when the nouns they quantify are identified.

> Many of Betty's friends go on picnics.
> They don't spend much of their time studying.
> A few of the serious students take books with them.
> They spend a little of their time studying.

14 **Quantity terms used with both uncountables and plurals**

a. *Some* is used in affirmative statements and in questions. It is not usually used in negative statements.

> We always take some fruit.
> Would you like some bananas?

b. *Any* is used in negative statements and in questions. It does not make a statement negative, however.

> I don't use any sugar.
> Do you want any cream?

c. *A lot of/lots of* are equivalent terms. They look different and they sound different, but they pattern the same way and they express the same meaning. They are used in all sentence types.

> Betty plays a lot of tennis.
> She has lots of fun in summer.

d. *No* indicates the absence of something. It is used to modify singulars as well as plurals and uncountables.

> There is no charge for swimming.
> There are no boats here.
> There is no entertainment at the lake.

15 *Quite* reverses the meaning of some of the above terms. For instance, *quite a little* means a rather large amount, and *quite a few* means a rather large number. *Quite a lot*, on the other hand, often means less than *a lot*.

> Few people go swimming in winter. (practically none)
> A few go in the spring. (perhaps four or five)
> Quite a few go in summer. (a whole beach full)

> few < a few < quite a few
> little < a little < quite a little

16 **Pronouns.** All of the quantity expressions in this lesson, excepting *no,* may be used as pronouns as well. The *of* is dropped after *lot* and *lots.* The pronoun for *no* is *none.*

> The Allens don't have much money but the Bakers have a lot.
> We need some paper. Do you have any?
> George has a few relatives in this country but Sue Liu has none.

17 **More about *the***

NO *THE*	*THE*
a. On first mentioning an unidentified person or thing	**a.** To identify a person or thing just mentioned
I see some boys and girls. ⟶	⟶ The boys are playing baseball.
I have a pen and a pencil. ⟶	⟶ The pencil is broken.
b. Before a singular proper name with or without a title	**b.** Before common nouns referring to specific known persons
Dr. Green is out. ⟶	⟶ The secretary said, "The doctor is out."
We study with Professor Baker. ⟶	⟶ Bill said, "The professor is late today."
c. Before the names of most countries (cf. IV, 7b)	**c.** Before names of countries which contain the words *Union* or *United*
Pierre comes from France. ⟶	⟶ He lives in the U.S.A. now.
Athens is the capital of Greece.	Moscow is the capital of the U.S.S.R.
d. Before the names of states, cities, or towns	**d.** Before one city only
Philadelphia is in Pennsylvania.	The Hague is the capital of Holland.
Boston is in Massachusetts.	
e. Before the names of streets	**e.** Before the common noun *street* when the referent has been specified
Sue Smith lives on Main Street. ⟶	⟶ It is the main street of College Town.
f. Before the name of a language when it is used without the word *language* following	**f.** Before the name of a language when the word *language* follows
Miss Liu speaks Chinese. ⟶	⟶ The Chinese language uses tone.
We are learning English. ⟶	⟶ The English language is spoken in India.
g. Before the names of games	**g.** Before the names of musical instruments
Betty plays tennis.	Mrs. Allen plays the piano.
Bill likes chess.	One of my friends plays the guitar.

Reflexive pronouns

a. *Forms*

PERSON	SINGULAR	PLURAL
1	myself	ourselves
2	yourself	yourselves
3	himself herself itself	themselves

b. *Uses*

1. Reflexive pronouns are used with a limited number of verbs to indicate that the subject and the object have the same referent.

   We entertain ourselves.
   They enjoy themselves.

2. They are also used to emphasize that the action of the verb is performed by the subject rather than by someone else as might be expected from the context.

   None of Betty's friends prepare lunch.
   She prepares it herself.

3. A reflexive preceded by *by* means *alone*.

   Bill usually studies by himself.
   Do you ever go to the movies by yourself?

4. Sometimes it has the additional meaning of *without assistance*. When used in this way it is often preceded by *all*, for emphasis.

   Bill cleans his room all by himself.

19 | **Two-word verbs** used in reference to clothing are the following:

put on (clothes):   dress oneself
take off (clothes):   remove them, undress
wear out (clothes):   use them until they are torn or shabby
try on (clothes):   put on for a very short time to see if they fit and are becoming

Also in this lesson

make out: succeed

20 | **Idioms with go**

a. Go + *ing*-form is a pattern used for expressing participation in an activity for the purpose of recreation.

go boating	go hiking	go riding
go fishing	go climbing	go driving
go wading	go skating	go dancing
go swimming	go skiing	go shopping

b. We also use the expressions *go for a walk, go on a picnic, go to the beach, go to a party.*

Pronunciation helps

a. Pronunciation of regular plurals (cf. II, 18c).

RULES	EXAMPLES
1. When the simple form ends in a sibilant sound, the plural form has one more syllable than the simple form has, and that syllable sounds like the verb *is*.	dishes sandwiches places
2. When the simple form ends in a voiced sound which is not a sibilant, the final sound of the plural form is voiced.	rooms shoes clothes
3. When the simple form ends in a voiceless sound which is not a sibilant, the final sound of the plural form is voiceless.	picnics drinks boats

Imitate your instructor's pronunciation of the examples. Be sure to pronounce the additional syllable after the sibilant sounds. Note that *clothes* has only one syllable.

b. *Irregular plurals.* It is particularly important to pronounce the vowel sounds of irregular plural forms clearly, because it is the vowel sounds which distinguish singular and plural forms. Imitate your instructor's pronunciation, paying particular attention to the contrasts *man* and *men*, *woman* and *women*. Note in the latter word that although the spelling difference is in the second syllable, the pronunciation difference is in the first.

c. *Advice* ends in a voiceless sibilant and *advise* ends in a voiced one. Listen to the difference in the pronunciation of these two words, and note the difference in spelling. *Advice* is a noun; *advise* is a verb.

d. Review the pronunciation of *the* (I, 16e).

22 **Punctuation**

Jack : What do you take with you?
Betty : We always take a lot of food : bread, meat, tomatoes, potato
chips, pickles, fruit, cake, and coffee .

a. Colons

A colon is used between a general statement and a long list of examples.
A colon is used after the name of each speaker when dialogue is
written without the use of quotation marks.

b. Indentation

Note in the model dialogues that none of the speakers' words are
written under their names. This type of indentation, used for play
writing, court reporting, and conversation lessons, greatly simplifies the
reading of dialogue. Use this style of punctuation when writing
dialogue for your assignments.

Exercises

a. Your instructor will read a word. Respond by repeating the word preceded by *a* if it is a countable and *some* if it is uncountable (§ 2).

> Instructor: book   Instructor: water
> Student: a book   Student: some water

1. course	6. place	11. tomato	
2. school	7. lake	12. fruit	
3. tennis	8. food	13. coffee	
4. picnic	9. bread	14. drink	
5. fun	10. meat	15. ice cream	

b. Continue as in exercise a (§ 2).

1. homework	6. luggage	11. chance
2. housework	7. average	12. change
3. assignment	8. privilege	13. mail
4. trouble	9. knowledge	14. information
5. problem	10. intelligence	15. advice

c. Your instructor will give you a generic term. If you can, mention one of the units that compose it. Use the expression *a piece of* [4] (§ 2).

> Instructor: equipment
> Student: A thermometer is a piece of equipment.

1. fruit	5. jewelry
2. furniture	6. clothing
3. mail	7. equipment
4. luggage	8. apparatus

[4] Several of the items may be used more than once.

d. Substitute the given words into the given sentence. Make all the necessary changes. Do not omit *the* (§§ 8, 9, 10).

The weather is fine.

1.	child	6.	old	11.	are
2.	are	7.	men	12.	teeth
3.	big	8.	is	13.	good
4.	fish	9.	small	14.	news
5.	is	10.	mouse	15.	people

e. Complete each of the following sentences with an appropriate expression from the lesson. Be sure to include the sign of the singular, *a/an,* wherever it is necessary (§ 5).

1. An appliance for smoothing clothing is called _____.
2. A party where tea is served is called _____.
3. The novels of Dickens are called his _____.
4. When we write compositions our teachers collect our _____.
5. Another name for spectacles is _____.
6. Visitors are often called _____.
7. A business firm is often called _____.
8. A young man is sometimes referred to as _____.
9. Your official documents of identification are called your _____
10. Beethoven's music is known as his _____.
11. We read the news in _____.
12. We drink water from _____.
13. Another word for alterations is _____.
14. My apartment has only two _____.
15. I can't have company because there isn't enough _____.

f. Answer the following questions using one of the quantity terms as a pronoun (§§ 3, 12, 16).

Instructor: Do you have any beer?
Student: Yes, I have a little.

1. Do you have any cigarettes?
2. Do you have any money?
3. Do you have any spare time?
4. Do you have any good friends?
5. Do you have any relatives in this country?

6. Are there any Americans in this class?
7. Are there any maps in this room?
8. Are there any pictures in this book?
9. Are there some lazy people in this class?
10. Are there some ambitious ones?

11. Is George having trouble with economics?
12. Is he having trouble with English?
13. Are you having trouble with English?
14. Do you have some knowledge of mathematics?
15. Do you have some problems for homework every night?

g. Substitute the given words into the given sentence and make the necessary changes. Include *much* or *many* in your responses (§§ 3b, 12b, 13).

We don't have much homework.

1. spare time	6. need	11. know
2. problems	7. want	12. people
3. trouble	8. advice	13. mathematics
4. friends	9. your advice	14. rules
5. money	10. those things	15. English

h. Continue as in exercise g but include *a few* or *a little* in your response (§§ 3a, 12a, 13).

Betty wants a little water.

1. sugar	6. matches	11. those tomatoes
2. spoons	7. soup	12. that cake
3. potatoes	8. pickles	13. those cookies
4. catsup	9. mustard	14. those delicious sandwiches
5. salt	10. slices of bread	15. ice cream

i. Repeat the sentence read by the instructor and follow it with another sentence about one of the items mentioned in the first (§ 17a).

> Instructor: I have a textbook and a workbook.
> Student: I have a textbook and a workbook.
> The workbook has drills in it.

1. Jack has a gray suit and a brown suit.
2. Bill has a record player and a radio.
3. There is a typewriter and a telephone on Professor Allen's desk.
4. There is a coat hanger and a file cabinet near his desk.
5. His secretary has a red pen and a blue one.

6. There are American students and foreign students in this university.
7. There is a YMCA and a Student Union Building on the campus.
8. There is a main reference room and an undergraduate reference room in the library.
9. A blond girl and a red-haired girl are working at a table in the reference room.
10. A fat boy and a thin lady are picking out their food in the cafeteria.

11. Boys and girls go dancing.
12. Young people and old people go on picnics in summer.
13. Students and professors go to football games.
14. Boys and men go fishing.
15. Girls and women go shopping.

j. Change the following sentences in such a way that you must use a reflexive pronoun in each. Do not change the meaning (§ 18).

> Instructor: No one is with me.
> Student: You're by yourself.

1. Bill studies alone.
2. He cleans his room; no one helps him.
3. He doesn't always use a mirror when he shaves.
4. Sometimes he cuts his face.
5. He should take better care.

6. On Sundays Betty often goes for a walk alone.
7. She always enjoys the walk.
8. On picnics her friends provide their own entertainment.
9. They sing songs for amusement.
10. After swimming they put on their clothes.

11. Nobody washes a cat.
12. Someone has to dress a baby.
13. We must help sick people.
14. No one helps us.
15. We are learning the reflexives without assistance.

k. Answer the following questions with complete sentences (§ 19).

1. When do you put on your pajamas?
2. When do you put on a warm coat?
3. When do you put on your clothes?
4. When do you put on your wristwatch?
5. When do you put on your glasses?

6. When do you take off your clothes?
7. When do you take off your sweater?
8. When do you take off your ring?
9. Do girls take off their wigs in class?
10. When do Betty's friends take off their shoes?

11. Do you usually try on a dress before you buy it?
12. Do you usually try on trousers before you buy them?
13. Do you usually try on socks (stockings)?
14. Do you try on shirts?
15. Do you try on ties?

16. What wears out if we walk a lot?
17. What wears out if we sit a lot?
18. What wears out if we swim a lot?
19. What wears out if we carry a lot of change?
20. What wears out if our shoes don't fit properly?

21. How are you making out in math? [5]
22. How are you making out in chemistry?
23. How are you making out in physics?
24. How are you making out in economics?
25. How are you making out in philosophy?

[5] Instructor: Use subjects you know your students are taking.

24 | **Assignments**

a. Write a ten-speech dialogue (five questions and five answers) between an American student and a foreign student in which the foreign student asks questions and the American student answers them. Give your students names. Include some uncountables and some plural forms. Write simple sentence patterns like those we have studied. Punctuate with colons (§ 22).

b. Write another ten-speech dialogue in which the American student asks questions and the foreign student answers them. Include some expressions of quantity used as pronouns (§ 16).

c. Copy the following paragraph. Write on each blank line *a, an, the,* or *x. X* means that no word is needed.

_____ first time I saw _____ American movie I didn't like it at all. _____ people in the film all seemed strange to me. They spoke _____ English, but it didn't sound like _____ language that I had learned at school. Besides, _____ cars in the picture all seemed too shiny and new, and _____ streets all looked too wide to be real, especially _____ Fifth Avenue in _____ New York. Now that I am living in _____ United States, I like American movies very much.

d. Substitute for the italicized words one of the following expressions: *little, quite a little, few, quite a few.* Make the necessary changes in sentence structure (§ 15).

1. *A rather large number of* students have trouble with economics.
2. It requires *a rather large amount of* reading.
3. George's adviser spends *a rather large amount of* time with him.
4. *Not many* advisers spend so much time with their students.
5. George spends *a rather large number of* hours a week studying.

6. He hasn't *much* hope of passing economics.
7. He doesn't understand *much* of the reading.
8. *A rather large number of* students attend the class.
9. He doesn't know *many* people in the class.
10. He worries *a rather large amount.*

11. Jack spends *a rather large amount of* money on clothes.
12. Bill doesn't spend *much* money on clothes.
13. Jack has *a rather large number of* suits.
14. Bill doesn't have *many* suits.
15. He spends *a rather large amount* on records.

REVIEW V

a. The following statements are all about Bill. We want to know the same things about Jack. Make the information questions that you would have to ask to get that information. The italicized words will determine your question word. (Reread II, 20b).

Instructor: Bill reads *magazines*.
Student: What does Jack read?

1. Bill eats *in the school cafeteria*.
2. He has classes *on Mondays, Wednesdays, and Fridays*.
3. He borrows *Betty's* textbook.
4. He likes the *mathematics* course.
5. He goes *home* on weekends.

6. Bill is taking *chemistry, mathematics, rhetoric, drawing, and P.E.*
7. He is studying for a *B.A. degree*.
8. He studies chemistry with *Betty*.
9. Every evening he listens to *music*.
10. He often thinks about *his mother*.

11. Bill is *downtown* right now.
12. He is *shopping for a tie*.
13. He is looking at *ties*.
14. He is talking to *a salesman*.
15. He is picking out a tie for *a friend*.

b. Precede each of the following with *in, on,* or *at* where appropriate. If none of these is appropriate, just repeat the word.

1. 1941	6. 1441 Broadway	11. home
2. 14th Street	7. the country	12. Sundays
3. 2 o'clock	8. downtown	13. noon
4. Tuesday	9. 4 o'clock	14. June 14th
5. Chicago	10. Japan	15. every day

c. Start with the given sentence and change it to accommodate the words in the list below. Be careful of your use of *the* and of verb forms and phrases.

The boys are playing basketball.

1.	tennis	6.	piano	11.	violin
2.	flute	7.	chess	12.	always
3.	music teacher	8.	the Smiths	13.	drums
4.	baseball	9.	cards	14.	bridge
5.	John	10.	the doctor	15.	now

LESSON

VI

FUTURE: SIMPLE AND CONTINUOUS TIME CLAUSES, ADJECTIVE PHRASES

Mrs. Allen is going to have a party next Sunday. She's going to invite Betty's friends. She's going to invite some of her husband's students too. She is making a list of guests right now. Later today she will write the invitations. Then she'll plan the games and the refreshments.

At this time next Sunday the Allens will be very busy. Mrs. Allen will be preparing refreshments and her niece will be helping her. Mr. Allen will be straightening up the living room and moving furniture. The guests will be arriving. There will be singing and dancing at the party. Everyone will have a good time.

Mrs. Allen is having her party now. Betty is about to introduce the guests. They'll talk for a while and then they'll play games. Let's listen to their conversation.

Betty: Jack, this is Bill Brown. Bill, this is Jack Jones. You're in the same chemistry class.

Bill: How do you do? [1]

Jack: Glad to meet you, [1] Bill. That's a pretty big class. You can't know everybody. Which lab section are you in?

Bill: Section H, at three o'clock. My table is in the back of the room near the assistant's desk.

Jack: I'm in that section too. Mine is the table by the door in the front of the room. That tall girl with red hair works on my right. Do you know her?

Bill: Yes, she's my friend's sister. She's very shy but she's friendly when she knows you. She's coming to the party later. She'll be here in a little while. I will introduce you when she arrives.

[1] *How do you do* and *glad to meet you* are phrases that people say when they are introduced. If you don't know these phrases you should learn them. People expect you to say them when you are introduced.

1 **Verb phrases for simple future.**   There are several ways of talking and writing about the future in English. Some of them can be used interchangeably; a few have specialized meanings in addition to simple future reference.

a. *Be + going to +* simple verb is probably the most common and unambiguous verb phrase used for future. It does not require an accompanying time expression although it may have one. Here are the patterns.

QW	AUX BE	SUBJECT NOUN/QW	VERB PHRASE			COMPLEMENT		
			Aux Be	Going To	Simple	Object	P	T
		Mrs. Allen	is	going to	have	a party.		
	Is	Mrs. Allen	——	going to	have	a party?		
		Who	is	going to	have	a party?		
When	is	Mrs. Allen	——	going to	have	a party?		

b. *Will* [2] *+* simple verb also indicates future. For some people it also suggests an additional idea of promise, determination, or inevitability. It does not require a time expression, but it may have one.

QW	AUX WILL	SUBJ N/QW	VERB PHRASE		COMPLEMENT		
			Aux Will	Simple	Object	P	T
		She	will	write	the invitations		later today.
	Will	she	——	write	the invitations		later today?
		Who	will	write	the invitations?		
When	will	she	——	write	the invitations?		

c. *Be + about to +* simple verb is a less common pattern. It refers only to the immediate future, just after speaking. No time expression is used with this verb phrase although the word *just* is often placed between *be* and *about to*: *We are just about to look at the pattern.*

QW	AUX BE	SUBJ N/QW	VERB PHRASE			COMPLEMENT
			Aux Be	About To	Simple	Object
		Betty	is	about to	introduce	the guests.
	Is	Betty	——	about to	introduce	the guests?
		Who	is	about to	introduce	the guests?
Whom [3]	is	Betty	——	about to	introduce?	
What	is	Betty	——	about to	do?	

[2] British speakers use *shall* in first person (I, we) in preference to *will*. Most Americans do not make this distinction.
[3] Here's a place to use *whom* if you really want to. Most people use *who*.

2 **Present tense for future time.** The presence of a future time expression—word, phrase, or clause—in a sentence whose verb is present indicates that the statement refers to a forthcoming event and not to a customary, repetitive, or ongoing activity (cf. II, 1; III, 1).

a. Simple and *s*-forms

SUBJECT	VERB	COMPLEMENT
		Time (Future)
The Bakers	arrive	tomorrow.
Richard	graduates	in June.
The next meeting	is	a week from today.

b. Continuous present

SUBECT	VERB	COMPLEMENT
		Time (Future)
The Bakers	are coming	tomorrow.
Richard	is graduating	in June.
The conference	is taking place	next month.

3 **Continuous future** (cf. III, 5–7) emphasizes ongoing activity at a very specific time in the future. The time must be expressed in the sentence or in a previous sentence in the same conversation.

QW	AUX WILL	SUBJECT N/QW	VERB PHRASE			COMPLEMENT		
			Will	Be	Ing	Object	P	Time
		Mrs. Allen	will	be	preparing	refreshments		at this time next week.
	Will	Mrs. Allen	——	be	preparing	refreshments		at this time next week?
		Who	will	be	preparing	refreshments		at this time next week?
When	will	Mrs. Allen	——	be	preparing	refreshments?		
What	will	she	——	be	doing			at this time next week?

4 **Future time expressions**

a. Words for future time are *soon, later, tomorrow.*

b. Phrases are numerous. There are many different types.

1. *Next* [4] week, next month, next year, next Friday

2. *In* a little while, in a few minutes, in two years [5]

3. *From now* comes at the end of the phrase: *a week from now, a month from now, a year from now*

4. *The . . . after*: the day after tomorrow, the week after next, the meeting after this one

5. *At* three o'clock tomorrow, at this time next week

c. Clauses are groups of words which function as units in a sentence (cf. II, 12). They have subjects, related verbs, and other sentence parts, and they are introduced by words called by various names in various grammars. We shall simply call them clause markers. The time clauses in this lesson are introduced by *when.*

1. *Sentence pattern with time clause*

SUBJ	VERB	COMPLEMENT				
			Time Clause			
			CM	S	V	C
She	is	friendly	when	she	knows	you.
I	will introduce	you	when	she	arrives.	

2. *Position.* The time clause may also be at the beginning of the sentence, before the subject (cf. IV, 3).

3. *Present verb in future time clause.* Note that the verbs in the time clauses are *s*-forms. Future verb phrases with *will* and *going to* are never used in time clauses.

---

[4] Notice that phrases with *next* are not preceded by *the* or by a preposition.
[5] These phrases refer to future time only when used with future or present verb phrases.

5 **Then: meanings and uses**

a. *Then* [6] is a time word which refers to a time previously mentioned. It usually comes at the end of a sentence.

> Mrs. Allen is going to have a party *next Sunday.*
> Betty will introduce Jack and Bill *then.*

b. *Then* is also a sequence signal, like *next.* When used in this way it comes at the beginning of the sentence.

> Later today she'll write the invitations.
> Then she'll plan the games and refreshments.

c. Note that *then* is not a connective. It does not connect sentences. A sentence beginning with *then* is often joined to a preceding sentence by a connective.

> They'll talk for a while *and* then they'll play games.

6 **Auxiliary *will*** is one of the modals (see XIV, 1b). The modals have no *s*-forms or *ing*-forms. They are always used with other verbs.

a. *Contractions with subject pronouns* [7] are regular and they are the usual forms.

> *I'll you'll he'll she'll it'll we'll they'll*

They never occur in sentence final position.

b. Contraction with *not* is irregular. The form is *won't.*

---

[6] In writing and in speaking be careful not to confuse *then* with *than* or *them.*
[7] See Pronunciation helps, § 11.

7   *You, indefinite.*   The pronoun *you* usually refers to the person or persons being spoken to. Sometimes, however, it refers to no particular person or persons; it just means anyone or everyone. This is mainly a colloquial expression. *You* is not generally used with this meaning in writing except of a very informal nature (see IX, 12a).

> You can't know everybody.
> She's friendly when she knows you.

8   *Which* [8] asks about one or more of a certain group.

> Which lab section are you in?
> Which table do you work at?

What is sometimes used in place of *which.*
Which is more precise but *what* is acceptable.

9   **More about place.**   Observe the following rules for specifying location within a certain area, or in reference to one's self.

RULES	EXAMPLES	
in before front and back	in the front of the room [9]	in front of me
	in the back of the room	in back of me
on before right and left	on the right	on my right
	on the left	on my left

> We drive on the right.
> We pass on the left.

---

[8] Note the spelling of this word. There is another word, *witch*, pronounced in the same way by many people, but it is not much used except on October 31st. If you are curious, look it up in a dictionary.
[9] Many rooms do not have a front and back. It is probably appropriate to use these expressions only in reference to classrooms and lecture halls.

10 **Possessive forms of nouns** end in *s*. They sound just like plurals but in writing they look different because they have apostrophes.

a. Not all nouns have possessive forms. Those that do refer to persons, animals, places, times, or money when followed by the word *worth*.[10]

George's parents   College Town's mayor   a dollar's worth of gasoline
his dog's name   yesterday's newspaper   ten dollars' worth of groceries

We do not make possessive forms of words like chair and table. We say *the legs of the chair* and *the top of the table*.

b. Possessive forms do not always express possession. They express a number of different kinds of relationships between the possessive form and the following noun.

c. Apostrophes are placed according to the following rules:

RULES	EXAMPLES
a. When the base form ends in *s* and it is a plural form, only an apostrophe is added.	the guests' coats the Allens' house two weeks' vacation
b. When the base form ends in *s* and it is a singular form, you may add either just an apostrophe or an apostrophe and *s*.	Jack Jones'[11] coat Jack Jones's coat
c. When the base form ends in any letter except *s*, an apostrophe plus *s* is added, regardless of whether the base is a singular or a plural form.	the assistant's desk Betty's friends men's coats children's voices Canada's resources

---

[10] There are a few other kinds, too, but they are not important to us now.
[11] Many people use this form in writing but pronounce an extra syllable in speech.

11 **Adjective phrases** are phrases which modify common nouns.

a. Form. They consist of a preposition and a noun with or without modifiers (cf. II, 12–15).

b. Order. In contrast to single word adjectives, phrases follow the words they modify.

a *tall* girl *with red hair*

c. Agreement. The verb of a sentence or clause agrees in number with the subject noun which is modified and not with a noun in the modifying phrase.

That *book* of poems *is* mine.
Those *poems* about nature *are* beautiful.

d. *The*. When an adjective phrase limits the meaning of the noun it modifies to one specific instance, the noun is preceded by *the*.

Books are very expensive.
The books for this course are very expensive.

Pronunciation helps

a. Contractions with *will* seem very difficult for some students to pronounce. Check your pronunciation with that of your instructor to make sure it is reasonably like that of a native speaker. *It'll* has two syllables. Other short forms with pronouns have only one. Do not confuse *won't* and *want*. *Won't* rhymes with *don't*.

b. *Will* after nouns is frequently shortened in speech though not in writing. *Jane will come later* sounds like *Jane-l come later.*

c. Wh-words are pronounced with an initial fricative [12] by some people, but many people pronounce them as though they were spelled with initial *w* only. They make no distinction in sound between *wear* and *where*, *weather* and *whether*, *witch* and *which*.

d. Possessive forms of nouns all end with *s* or an apostrophe. The apostrophe does not represent a sound. The *s* is pronounced as in plurals (V, 21). With *s*-ending base words, many people choose the more formal pattern for writing and the less formal one for speech.

They write: *Jack Jones' coat.*   They say: *Jack Jones-is coat.*

[12] A fricative is a kind of blowing sound.

13 Punctuation

Every ⊙

one will have a good time.

Let's listen to their con ⊙
versation.

Jack ⊙ this is Bill Brown.

Glad to meet you ⊙ Bill.

Tell me ⊙ Bill ⊙ which section
are you in?

a. Apostrophes

See § 10c.

b. Hyphens

A hyphen is used at the end of a line to indicate that a word has been broken. Words are divisible only at syllable boundaries and it is sometimes difficult to know just where the syllable boundaries are. If you are not absolutely sure, either look the word up in a dictionary or write the whole word on the next line.

c. Commas

When speech is recorded in which one person addresses another by name, the name is set off from the rest of the sentence by a comma or commas. This kind of statement is called *direct address*.

14 A question about the future.
With so many ways of expressing the future, how does a learner know which to choose?

It isn't easy. In many situations *going to* and *will* are equivalent. In other cases there are subtle differences of which the learner is unaware. It is wise to avoid using present tense for future time (§ 2), as it is not always appropriate. You need to understand it when you hear it, however.

15 Exercises

a. Bob does the following things every day. Tell what he is going to do tomorrow (§ 1a).

1. Bob gets up at 7 o'clock.
2. He takes a shower.
3. He doesn't shave.
4. He puts on his clothes.
5. He doesn't wear a tie.

6. He eats breakfast.
7. He puts on his jacket.
8. He doesn't wear a hat.
9. He rides his bicycle to school.
10. He attends his first two classes.

11. He has a cup of coffee at the Student Union.
12. He meets his girl friend there.
13. They go to the library together.
14. They stay there for an hour.
15. They leave before noon.

b. Tell the class what you are going to do at some other time. Include the given time expression (§§ 1a, 4).

> Instructor: this afternoon
> Student: I am going to go to the bank this afternoon.

1. tomorrow
2. next Sunday
3. later
4. the day after tomorrow
5. next week

6. in half an hour
7. ten minutes from now
8. next year
9. the day after tomorrow
10. later today

11. when I finish this course
12. when the bell rings
13. half an hour from now
14. in three days
15. when I get my degree

c. Repeat the following sentences, using contractions wherever they are appropriate (§§ 1b, 6a, 12).

1. Betty will introduce the boys.
2. She will talk to them.
3. I know she will.
4. They will talk about chemistry class.
5. I know they will.

6. Jack will ask Bill a question.
7. He will ask Bill which section he is in.
8. Bill will answer.
9. I know he will.
10. We will all hear him answer.

11. I will hear him answer.
12. You will hear him answer.
13. Mr. Allen will not hear him answer.
14. Mrs. Allen will not hear him answer.
15. They will be busy.

d. Answer the following questions with short responses (§ 2).

1. Where are you eating dinner tonight?
2. Who are you eating with?
3. What are you doing after dinner?
4. Who are you studying with?
5. Which courses are you working on?

6. Where are you going after class?
7. What are you doing then?
8. What are you doing at 3 o'clock this afternoon?
9. When are you going to the library?
10. When are you writing to your parents?

11. What are you going to do in June?
12. Where are you going to go?
13. Who are you going with?
14. When do you get your degree?
15. What will you do then?

e. Answer the following questions with complete statements. Include the time in your answer. You may put it at the beginning or at the end.

Instructor: What will you be doing at eleven thirty tonight?
Student: At eleven thirty tonight I'll be going to bed.

1. What will Professor Allen be doing at seven o'clock Sunday evening?
2. What will Mrs. Allen be doing?
3. What will Betty be doing?
4. What will the guests be doing?
5. What will you be doing?

6. What will you be studying at this time next year?
7. Which English course will you be taking?
8. Whose class will you be in?
9. Where will you be living?
10. Who will you be living with?

Many people work at night. At midnight tonight

11. What will the bakers be doing?
12. What will the printers be doing?
13. What will the railroad engineers be doing?
14. What will the airplane pilots be doing?
15. What will the serious students be doing?

f. In the following questions *you* means anybody or everybody. Answer the questions using *you* in the same way (§ 7).

1. Where do you pay your tuition?
2. Where do you get your ID card?
3. Who do you see about your schedule?
4. Who do you go to for advice?
5. Where do you go when you're sick?

6. Where do you cash a check?
7. Where do you buy a stamp?
8. Where do you catch a bus?
9. Where do you buy football tickets?
10. Who do you buy them from?

11. What do you do when you miss the bus?
12. Where do you buy tennis shoes?
13. Who do you see for an appointment?
14. When do you find out your grades?
15. Which English course do you take after this one?

g. There are several people pictured on page one of this book. Ask questions about them. Use *which.* Answer the questions.

>Student 1: Which girl has red hair?
>Student 2: Jane.

h. There are quite a few students in this class. Ask your neighbor a *which*-question about one of them. See if he can answer.

>Student 1: Which student is wearing a blue sweater?
>Student 2: Pierre.

i. To each of the following questions make a response which is a word, a phrase, or a clause that indicates some future time (§ 4).

>Instructor: When are we going to have lunch?
>Student: An hour from now.

1. When will we put our homework on the board?
2. When will we have dictation?
3. When will this class be over?
4. When will we have another class?
5. When will we have a holiday?

6. When does the next semester begin?
7. When is it going to get colder?
8. When will it snow?
9. When will it get warmer?
10. When will we have hot weather?

11. When will you get your degree?
12. When will you start to work?
13. When are you going to go home (to your country)?
14. When are you going to get married?
15. When are you going to come back to visit the United States?

j. Tell the class about two things that you usually do in succession. Use the word *then* to begin your second sentence (§ 5b).

> I take a shower when I get up.
> Then I put on my clothes.

k. Add to each of the following sentences a time clause beginning with *when.* Say the complete sentence (§ 4c).

> Instructor: I am going to the movies.
> Student: I am going to the movies when I finish my homework.

1. Mrs. Allen will invite Jack and Bill.
2. Betty will introduce the guests.
3. Jack will meet Bill.
4. They will talk about their chemistry class.
5. Bill will introduce Jane.

6. I am going to read a novel.
7. I am going to learn French.
8. I am going to take a trip to Washington.
9. I am going to buy a camera.
10. I am going to take pictures.

11. Mr.[13] _____ is going to make a lot of money.
12. Mr. _____ is going to buy a new car.
13. Ms. _____ is going to be very famous.
14. Mrs. _____ is going to be very happy.
15. Miss _____ is going to get married.

[13] Instructor: Fill in names of your students.

I. To each of the following sentences, add an adjective phrase which limits the meaning of the word it modifies in such a way that the noun must be preceded by *the*.

> Instructor: Workbooks are unavailable.
> Student: The workbooks for this course are unavailable.

1. Books are expensive.
2. Students are well-prepared.
3. Homework is endless.
4. A teacher corrects errors.
5. Oral exercises are helpful.

6. Windows break easily.
7. Stairs make me tired.
8. A lock is jammed.
9. Chairs are uncomfortable.
10. A lamp is broken.

11. Music is soothing.
12. Plays are entertaining.
13. Novels teach us history.
14. Newspapers tell us the news.
15. Advertisements convince us.

m. Combine each of the following pairs into one sentence by making the second sentence into an adjective phrase which modifies a common noun in the first sentence.

> Instructor: There is a tall girl in my chemistry class.
> She has red hair.
> Student: There is a tall girl with red hair in my chemistry class.

1. The desk is small. It's in the front of the room.
2. The sentence patterns are easy. They are on the blackboard.
3. The lighting is not very good. It is in the hall.
4. The seats are not movable. They are in this room.
5. The windows are dirty. They are on the right.
6. There are three girls in this class. They are from China.
7. Jack likes a girl. She is in his chemistry class.
8. A girl likes him. She is in his math class.
9. Bill reads many books. They are about photography.
10. We use theme paper. It has lines on both sides.
11. Professor Baker is an elderly man. He is from New England.
12. He has an old-fashioned typewriter. It has a loud bell on it.
13. Professor Miller is a young man. He is in his thirties.
14. He gives many free lectures. They are for the townspeople.
15. He is going to give a lecture tonight. It will be on the cost of living.

n. Pronounce the possessive form of each word which has one. If the given word does not ordinarily have such a form, say "no possessive" (§§ 10, 12d).

> Instructor: John   Instructor: desk
> Student: John's   Student: no possessive

1.	horse	6.	car	11.	women
2.	hour	7.	chair	12.	Alaska
3.	man	8.	today	13.	room
4.	month	9.	telephone	14.	shoes
5.	mouse	10.	quarter	15.	shirt

16 Assignments

a. Write a paragraph about what you are going to do next vacation. Tell several details and include the word *then*. Include at least one time clause. Do not use the word *plan*.

b. Write five information questions to ask your classmates about their future activities. Include time clauses in at least two of your questions.

c. Copy the following sentences, filling each blank with *will* or *be going to*. Use *will* for promise, determination, or inevitability.

1. When the professor arrives, the lesson _____ begin.
2. Professor Allen _____ have dinner with a friend this evening.
3. Bill says to Betty: I _____ help you with your math assignment.
4. Jack _____ go home this week end.
5. He is determined he _____ come back Sunday night.

6. I _____ go to Chicago next weekend.
7. I _____ take the train that leaves at 5:20.
8. I _____ arrive in Chicago at 8 o'clock.
9. When I go to Chicago, I _____ buy theater tickets for you.
10. I _____ get the best tickets available.

11. Betty _____ play tennis on Saturday.
12. She _____ win. She always wins.
13. George _____ go swimming on Saturday.
14. He (neg.) _____ go boating.
15. He is sure that he _____ be home by 5 o'clock.

REVIEW VI

a. Substitute the given words into the following sentence. Make only the changes that are necessary.

Mr. Lee writes letters on Sunday afternoons.

1. Mrs.	11. book	21. pair of shoes
2. Smith	12. next week	22. wears out
3. tomorrow	13. buy	23. his wife
4. a letter	14. car	24. needs
5. now	15. every year	25. in a week or two
6. story	16. a month from now	26. a new handbag
7. next month	17. Mr. Jones	27. every season
8. every month	18. station wagon	28. wants
9. reads	19. in two months	29. coat
10. Harry	20. every six months	30. soon

b. Starting with the sentence *Jack is going to go on a camping trip next summer*, compose a paragraph in which you tell what he is going to take, wear, do, and so forth. Tell who is going with him, what they are going to see, and when they are going to come back.°

c. Fill in the blanks in the following story with appropriate expressions. Most of them will be two-word verbs.

Betty plays a lot of tennis. She _____ her tennis

shoes very quickly. Today she is going to _____ for

a new pair. She will _____ several pairs before

she _____ the pair she likes. While she is in the

shoe store she will probably _____ some dancing

shoes, too, but she won't buy them today.

° Instructor: This can be done as an oral exercise with each person in the class contributing at least one sentence.

SIMPLE PAST: REGULAR AND IRREGULAR
WHILE, WHEN, AGO

Bill introduced Jack and Jane at Mrs. Allen's party last Sunday. They talked about their studies and about their hobbies. They sang folk songs while Mrs. Allen played the piano. They played records and danced in the large room in Mrs. Allen's basement. They ate ice cream and drank cokes and had a good time. When the party was over, Jack took Jane home.

George came to this country a year ago. He didn't know much English then but he worked hard and studied every day and now he speaks well and understands everything. He was one of Mr. Allen's best students. He was going to major in history but he changed his mind. He's in sociology now.

The foreign students of this university went on a bus trip to the TVA last spring. They visited several campuses on the way. They stopped in Kentucky and saw the famous racetrack there. They observed experimental farms in the Tennessee Valley and they listened to lectures about farming and soil conservation. They stayed overnight with American families.

1   **Simple past** expresses a one-time completed past event.

2   **Regular past tense forms** end in *ed*. They are made from the simple forms in the following ways:

RULES	EXAMPLES	
a. When the simple form of a verb ends in *e*, only *d* is added.	change dance	changed danced
b. When a one-syllable verb ends in a single consonant (excepting *c, w, x,* or *y*) preceded by a single vowel, the final consonant is doubled and *ed* is added.	plan shop stop	planned shopped stopped
c-ending verbs add *k* before the suffix.	picnic panic	picnicked panicked
c. When a verb of more than one syllable ends in a single consonant preceded by a single vowel, the final consonant is doubled when the final syllable is stressed.	omít occúr	omitted occurred
The final consonant is not doubled when the final syllable is unstressed.[1]	vísit lísten	visited listened
d. When the simple form of a verb ends in *y* preceded by a consonant, the *y* is changed to *i* and *ed* is added.	try hurry study	tried hurried studied
e. All other regular past tense verbs are formed by adding *ed* to a simple form.	look talk stay	looked talked stayed

[1] In British English, *l* in this position is doubled: trável – travelled

3 **Irregular past tense forms** must be memorized because they are not related to simple forms in any predictable way. There are approximately 150 of them in all, and many are among the most frequently used words in the language. In the following lists the less common ones are marked *. These need be learned for recognition only, whereas the others will be needed in everyday speech.

Many irregular past forms differ from the simple forms in their internal vowel sounds only. Others also differ in their final consonant sounds. They are presented here in groups meant to facilitate memorization.

a. **Verbs with no special past tense forms.** The simple forms are used to express both present and past events.

bet	cost	let	set	spread
bid	cut	put	shed	*thrust
*burst	hit	quit	slit	*wed
*cast	hurt	*rid	split	wet

b. **Final consonant change only.** The past forms end in *t*.

Simple	Past		Simple	Past
bend	bent		*rend	rent
build	built		send	sent
*dwell	dwelt		spend	spent
lend	lent			

c. **Vowel and consonant changes.** All the following past forms rhyme though the spellings differ. Note which two are spelled with *a*.

Simple	Past		Simple	Past
bring	brought		*seek	sought
buy	bought		teach	taught
catch	caught		think	thought
fight	fought			

d. Vowel change [i] to [ɛ]

Simple	Past	Simple	Past
bleed	bled	kneel	knelt
breed	bred	lead	led
creep	crept	leave	left
deal	dealt	mean	meant
dream	dreamt	meet	met
feed	fed	read	read [2]
feel	felt	sleep	slept
flee	fled	sweep	swept
keep	kept	weep	wept

e. Vowel change [ɪ] to [ʌ]

Simple	Past	Simple	Past
*cling	clung	stick	stuck
dig	dug	sting	stung
*fling	flung	string	strung
*sling	slung	swing	swung
slink	slunk	win	won
spin	spun	wring	wrung

f. Vowel change [ai] to [au]

Simple	Past	Simple	Past
bind	bound	grind	ground
find	found	wind	wound

[2] Note that the spelling is the same as for the simple form. See Pronunciation helps.

g. Miscellaneous vowel changes

Simple	Past	Simple	Past
come	came	shine	shone [5]
hang	hung [3]	*shoe	shod
hear	heard	shoot	shot
hold	held	sit	sat [6]
light	lit [4]	slide	slid
lose	lost	stand	stood
run	ran	strike	struck
say	said	tell	told
sell	sold		

h. Other irregular past forms

Simple	Past	
lay	laid	} These are irregular in spelling only.
pay	paid	
have	had	} These have each lost a consonant.
make	made	

[3] When *hang* means to put to death by hanging, the past form is *hanged*.

[4] *Light* also has a regular past form *lighted*. Both forms are used. *Lit* is the older form.

[5] This verb is irregular only when it means to send off light, as in *the sun shines*. When it means to polish, as in *John shines his shoes every day,* the past form is regular.

[6] Do not confuse *sit* with *set*. *Sit* means to take a seat. *Set* means to place an object somewhere.

4 **Verbs with special past participle forms.** Soon we will look at some sentence patterns which require the use of past participles. All regular verbs, and all those listed in § 3 above, do not have special participial forms. The past form and the participle are identical.[7] The verbs listed here are the only ones with special past participle forms.

a. Regular vowel changes, [ɪ] to [æ] to [ʌ] (*i, a, u*)

Simple	Past	Participle
begin	began	begun
drink	drank	drunk
swim	swam	swum
ring	rang	rung
shrink	shrank	shrunk
sing	sang	sung
sink	sank	sunk
spring	sprang	sprung
stink	stank	stunk

---

[7] The two exceptions to this statement are *come* and *run*. For these verbs the past participles are identical with the simple forms.

b. *N-ending participles.* All the following verbs have participles ending with the sound [n], though a few are spelled with a final silent *e*.

Simple	Past	Participle	Simple	Past	Participle
awake	awoke	awaken	lie [10]	lay	lain
be	was/were	been	ride	rode	ridden
bear	bore	born/borne [8]	rise [11]	rose	risen
beat	beat	beaten	see	saw	seen
bite	bit	bitten	sew	sewed	sewn
blow	blew	blown	shake	shook	shaken
break	broke	broken	show	showed	shown
choose	chose	chosen	*slay	slew	slain
do	did	done	*smite	smote	smitten
draw	drew	drawn	sow	sowed	sown
drive	drove	driven	speak	spoke	spoken
eat	ate	eaten	steal	stole	stolen
fall	fell	fallen	*stride	strode	stridden
fly	flew	flown	strive	strove	striven
forget	forgot	forgotten	swear	swore	sworn
forgive	forgave	forgiven	swell	swelled	swollen
*forsake	forsook	forsaken	take	took	taken
freeze	froze	frozen	tear	tore	torn
get	got	gotten [9]	throw	threw	thrown
give	gave	given	*tread	trod	trodden
go	went	gone	wear	wore	worn
grow	grew	grown	weave	wove	woven
hide	hid	hidden	write	wrote	written
know	knew	known			

[8] The past participle of *bear* is spelled in two ways, both pronounced the same. When *bear* means to give birth, the past participle is *born;* in other cases it is spelled *borne. George was born in Greece. The expense of his trip to America was borne by his uncle.*

[9] *Got* is used as the participle in British English.

[10] Do not confuse *lie, lay, lain* with *lay, laid. Lie* means to recline on a bed or other surface. *Lay* means to place an object on a surface. The difference is similar to that between *sit* and *set. After class I lay my books on my desk. Then I lie down and take a nap.* However, when *lie* means to tell an untruth, the verb is regular and the past form is *lied* (see § 2a).

[11] Do not confuse *rise* with the regular verb *raise.* Rising is a voluntary movement upward. To raise means to lift something up. *In America students do not rise when the teacher enters the room. On hot days we raise the windows.*

5 **Patterns for past events**

a. With *be* as main verb (cf. I, 2–4), the patterns are the same as those for *be* present, but with past forms. No auxiliary is used with verb *be*.

QUESTION PHRASE [12]	VERB BE	SUBECT NAME/QW	VERB BE (NOT)	COMPLEMENT	
				Noun Phrase	Place Phrase
		George	was	the best student	in Mr. Allen's class.
	Was	George	——	the best student	in Mr. Allen's class?
		Who	was	the best student	in Mr. Allen's class?
In whose class	was	George	——	the best student?	
In which class	was	George	——	the best student?	
		He	wasn't	a good student	in economics.

b. With all other verbs (cf. II, 2–6), the word order is the same as for simple present. In affirmative statements the verbs are past forms. In negatives and questions the auxiliary *do* is a past form, *did,* and the main verb is a simple form.

QW	AUX DO PAST	SUBJECT	VERB		COMPLEMENT		
			Aux Do	Main	O	P	T
		George		came		here	a year ago.
		He	didn't	know	much English		then.
	Did	he		study			every day?
What	did	he		study?			
		Who		helped	George?		

6 *Ago* is used only with the simple past tense. It refers to a specific time in the past, counting backward from the present. It comes at the end of the time phrase instead of at the beginning. *Ago* is the only word that can be used in this way. Do not use *before*.

George came to this country a year ago.
Miss Liu moved to College Town three months ago.

---

[12] The question-word slot can also be filled by a phrase. See X, 4–6.

7 **Time clauses** (cf. VI, 4c) in past time sentences are often introduced by *before, after, while, when.*

a. *Before/after* express a simple sequence relationship.

SUBJECT	VERB	COMPLEMENT				
		Object	TIME CLAUSE			
			CM	S	V	P
George	didn't know	English	before	he	came	here.
He	learned	it	after	he	arrived.	

b. *While/when.* *While* emphasizes the passage of time, duration. It contrasts with *when,* which can refer to punctual action, though in informal language *when* is often substituted for *while.*

C . . .				S	V	. . . C	
TIME CLAUSE						O	P
CM	S	V	C				
While	Mrs. Allen	played	the piano,	Betty	served	the refreshments.	
When	the party	was	over,	Jack	took	Jane	home.

8 ***Was/were going to* + simple verb** is a verb phrase for expressing unfulfilled plans. It is often followed by *but* and an independent clause explaining why the plan was abandoned.

S	V	C	CONNECTIVE
George	was going to major	in history	but
he	changed	his mind.	

9 ***One of*** introduces a noun phrase which includes a plural noun. The *of* indicates that *one* is part of a group.

a. The plural noun is always modified.

> one of my friends
> one of the best students

b. When the phrase is the subject of a clause, the verb form is singular. It agrees with *one*.

> One of the guests *was* late.
> One of the boys *is* playing the guitar.

c. The possessive *of* is used with this type of phrase to avoid an ambiguous construction.

> at the home of one of my friends
> in the office of one of the deans
> for the benefit of one of the children

10 ***None of*** differs from *one of* in two ways:

a. It may be followed by a plural or by an uncountable.

> none of Betty's friends
> none of the food

b. When the phrase is the subject of a clause, the verb agrees in number with the noun which follows *of*.

> None of Betty's friends *like* to go boating.
> None of the food *is* left.

11 *In*, *on*, and *at* again

	RULES	EXAMPLES
a.	*In* often indicates the position of something surrounded.	in the cafeteria in the laboratory in the dormitory
	On often indicates contact with a surface.	the books on the shelf the sentences on the blackboard
	At is often used in expressions of position to indicate proximity.	the blond girl at the table someone at the door

	RULES	EXAMPLES
b.	*In* is also used to indicate one's course of study, profession, or business.	in engineering in government in medicine in commerce

Pronunciation helps

a. Regular past forms

RULES	EXAMPLES	
When the simple form of a verb ends in a *d* or *t* sound, the past form has one more syllable than the simple form has. Listen to the examples and imitate your instructor's pronunciation.	want	wanted
	wade	waded
	omit	omitted
	benefit	benefited
When the simple form ends in a voiceless sound other than *t*, the past form is pronounced with a final *t* sound and the number of syllables in the past form is the same as that in the simple form; i.e., the *e* is not pronounced.	talk	talked
	dance	danced
	work	worked
	introduce	introduced
When the simple form ends in a voiced sound other than *d*, the past form is pronounced with a final *d* sound and the number of syllables is the same as the number in the simple form.	play	played
	change	changed
	study	studied

b. Irregular past forms are characterized by vowel changes. It is very important to master the vowel sounds of the irregular verbs so that you will be understood. Your instructor will go through the lists with you. Ask about any form of which you are not sure.

Some of the irregular verbs have silent letters, i.e., letters which are not pronounced. The main ones are the *k* before *n* (*kneel*), the *w* before *r* (*write, wring*), and the *gh* in *light* and in past forms such as *bought* and *taught*.

A few of the most common past forms seems to be consistently mispronounced by many students. Check your pronunciation against these:

heard rhymes with *bird*   *read* sounds like *red*
meant rhymes with *went*   *said* rhymes with *red*

c. Contractions

Wasn't has two syllables. It is pronounced as if there were a vowel between the *s* and the *n* (waz-int).

Weren't is usually pronounced as one syllable. The second *e* is silent.

Didn't has two syllables. The second syllable does not have a true vowel sound but rather what is called a syllabic *n*. The second *d* is not released. Imitate your instructor's pronunciation (did-nt).

13 Punctuation

While Mrs. Allen played the piano ⊙ the students danced.
The students danced while Mrs. Allen played the piano.

When the party was over ⊙ Jack took Jane home.
Jack took Jane home when the party was over.

When a time clause precedes the subject, it is usually separated from the main clause by a comma. No comma is used when the time clause is placed at the end.

14 Exercises

a. Student 1: Ask your neighbor an information question suggested by the instructor's words. Begin your question with *when* (§ 5b).

Student 2: Give a short response to the question using the word *ago* (§ 6).

> Instructor: arrive.
> Student 1: When did you arrive?
> Student 2: Five minutes ago.

1. graduate from high school
2. apply for admission
3. get your visa
4. say good-bye to your family
5. leave home
6. meet the dean
7. register
8. buy your notebook
9. buy your textbook for this course
10. see your consul
11. get a letter from home
12. eat lunch (breakfast, dinner)
13. have your hair cut
14. buy those shoes
15. learn to dance

b. Change the following sentences to indicate that the action occurred once in the past (§§ 1–3).

> Instructor: I always get up at seven.
> Student: I got up at seven this morning.

1. I take a shower every morning.
2. I don't always shave.
3. I drink orange juice while I dress.
4. I have coffee and rolls for breakfast.
5. I smoke a cigarette after breakfast.
6. I put on my jacket.
7. I pick up my books.
8. I hurry to class.
9. The class begins promptly at eight.
10. I am never late.
11. I read when it is my turn.
12. I answer questions when the instructor calls on me.[13]
13. I write my homework on the board.
14. I take dictation.
15. I usually do quite well.

[13] This item is best changed to the singular for one-time past.

c. Answer the following questions with complete statements. Include time phrases or clauses where they are appropriate (§§ 1–7).

> Instructor: Did you ever visit a zoo?
> Student: Yes, I visited a zoo last summer.

1. Did you ever take a trip on a plane?
2. Did you leave in the morning or in the afternoon?
3. What time did you get on the plane?
4. Did you choose a seat in the front of the plane or in the back?
5. Did you fasten your seat belt when you sat down?

6. Did the hostess hang up your coat?
7. Did she bring you some coffee?
8. Did she offer you any food?
9. Did she make you comfortable?
10. Did you thank her?

11. When did you land?
12. What did you do then?
13. Where did you go?
14. Were you tired?
15. Did you enjoy your trip?

d. Give short responses to the following questions, using contractions where they are appropriate (I, 8 and § 5b).

1. Was it hot (cold) last night?
2. Did it rain?
3. Did it snow?
4. Were there stars in the sky?
5. Were they bright?

6. Who went to a football (basketball, baseball) game last week?
7. Was it a good game?
8. Were there many people there?
9. Did your favorite team win?
10. Was anyone hurt?

11. Did George come to this country five years ago?
12. Did he know a lot of English when he came?
13. Was he a good student in English?
14. Was he a good student in economics?
15. Is he in engineering now?

e. Student 1: Ask your neighbor what field he is in.
Student 2: Answer, using the pattern "I am in _____."
Student 1: Ask your neighbor what his father does.
Student 2: Answer, telling the trade or profession of your father or some other relative.
Practice the pattern "My father is in _____" (§ 11b).

f. Following is a list of simple forms of nouns. State for each the form which must be used after the expression *one of*. Use a possessive pronoun where it is appropriate (§ 9).

Instructor: boy   Instructor: brother
Student: one of the boys   Student: one of my brothers

1.	table	6.	cousin	11.	map
2.	box	7.	room	12.	aunt
3.	man	8.	piece	13.	picture
4.	foot	9.	friend	14.	neighbor
5.	fence	10.	church	15.	eye

g. Look around you and make a statement about something or someone in this room. Begin your sentence with *one of*.

Instructor: One of the windows is open.[14]

h. Using the word given by your instructor, make a simple sentence beginning with *none of* and including the verb *be*.

Instructor: fruit
Student: None of the fruit is ripe.
Instructor: apple
Student: None of the apples are ripe.

1.	equipment	6.	suitcase	11.	news
2.	test tube	7.	umbrella	12.	people
3.	furniture	8.	clothing	13.	advice
4.	chair	9.	sweater	14.	oil
5.	luggage	10.	money	15.	package

[14] Instructor: Make a true statement. Encourage your students to make only true statements.

i. Make a sentence suggested by the two given words. Use *in, on,* or *at* in your sentence (§ 11a).

>Instructor: eat — cafeteria
>Student: I eat in a cafeteria.

1. write – white paper
2. cigarettes – pocket
3. hat – head
4. family – table
5. bus – railroad station
6. study – library
7. stamp – envelope
8. candy – mouth
9. bandage – arm
10. salesman – door
11. swim – pool
12. pencil – floor
13. secretary – desk
14. book – shelf
15. milk – glass

i. Combine each of the following pairs of sentences into one sentence. Do this by changing one of the given sentences into a time clause. This will sometimes require omitting a few words. Choose carefully from *before, after, while,* and *when* (§ 7).

>Instructor: The foreign students visited the TVA.
>Then they stayed overnight with American families.
>Student: After the foreign students visited the TVA, they stayed overnight with American families.

1. Bill picked up the receiver.
   Then he dropped a dime in the coin box.

2. Bill dropped a dime in the coin box.
   Then he dialed the operator.

3. Bill was talking to his mother.
   There was a strange noise in the telephone.

4. Bill called his mother after 9 p.m.
   The charge was less.

5. He talked for three minutes.
   Then he hung up.

6. George came to this country.
   He didn't know how to study.

7. He listened to the radio.
   He studied at the same time.

8. He got a low grade on a test.
   Then he went to his adviser.

9. His adviser told him how to study.
   He listened.

10. Now he studies without the radio.
    He doesn't listen to the radio and study at the same time.

11. We don't listen carefully.
    We don't understand.

12. We listen carefully.
    We understand.

13. Our teacher shows us our mistakes.
    Then we correct them.

14. Bill works in the chemistry laboratory.
    He talks to Betty during that time.

15. Jack does his experiments in the chemistry laboratory.
    He talks to Jane during that time.

k. Tell the class about something that you planned to do but didn't. Be sure that your sentence is complete (§ 8).

> Instructor: I was going to prepare a quiz but I didn't have time.

l. Make an information question from each of the following statements. Substitute question words for the italicized words (§§ 1–5).

1. *Mrs. Allen* had a party last Sunday.
2. Jack met *Jane* there.
3. Jack met Jane *at Mrs. Allen's party*.
4. They *danced* in the basement.
5. Jack took Jane home *after the party*.

6. George came to this country *a year ago.*
7. He spoke *Greek* then.
8. *He* speaks English now.
9. He was *Mr. Allen's* best student.
10. He changed his mind about his major field *after he got here.*

11. The foreign students went to the TVA *last spring.*
12. They went with a *man from the YMCA and a lady from the YWCA.*
13. They saw *the famous race track in Kentucky.*
14. They listened to *lectures about farming.*
15. They stayed overnight with *American families.*

m. *Spelling bee.* Pronounce and spell the past forms of the following verbs.

teach	buy	tear	travel	draw	weave
reach	tie	grow	feed	find	break
choose	sleep	speak	hang	go	come
lose	hold	fall	help	swear	try
drink	light	wear	shake	omit	plan
think	know	take	hide	change	say
win	swing	lie	ride	want	eat
pin	bring	lay	swim	read	throw
build	shoot	die	play	kill	sew
cost	run	work	see	steal	mean

Assignments

a. Write a paragraph of from six to ten sentences telling what you did last Sunday. Include one statement about something you planned to do but didn't. Include at least one time clause beginning with *while*.

b. Write a paragraph in which you describe a trip that you took for pleasure. Tell where you went, who you went with, what you saw, and what you did. Include the word *ago* in your introductory sentence. Use the sentence patterns from Lessons I–VII.

c. Write one statement to explain each of the following situations (§ 9c).

1. You went for a ride in a car.
   The car belonged to one of your friends.

2. You sat and talked in the evening.
   You were in a yard.
   The yard belonged to one of your neighbors.

3. You went to a party.
   It was in a private home.
   The home belonged to one of your professors.

4. At an adviser's suggestion you changed your major.
   The adviser is one of many.

5. You bought a present for a lady.
   She is married to one of your brothers.

6. You borrowed a book about photography.
   It came from a private library.
   The library belongs to one of your professors.

7. A friend of yours married a girl.
   Her father knows your father.
   The two men are friends.
   Your father has many friends.

8. You have two married sisters.
   They each have a son and a daughter.
   You are very fond of one of the boys.

9. You like the work of a certain author.
   His name is John Steinbeck.
   He is an American. He is one of the best authors.

10. You work in a laboratory.
    It is part of this university.
    This university has many laboratories.

REVIEW VII

a. Show the relationship between the pairs of words below by use of an apostrophe form or the word *of*. Make each answer specific by adding *the* where necessary.

> Instructor: table – top
> Student: the top of the table

> Instructor: John – uncle
> Student: John's uncle

1. car – color
2. horse – tail
3. chair – legs
4. book – pages
5. top – box
6. man – gloves
7. wife – Mr. Smith
8. news – today
9. bus – windows
10. book – teacher
11. student – vacation
12. month – journey
13. car – Mr. Jones
14. university – president
15. telephone number – store

b. Substitute the given word or words in the sentence below and make all the necessary changes.

The foreign students went to Tennessee.

1. Chicago
2. a walk
3. a picnic
4. tomorrow
5. skating
6. the day before yesterday
7. September
8. every Saturday
9. have classes
10. right now
11. party
12. every month
13. January 1st
14. will
15. ago
16. Bill
17. two weeks from now
18. home
19. New York
20. fly
21. visit
22. cousin
23. Thursday
24. last week
25. his mother
26. in Westview
27. when she was sick
28. ago
29. right now
30. was going to

c. Fill in the blanks in the following story with appropriate forms of two-word verbs.

John _____ at 7 o'clock yesterday. He _____ his pajamas and _____ his clothes. He _____ a green tie to wear with his brown suit. Then he _____ a telephone number and _____ his friend. He _____ the receiver and dialed the number but there was no answer so he _____.

VIII

USED TO, HAVE TO, EXPLETIVE *IT*
NOUNS THAT MODIFY NOUNS

When George was a very little boy, he lived on a farm in the country. It was his grandfather's vegetable farm and George used to feed the chickens and fill their water pans early in the morning. Then he played in the fields with his brothers until noon. They used to pick blackberries and dig for worms and chase rabbits out of the carrots. After dinner it was too hot to work or play. Everyone took a nap for two or three hours.

It was pleasant to live on the farm but it was impossible for George to stay there after he became old enough to go to school. It was three miles to school and that was too far for George to walk. He had to go to live with his uncle who had a shoe store in town, not far from the school.

1 **Used to** [1] + **simple verb** expresses past custom, habit, or repeated action in the past which no longer occurs (cf. II, 1). Questions and negatives are made with the auxiliary *do*, as in the simple past (VII, 5b).

2 **Patterns for past custom**

QW	AUX DO (NOT)	SUBJECT	VERB (NOTE FORMS)	COMPLEMENT		
				Object	Place	Time
		Who	used to [2] feed	the chickens	on the farm	in the morning?
		George	used to feed	the chickens	on the farm	in the morning.
	Did	George	use to live		on a farm?	
	Didn't [3]	George	use to live		in town?	
What	did	George	use to do			in the morning?

3 **Any more** is an adverbial expression used in negative statements and questions indicating that a condition or situation which previously existed no longer exists. It is often used in sentences with *used to* to show contrast with past custom.

George used to be in Professor Miller's economics class, but he isn't any more.
Doesn't he take economics any more? No, not any more.

---

[1] Do not confuse this phrase with the expression *be used to*. They are entirely different both in pattern and in meaning. (See X, 9.)
[2] See Pronunciation helps (§ 13a).
[3] *Use to* is seldom used in negative statements.

4 *Have to*[4] **+ simple verb** expresses necessity. (See also XIV, 1e.) Questions and negatives are formed with the auxiliary *do*. When *have* is used in this way, it is never combined with any other word in a contraction.

5 **Patterns with** *have to*

a. Affirmative statements

SUBJECT	VERB			COMPLEMENT		
	Aux	Have To	Simple	Object	Place	Time
We		have to	study	English	at home	every night.
George		has to	study	math.		
He		had to	live		in town	when he went to school.
He	will	have to	return		to Greece	when he gets his degree.

b. Negative statements

SUBJECT	VERB			COMPLEMENT		
	Aux + Not	Have To	Simple	Object	Place	Time
We	don't	have to	study	French.		
George	doesn't	have to	study	economics.		
He	didn't	have to	walk	three miles	to school.	
He	won't	have to	stay		in America	after he graduates.

c. Yes/no questions

AUX (NOT)	SUBJ	VERB		COMPLEMENT		
		Have To	Simple	Object	Place	Time
Do	we	have to	study	English	at home	every night?
Does	George	have to	study	math?		
Did	George	have to	live		in town	when he went to school?
Will	he	have to	return		to Greece	when he graduates?

[4] See Pronunciation helps (§ 13b).

d. Information questions

QW	AUX	SUBJ	VERB		COMPLEMENT		
			Have To	Simple	Object	Place	Time
		Who	has to	study	English?		
What	do	we	have to	study?			
What	does	George	have to	study?			
Where	did	George	have to	live			when he went to school?
When	will	he	have to	return		to Greece?	

6 *It* is not always a personal pronoun. Sometimes it is a kind of expletive (cf. III, 11). It doesn't really refer to anything at all; it just fills a position in a sentence pattern.

a. Impersonal *it* is used in statements about time, weather, distance, and identification. Note the following uses of impersonal *it*. Memorize the examples.

TIME
Is it late? No, it's early.
What time is it? It's two o'clock.
What day is it? It's Wednesday.

WEATHER
What's it like out? It's pretty cold.
Is it raining? No, but it looks like rain.

DISTANCE
How far is it to George's school? It's about three miles.[5]
How long does it take to get there? It takes a long time.

IDENTIFICATION
Is that Mr. Allen? Yes, it is. (Cf. I, 3b.)

Someone is at the door.
Who is it? I don't know who it is.

There was a telephone call for you this afternoon.
Who was it? It was Jack Jones.

---

[5] Note that the word *far* does not occur in the answer when the distance is stated.

b. Anticipatory *it* fills the subject position of a sentence which has an adjective and an infinitive [6] in the complement position.

SUBJ	VERB	COMPLEMENT			
It		Adj	Infinitive	Place	Time
It	was	pleasant	to live	on the farm.	
It	was	impossible	to stay	there	while he went to school.

 Very/too/enough

a. *Very* is an intensifier.[7] It strengthens the meaning of the word which immediately follows it. It precedes adjectives and other words referring to time, frequency,[8] quantity, distance, manner, and condition.

George was *very* little.
The school was *very* far from the farm.

b. *Too* [9] does not intensify. It has a more specific meaning than *very*. *Too* is used when some action, either expressed by an infinitive or implied, is impossible as the result of the condition described by the word which follows *too*.

It was *too* hot to work. (It was impossible to work.)
Three miles was *too* far to walk. (It was impossible for George to walk three miles.)

A native speaker does not always express what is impossible but the use of *too* implies the impossibility.

My professor speaks *too* fast. (It is impossible for me to understand him.)
Don't work *too* hard. (Don't work so hard that it is impossible ·for you to enjoy life.)

---

[6] See § 8 and Lesson XVI, 3b.
[7] Classified as an adverb in traditional terminology.
[8] Not all adverbs of frequency are intensified.
[9] Note the spelling. Do not confuse *too* with *to* or *two*. They all sound the same.

c. *Enough* means a sufficient amount. It is used when the action expressed by the infinitive after *enough* is made possible by the situation described by the word which precedes *enough*. A negative statement, of course, has the opposite meaning.

> George was old *enough* to go to school.
> He wasn't strong *enough* to walk six miles every day.

Note that *enough* follows the word it modifies, whereas *very* and *too* precede. *Enough* is also used with nouns, in which case it may precede or follow without any difference in meaning.

> George's uncle had *enough* room in his house for George.
> George's uncle had room *enough* in his house for George.

d. Be very careful in choosing between *too* and *very*. Don't be like the student who said in his farewell speech at his graduation banquet that he had made *too many good friends in the United States.* No one can have too many good friends anywhere, although it might be possible to have too many friends to invite to your house at one time. If you have that many good friends you are a lucky person indeed!

8 **Infinitives which limit.** A unit consisting of the word *to* and a simple verb is called an infinitive. Infinitives are used in many different ways. In this lesson we have examples of infinitives which limit the meaning of the words they follow.

a.

S	V	COMPLEMENT		
		Adj/Adv	Infinitive	Place
It	was	too hot	to work.	
It	was	too far	to walk.	
George	wasn't	old enough	to walk	to school.

b. It is not too hot to play cards or to go swimming or to go on a picnic. It is only too hot to work.

9 **For-phrases which limit.** Adjectives and adverbs are also limited by *for*-phrases; *this lesson is hard for me* (but not for anyone else). When both an infinitive and a *for*-phrase limit the meaning of a word, the *for*-phrase always precedes.

S	V	COMPLEMENT		
		Adj	For-Phrase	Infinitive
These rules	are	easy	for you	to understand.
They	are	hard	for you	to remember.

 Accompaniment. Prepositional phrases beginning with *with* frequently indicate accompaniment. They are placed after an intransitive verb (IV, 10), an object, or a place expression.[10]

S	V	O	(WITH-PHRASE)	P	(WITH-PHRASE)	T
George	lived			in town	with his uncle	many years ago.
He	played		with his brothers	in the fields		when he was young.
He	took	his dog		to town	with him	when he went.
He	took	his dog	with him	to town		when he went.

[10] In literature they are sometimes placed in other positions for special effects.

Nouns that modify nouns

a. When two common nouns occur in sequence, the first one modifies the second. A noun which modifies is usually a simple form, even when the modified noun is plural.[11]

a vegetable farm water pans
a carrot patch duck eggs
a shoe store blackberry bushes

b. Proper nouns which are plural forms are sometimes used in modifying position.

a United States citizen United Nations observer groups

Duration of a condition or activity may be expressed in many ways. Two prepositions frequently used for this purpose are *for* and *until*.

a. *For* introduces a phrase. It is often followed by a cardinal number or by *a*.

for two or three hours for a little while
for six days for a long time

b. *Until* introduces a phrase or a clause. The time stated marks the end of the duration.

until noon until dinner was ready
until dinner time until he ate dinner
until twelve o'clock until his grandmother called him

---

11 You may see some exceptions to this rule, for the pattern seems to be changing. For instance, the library has a *Periodicals Room* and the engineering college has a *Materials Testing Laboratory*. We can still say, however, that it is always correct to use a simple-form noun in modifying position, and that it is frequently wrong to use a plural.

13 **Pronunciation helps**

a. *Use to* is pronounced as one word with voiceless *s* (as in the noun *use*) and a reduced vowel in *to*. *Used to* and *use to* sound exactly the same. Imitate your instructor's pronunciation of the following phrases:

used to say	used to do	used to smile
used to see	used to be	used to laugh

b. *Have to* also has a special sound. The *have* of *have to* sounds like *half* and the *o* of *to* is somewhat reduced. Imitate your instructor's pronunciation of the following phrases:

have to breathe	have to sleep	have to come
have to eat	have to grow	have to go

c. **Nouns in sequence.** When one noun modifies another, the stronger stress is on the first. Listen to your instructor pronounce the following examples.

végetable farm	fárm house	dúck eggs
chícken feed	shóe store	bláckberry bushes

14 Exercises

a. Student 1: Ask your neighbor about his habits before he came to the United States and about his habits now.

Student 2: Answer the question with a complete sentence (§ 2).

Instructor: do on Sundays
Student 1: What did you use to do on Sundays and what do you do now?
Student 2: I used to visit my friends on Sundays, but I study now.

1. get up
2. eat for breakfast
3. drink for breakfast
4. wear to school
5. live with
6. do in summer
7. do on holidays
8. do for exercise
9. go on vacation
10. do for relaxation
11. eat for a snack
12. watch on TV
13. study with
14. write letters
15. go to bed

b. Student 1: Ask your neighbor about what he has to do.

Student 2: Give a negative answer. Do not give a short response (§ 5).

Instructor: hand in a report
Student 1: Do you have to hand in a report?
Student 2: No, I don't have to hand in a report.

1. make your bed
2. cook your meals
3. wash your dishes
4. do your own laundry
5. clean your room
6. get up at six
7. write up your experiments
8. take P.E.
9. write to your girl friend
10. get your visa extended
11. have an ID card
12. look up many words
13. go to the hospital
14. take an entrance exam
15. shave every day

c. Tell the class about something that you used to do but you don't do any more. Be sure to use the term *any more* in your statement.

I used to go dancing a lot, but I don't any more.

d. Answer the instructor's questions with complete sentences (§ 5).

1. Before you came to this country, did you have to fill out an application form?
2. Did you have to obtain a visa?
3. Did you have to show proof of funds?
4. Did you have to request a housing assignment?
5. Did you have to advise the school of your date of arrival?

6. Before you started classes, did you have to prepare your study schedule?
7. Did you have to have your schedule approved?
8. Did you have to register?
9. Did you have to pay fees?
10. Did you have to get an ID card?

11. When you started classes, did you have to find the right lecture rooms?
12. Did you have to learn your teachers' names?
13. Did you have to buy the textbooks for your courses?
14. Did you have to get notebooks and pens and pencils?
15. Did you have to find out where the library is?

e. Ask and answer questions about the following. Be sure to use the expletive *it* and the idioms [12] from the lesson (§ 6).

1. the day of the week
2. the time of day
3. the weather today
4. the weather yesterday
5. the climate of a country
6. the distance to a country
7. the length of time necessary to travel to a country
8. the distance from campus to a student's room
9. the length of time to go there
10. the distance from New York to San Francisco

---

[12] An idiom is a special way of saying something which does not fit a usual pattern.

What questions would you ask in the following situations?

11. You want to know who is on the telephone.
12. You want to know who is at the door.
13. You want to know the time.
14. You want to know the day of the week.
15. You want to know about the weather.

f. Express the following ideas in good idiomatic sentences which include *very* or *too* (§ 7).

> Instructor: This exercise is important.
> Student: This exercise is very important.
>
> Instructor: We must not omit this exercise.
> Student: This exercise is too important
> to omit.

1. It is hot today.
2. It is impossible to work today because of the heat.
3. It is cold in Canada in September.
4. It is impossible to go swimming there then.
5. It is impossible to swim across Lake Michigan because of its size.

6. George is a good student.
7. He works hard.
8. His adviser is busy. He can't see George until Friday.
9. George comes from a large family.
10. His little brother is only ten. He can't go to college yet.

11. Most foreign students aren't happy when they first come here.
12. They are homesick.
13. They think that Americans work hard and do not play enough.
14. They learn American ways quickly.
15. They make many friends while they are here.

g. Express the following ideas in sentences which include the word *enough* (§ 7).

> Instructor: Bill can drive fast.
> He'll get there in time.
> Student: Bill can drive fast enough to get there in time.

1. Richard has many credits. He will graduate in June.
2. Bill has some money. He can go home this weekend.
3. Jack studied thoroughly. He got an A in his chemistry quiz.
4. Betty wasn't well. She couldn't go to the ball game on Saturday.
5. Mrs. Allen is very pretty. She could win a beauty contest.
6. Professor Baker makes a lot of money. He drives a Mercedes.
7. Professor Miller doesn't make much money. He doesn't drive a Mercedes.
8. One semester is not very long. You can't learn a language in that time.
9. Ten minutes is plenty of time for a quiz.
10. Our instructor doesn't have much paper. He can't give everyone a piece.
11. Betty didn't finish her assignments. She didn't have time.
12. Bill doesn't play his radio loud. It doesn't disturb the other boys in the house.
13. Jack wants to invite Jane to a dance. He doesn't have the necessary money.
14. Richard can vote. He is twenty-three.
15. Mr. Allen has a lot of work. It will keep him busy for a long time.

h. Combine each of the following pairs of sentences into one sentence which includes *too, very,* or *enough* limited by an infinitive. When it is appropriate, include a *for*-phrase as well.

> Instructor: Sue's suitcase was heavy. She couldn't carry it.
> Student: Sue's suitcase was too heavy for her to carry.

1. An unabridged dictionary is large. You can't lift it.
2. A pocket dictionary is small. You can carry it.
3. This book is difficult. I can't understand it.
4. The exercises are easy. Anyone can do them.
5. Five a.m. is early. Some students get up then.

6. Two a.m. is late. Some students go to bed then.
7. The radio is turned low. I can't hear it.
8. It is dark here. I can't read.
9. The paper is thin. It is hard to write on it.
10. This cardboard is thick. It is hard to cut.
11. A Mercedes is expensive. A student can't buy one.
12. A Volkswagen is small. You can park it anywhere.
13. Michael Miller is young. He is a professor, however.
14. Professor Allen is young. He can't retire.
15. Professor Baker is old. He can retire.

i. Add a phrase which expresses accompaniment to each of the following sentences. Be sure to put it in an appropriate position in the pattern (§ 10).

> Instructor: I played tennis this afternoon.
> Student: I played tennis with Mr. Brown this afternoon.

1. George used to play in the fields when he was very little.
2. He went to school when he got older.
3. He didn't take his dog to school.
4. He doesn't live in Greece now.
5. He lives in College Town.

6. Bill often goes to concerts on Friday evenings.
7. He spends most weekends in Westview.
8. He usually gets a ride to Westview.
9. Sometimes he takes Betty when he goes home.
10. Occasionally his roommate goes.

11. Mrs. Allen usually goes to church on Sunday.
12. Betty often goes too.
13. Jack doesn't; he goes to a different church.
14. George goes to the Greek church.
15. After church Mrs. Allen usually goes for a walk.

j. What do we call the following? Answer by giving the noun and its modifiers. Be careful to distinguish singular and plural (§ 11).

> Instructor: a farm where vegetables are grown
> Student: a vegetable farm

> Instructor: stores where shoes are sold
> Student: shoe stores

1. cream that we put in our coffee
2. soup that has vegetables in it
3. salad made of different kinds of fruit
4. watches that we wear on our wrists
5. coats that are worn in winter
6. a lamp that we use on a desk
7. a table that is placed beside a bed
8. a radio that is placed on a table
9. a camera that takes moving pictures
10. covers that we put on books
11. a book from which we study history
12. a factory that produces dresses
13. glass that is used for making windows
14. a ticket that we need to ride on a bus
15. cups that are made of paper

k. Make the following word groups into time phrases or clauses by preceding each with *until* or *for*, whichever is appropriate (§ 12).

1.	three hours	6.	Monday	11.	Friday night
2.	two o'clock	7.	twenty minutes	12.	two weeks
3.	several days	8.	a short time	13.	a few days
4.	next week	9.	this evening	14.	quite a while
5.	George comes	10.	half an hour	15.	we understand

15 Assignments

a. Write a paragraph in which you tell about some of the things you used to do and some of the things you had to do when you were a child.

b. Write a paragraph about the climate of your country. Use *it* as a function word and include the words *very, too,* and *enough.*

REVIEW VIII

a. Repeat and complete the following fragments with the information given. Use only present-form verbs, not past (VII, 9).*

> Instructor: One of Professor Allen's students . . . (sick)
> Student: One of Professor Allen's students is sick.

1.	One of George's grandfathers . . .	(farm)
2.	One of George's brothers . . .	(Greece)
3.	One of George's uncles . . .	(shoe store)
4.	One of Professor Allen's nieces . . .	(live with him)
5.	One of Jane's teachers . . .	(write books)
6.	One of Bill's parents . . .	(Westview)
7.	One of the librarian's duties . . .	(helping students)
8.	One of the cashier's jobs . . .	(making change)
9.	One of Betty's favorite places . . .	(Lake-of-the-Woods)
10.	One of the girls in the story . . .	(red hair)
11.	One of the boys in the story . . .	(glasses)
12.	One of the professors in the story . . .	(teach chemistry)
13.	One of Mrs. Allen's friends . . .	(paint pictures)
14.	One of Bill's brothers . . .	(doctor)
15.	One of Jack's uncles . . .	(lawyer)

b. Substitute the word that your instructor gives for a similar term in the original sentence and make the necessary changes in verb tenses. Be sure that each sentence is complete.

> Jack watches TV in the evening.

1.	every	6.	doesn't	11.	going to
2.	Monday	7.	seldom	12.	right now
3.	yesterday	8.	right now	13.	in a little while
4.	twice a week	9.	about to	14.	until
5.	very often	10.	when he finishes	15.	frequently

---

* Instructor: Listen carefully for all the *s*'s: . . . Allen's students *is*

c. Same as b above.

Betty washes her hair once a week.

1. Saturdays
2. last night
3. the day after tomorrow
4. about to
5. was going to

6. twice a month
7. used to
8. before she went to the party
9. always
10. last Tuesday

11. next Saturday
12. have to – quite often
13. right now
14. isn't
15. always – herself

CONTINUOUS PAST
COMPOUND SENTENCE PATTERNS
ADJECTIVE CLAUSES

Saturday was a very busy day at the dormitory where Jack lives. The boys were preparing for their annual Parents' Day celebration. Everyone who lives in the dorm had to participate. Each boy had a special job to do; no one was excused. When Betty walked past the dorm in the morning, one boy was holding a ladder and another was painting "WELCOME" on a sign over the front door. The others were working inside. Some were decorating the dining hall and others were planning entertainment. Jack was working with the decorating committee and his roommate was, too. He didn't know much about decorating and his roommate didn't either, but they learned from the other boys who were on the committee with them.

Many of the boys' parents visited the dorm on Sunday and enjoyed the celebration. The ones who didn't come this Sunday will visit their sons on another Sunday. Sunday is the only day when parents visit their sons. Jack's roommate's parents are going to come next Sunday, but there won't be any entertainment then.

1   **Continuing past action** is expressed by a verb phrase made from a past form of *be* plus an *ing*-form (cf. III, 1). The resulting tense has many names. We shall call it the *continuous past*.

2   **Time expression essential.** Sentences having continuous past verb phrases must also include expressions of specific time, unless the time has already been expressed in a previous sentence. The time expression may be at the beginning or at the end of the sentence.

T	S	V	O	P	T
	The boys	were decorating	the dorm		all day Saturday.
	One boy	was painting	a sign	on the door	when Betty passed.
While they were decorating,	Bill	was studying		in the library.	

3   *While* **and** *when* **again** (cf. VII, 7b). Remember that *while* suggests a period of time whereas *when* is usually used in relation to a punctual activity, one which takes very little time. Thus *while* often introduces clauses having continuous tenses, as these stress duration.

4   **Patterns for continuous past sentences** are exactly the same as those for continuous present (III, 5–7) except that they must include time expressions, as explained above. Non-action verbs which do not occur in continuous present are not used in continuous past either (III, 8).

5   **New patterns for compound sentences** (cf. II, 11). When two statements have different subjects but the same predicates, they are sometimes combined to make a compound sentence. The predicate is reduced to the first auxiliary of the verb phrase.

a. *Too* is added when the statements are affirmative.

CONN	S	V	P	TOO
	Jack	was working	in the dorm	
and	his roommate	was	. . .	too.

b. *Either* is added when the statements are negative.

CONN	S	V	C	**EITHER**
and	Jack his roommate	didn't know didn't	about decorating . . .	either.

c. *Do* is the auxiliary used when the original verb is a simple present or past form.

CONN	S	V	P	TOO
and	Bill George	lives does	in a private room . . .	too.

CONN	S	V	O	T	TOO
and	Jack's father his mother	visited did	campus . . .	on Sunday	too.

d. *Used to* and *have to* are also replaced by *do*.

CONN	S	V	P	T	TOO
and	George his brothers	used to play did	in the fields . . .		too.
and	He his classmates	has to work do	in the laboratory . . .	now	too.

e. *But* is the connective when the predicates contrast, affirmative and negative. Nothing follows the second verb.

CONN	S	V	C
but	Jack and his roommate the other boys	didn't know did.	about decorating
but	Jack's father his roommate's father	came didn't.	on Sunday

6 **So and *neither*** are sometimes used instead of *too* and *either*, but the sentence pattern is completely different. These words immediately follow the connective and the word order of the second clause is inverted.

BASIC WORD ORDER			CONN	INVERTED	
S	V	C		V	S
Jack	was working	with the committee	and so	was	his roommate.
Jack	didn't know	about decorating	and neither	did	his roommate.

7 **Clauses that modify nouns/pronouns.**[1] In a previous lesson (VI, 11b) we learned that phrases which modify nouns immediately follow the nouns they modify. Nouns and their substitutes are also modified by clauses. There are different types. Note these examples from the model paragraphs.

a. The clause has a clause marker and a subject.

N/P	MODIFYING CLAUSE		
	Clause Marker	S	V
the dorm	where	Jack	lives
the day	when	parents	visit

b. The clause marker is also the subject of the clause.

N/P	MODIFYING CLAUSE			
	S/CM	V	P	T
everyone	who	lives	in the dorm	
the other boys	who	were	on the committee	
the ones	who	didn't come		last Sunday

8 ***The*** again. When a modifying clause limits the referent of a modified noun to one specific identified instance, the noun is preceded by *the*.

	S	(MODIFIER)	V	C
General:	Any dorm	where boys live	is	noisy.
Specific:	The dorm	where Jack lives	is	noisy.

[1] These are sometimes called adjective clauses.

9 *Each/every/all*

a. *Each* directs attention to the separate members of a group.

Each boy had a special job to do.

b. *Every* emphasizes the unity of the group. The members have something in common.

Every boy had to participate.

c. *Each* and *every* are singular. They are followed by singular nouns and singular verb forms.

Each boy has his special job to do.
Every boy has to participate.

d. *All* means whole, entire. It stresses completeness. It is used before plurals and uncountables. The verb form agrees with the noun which follows *all*.

All (of) [2] the boys work hard.
All (of) the work is done in one day.

e. *Not all* means part.

Not all (of) the boys were on the committee.
Not all (of) the parents visited the dorm.

10 **Compound words** are formed from *some, any, no* (V, 14) and *every*.

someone	anyone	no one [3]	everyone
somebody	anybody	nobody	everybody
something	anything	nothing [4]	everything
somewhere	anywhere	nowhere [4]	everywhere

---

[2] *Of* is optional.
[3] *No one* is always written as two separate words, but it patterns as a compound (cf. XV, 9b).
[4] See Pronunciation helps (§ 14).

Any again. Besides being an expression of quantity (V, 14), *any* may mean *it doesn't matter which or who*. This is the usual meaning of *any* when it occurs in affirmative statements.

Parents may visit their sons any Sunday.
Any father may visit his son's room.
Anyone can learn to decorate.

12 **One** is a cardinal number, but it also has other uses.

a. The indefinite personal pronoun *one* means any person or every person (cf. VI, 7). This use of *one* is quite formal. You will see it in writing and hear it in lectures, but it is seldom used in conversation.

One must eat to live.
One can't know everything.

b. To avoid repetition, *one* is often substituted for a noun or a noun phrase. When used in this way, it has a plural form *ones*.

The dorm where Jack lives has *an annual Parents' Day celebration*.
Not every dorm has *one*.

Many of the boys' *parents* visited the dorm on Sunday.
The *ones* who didn't will visit another time.

c. **Ones** is not used immediately following plural demonstratives, quantity expressions, or possessives. It is used when another modifier stands between. Observe the examples.

Salesman:	Do you need any ties?
Bill:	Yes, I need two.
Jack:	I need a couple too.
Salesman:	Do you like this one?
Bill:	No, I don't like that one but I like this one.
Salesman:	Do you like these?
Jack:	I like the brown ones but I don't like the blue ones.
Salesman:	How about these gray ones?
Betty to Jane:	Do you like Bill's new ties?
Jane:	I like his gray one but I don't like his brown ones.

13 *Other* is both an adjective and a pronoun.

a. As an adjective it has two forms: *another* before singular nouns, *other* before plurals and uncountables.

another boy	other boys	other advice
another day	other days	other information

b. As a pronoun it replaces singulars with *another* and plurals with *others*.

S	V	O
One boy	was holding	a ladder,
another	was painting	a sign,
others	were planning	entertainment.

c. *The other/the others* refer to the remaining one/ones of a group.

> ... the other boys on the committee (all except Jack)
> ... the others were working inside (all except those at the door)

d. Never use *the* before *another*.

14 **Pronunciation helps**

a. The compound words (§ 10) are all stressed on the first syllable.

> sómeone ányone nó one éveryone

b. Compounds with *no* all have the full vowel excepting *nothing*. The *o* of *nothing* sounds like the *u* in *nut*.

c. Be careful in reading *nowhere* to remember that the *w* belongs to *where* and not to what precedes it.

15 Punctuation

The dorm where Jack lives is large.
Everyone who lives there is a student.
The day when parents visit is Sunday.

Note that there are no commas in these sentences. Adjective clauses of the types in this lesson are never separated from the rest of the sentence by any mark of punctuation.

16 Avoid this common error.

When using a clause to modify a noun, be careful not to include an object or place which the clause marker represents.

This is a new watch.   My uncle bought (it) for me.
This is the new watch (which) my uncle bought   for me.

Smith Hall is a dorm.   Jack lives (there.)
Smith Hall is the dorm (where) Jack lives.

17 Exercises

a. Combine each of the following pairs of sentences into one sentence including a time clause beginning with *while* or *when*. All of the sentences can be done at least two ways. Be careful in your choice of clause marker (§ 3).

> Instructor: I was taking a shower. The phone rang.
> Student 1: While I was taking a shower, the phone rang.
> Student 2: I was taking a shower when the phone rang.
> Student 3: The phone rang while I was taking a shower.

1. Jack and Jane were walking home from school. It began to rain.
2. George was talking to Mrs. Allen. Betty got home.
3. Jack was sleeping. His roommate returned.
4. Someone called Bill on the telephone. He was taking a shower.
5. Betty's escort arrived. Betty was waiting.

6. Mrs. Allen was peeling potatoes. She cut herself.
7. Mr. Allen was reading the Sunday newspaper. He fell asleep.
8. Jane was waiting for a bus. One of her friends came along with a car.
9. My roommate turned the radio on. I was reading a magazine.
10. Betty slipped and fell. She was playing tennis.
11. Professor Baker was working in his garden. His wife called him to lunch.
12. Professor Miller was washing his car. He noticed a scratch on it.
13. Mr. Jones was playing golf. He lost his watch.
14. Jack was watching TV. He got a headache.
15. I was trying to finish the exam. The bell rang.

b. Student 1: Ask your neighbor what he was doing at a specific past time. Mention the hour and the day.

Student 2: Answer the question. Include the time, for practice. Put the time at the beginning of your statement (§§ 1, 2).

> Student 1: What were you doing at 6:30 this morning?
> Student 2: At 6:30 this morning I was sleeping.

c. Student 1: Ask your neighbor what he was doing when another action took place.

Student 2: Answer the question. Include the time in your sentence also (§§ 1–4).

> Student 1: Where were you living when you bought that car?
> Student 2: When I bought this car, I was living in London.

d. Combine each of the following pairs of sentences into one compound sentence using the connective *and* and completing your sentence with *too* or *either* when appropriate. Make the necessary changes in the second part of your sentence (§ 5).

1. Jones is studying engineering. Smith is studying engineering.
2. Jones doesn't take calculus. Smith doesn't take calculus.
3. Jones isn't going to graduate this year. Smith isn't going to graduate this year.
4. Jones likes music. Smith likes music.
5. Jones has a tape recorder. Smith has a tape recorder.

6. New York is a large state. Texas is a large state.
7. New Jersey isn't very large. Massachusetts isn't very large.
8. Illinois is a farm state. Iowa is a farm state.
9. Oregon is on the west coast. California is on the west coast.
10. Nevada isn't heavily populated. Arizona isn't heavily populated.
11. The *New York Times* is an excellent newspaper. The *London Times* is an excellent newspaper.
12. Businessmen read the *Wall Street Journal*. Stockbrokers read the *Wall Street Journal*.
13. Literary magazines don't contain many pictures. *The Reader's Digest* doesn't contain many pictures.
14. *Time* is a news magazine. *Newsweek* is a news magazine.
15. TV stations carry a lot of advertising. Radio stations carry a lot of advertising.

e. Using the items in exercise d, give the pattern with *so* or *neither* (§ 6).

f. Make one complex sentence from each of the following pairs. Construct your sentence in such a way that the information in the second sentence becomes a clause which modifies and specifies a noun in the first one. Use *where* and *when* as clause markers. Make the necessary changes in the articles (§§ 7a, 8).

> Instructor: Smith Hall is a dormitory. Jack lives there.
> Student: Smith Hall is the dormitory where Jack lives.

1. Mr. Smith just bought a rooming house. Bill Brown is living there.
2. There is a swimming pool. Betty goes swimming there.
3. The College Shop is a clothing store. Bill buys his ties there.
4. Chicago is a city. Jack was born there.
5. This is a classroom. We practice English here.

6. Sunday is a day. Parents visit their sons then.
7. Thursday is a weekday. Bill doesn't have classes.
8. Three o'clock is a time. The boys have their chemistry class then.
9. April is a month. Flowers begin to bloom then.
10. Summer is a season. People go on picnics then.

11. Westview is a town. Mrs. Brown lives there.
12. Seven o'clock is a time. Jack gets up then.
13. This is a chemistry laboratory. The students do their experiments here.
14. June is a month. Richard will graduate then.
15. Lincoln Hall is a large building. We take our placement exams there.

g. Here are some simple sentences about the people in the model paragraphs. Make complex sentences of them by adding to each a clause beginning with *who*. Don't forget to change the articles (§§ 7b, 8).

> Instructor: Jack is a student.
> Student: Jack is the student who likes movies.

1.	Mr. Allen is a professor.	(English)
2.	Mrs. Allen is a nice lady.	(party)
3.	Mr. Miller is a professor.	(economics)
4.	Mr. Baker is a professor.	(chemistry)
5.	George's grandfather is an old man.	(used to – farm)
6.	George's uncle is a businessman.	(shoe store)
7.	George's adviser is a young man.	(helped George)
8.	George is a bright boy.	(Greece)
9.	Jack is a happy-go-lucky boy.	(dorm)
10.	Jack's roommate is a blond boy.	(decorating committee)
11.	Bill is a serious student.	(private room)
12.	Richard is a senior.	(graduates in June)
13.	Betty is an active girl.	(tennis)
14.	Jane is a tall girl.	(red hair)
15.	Mrs. Brown is a woman.	(Westview)

h. Suppose that you are shopping for sport shirts. Tell the clerk what you want by substituting the given words into the following sentence. Use a form of *one* wherever it is appropriate (§ 12).

> I want this one.

1.	that	6.	those	11.	four
2.	the green	7.	the brown	12.	the expensive
3.	two	8.	several	13.	a three-dollar
4.	these green	9.	a few	14.	two short-sleeved
5.	a large	10.	some blue	15.	this

i. Give a negative response to the instructor's question. Include the word *another* as a modifier (§ 13a).

> Instructor: Is that the tie that Betty picked out?
> Student: No, she picked out another tie.

1. Is that the shirt you bought in the College Shop?
2. Is that the suit you are going to wear tonight?
3. Is that the only pair of shoes you have?

4. Is that the dorm where Jack lives?
5. Is this the restaurant where we're going to eat?
6. Is this the church where Mrs. Allen goes on Sundays?

7. Are we going to take this bus?
8. Are we going to the art museum?
9. Are we going to Central Park?

10. Does Harry go to City College?
11. Does Bill's brother go to Westview School?
12. Does Jack's uncle work in the First National Bank?

13. Does Jane live all by herself?
14. Did Jack take Jane to the movies last night?
15. Is George the only foreign student you know?

j. Change the following sentences so that some form of *other* is used as a pronoun (§ 13b).

> Instructor: Some parents came; other parents didn't.
> Student: Some parents came; others didn't.

1. The first two lessons are short; the other lessons are long.
2. This exercise is easy; some of the other exercises are hard.
3. Do the first ten problems; don't do the other problems.
4. Jack answered some of the questions; he didn't answer the other questions.
5. Some students have classes on Saturdays; other students don't.
6. I bought a newspaper in the morning; I bought a newspaper in the evening.
7. There were pictures on the front page; there was one on page four.
8. I heard one report on the radio; I heard a different report on TV.
9. One reporter blamed the driver; one blamed the pedestrian.
10. Some people believe the radio report; some believe the TV report.

11. Some drivers are careful; some drivers aren't.
12. Some pedestrians watch the traffic; some don't.
13. Some cars have good brakes; some cars don't.
14. Some accidents could be prevented; some accidents couldn't.
15. Some people obey traffic regulations; some people don't.

k. Use *the other* or *the others* to indicate the remaining items of a group (§ 13c).

> Instructor: One of my two sisters is married. (single)
> Student: The other is single.

1. One of my two dogs is a terrier. (hound)
2. Two of my five fish are mollies. (goldfish)
3. One of my two cats is male. (female)
4. Two of my three birds are parrakeets. (canary)
5. My niece has a pony. One of its feet is white. (brown)

6. All my five cards are red. Three are hearts. (diamonds)
7. All my five cards are black. Four are spades. (clubs)
8. One of my two cards is a king. (queen)
9. Only four of my thirteen cards are black. (red)
10. I have two packs of cards. One is on the table. (drawer)

11. One of the four tennis courts is occupied. (free)
12. Two of the free ones are concrete. (clay)
13. Two of these three rackets are in good shape. (broken)
14. Jack won two out of four games. (lost)
15. Tennis is the only game Betty likes.

18 **Assignments**

a. Copy the following sentences, filling each blank with *each, every, all,* or a compound of *every* (§ 9).

1. _____ student in this class has a special assignment.
2. _____ student must hand in a paper on Friday.
3. When _____ the papers are in, we will have a quiz.
4. The instructor discussed errors with _____ student individually.
5. Then he asked _____ to write a paragraph.
6. _____ the paragraphs were interesting.
7. We study almost _____ day.
8. _____ time we study we learn something.
9. We'll never know _____.
10. Nobody in America works all summer; _____ takes a vacation.
11. _____ needs some relaxation in the summer.
12. Do _____ the people in your country take vacations?
13. Not _____ the parents went to the Parents' Day celebration.
14. _____ father who went visited his own son's room.
15. _____ parent who went enjoyed the celebration.

b. Copy the following sentences, filling the blanks with the appropriate tense of the verb in parentheses. It will be simple or continuous past.

1. Jane   (look)   out the window when the accident   (happen) .
2. She   (see)   a traffic light turn red.
3. She   (hear)   brakes screech.
4. She   (know)   the driver   (try)   to stop his car.
5. Many people   (watch)   when the two cars collided.
6. Bill   (shine)   his shoes this morning, and he   (spill)   some shoe polish on the floor.
7. He   (try)   to clean it up but he couldn't.
8. While he   (work)   in the chemistry lab, he   (remember)   the shoe polish on the floor.
9. He   (ask)   the lab assistant for some cleaning fluid.
10. When he got home, his landlady   (wash)   the floor.

c. Write a ten-speech dialogue of five questions and five answers, all in the continuous past. Be careful to punctuate correctly (V, 22) and to include the essential time expressions (§ 2).

REVIEW IX

a. Copy the following sentences, adding *no* or *not* in each blank space. Do not add any other words.

1. The Flysafe Airline has _____ accidents.
2. In bad weather, _____ planes fly.
3. They do _____ leave the ground.
4. _____ many airlines have such a good record.
5. But people are _____ happy when the planes don't fly.

6. George is _____ taking economics now.
7. He has _____ trouble with his other courses.
8. He does _____ need any help with them.
9. He has _____ need for help.
10. He has _____ worries about grades now.

11. Bill eats _____ breakfast on Mondays.
12. He does _____ get up very early.
13. He has _____ time to waste.
14. He does _____ want to be late to class.
15. His professor would _____ like that.

b. Keeping in mind that nouns which modify other nouns must be simple forms, what would you call the following?

> Instructor: a book which cost ten dollars
> Student: a ten-dollar book

1. a truck which weighs two tons
2. a vacation which lasts two weeks
3. a poem of sixteen lines
4. a check worth two hundred dollars
5. a trip covering one thousand miles
6. a bicycle which has five speeds
7. men who sell cars
8. buildings with five stories
9. compositions of three hundred words
10. a meal of four courses
11. a roast which weighs five pounds
12. a cake with three layers
13. flour for all purposes
14. a garage for two cars
15. a car with four doors

c. Make complete sentences from the following beginnings. Be sure to include all the required structures (sentence parts) for each.

1. I was going to . . .
2. I am going to . . .
3. I was thinking about . . .
4. I have to . . .
5. I used to . . .
6. I am about to . . .
7. There are . . .
8. There isn't . . .
9. I know the man who . . .
10. This is the place where . . .
11. Jane is the girl . . .
12. While the foreign students were traveling through Tennessee, . . .
13. Three years ago . . .
14. Won't you . . .
15. Isn't it . . .

LESSON

HOW: QUESTION AND ANSWER PATTERNS
CAUSATIVES: HAVE, MAKE, GET

Michael Miller, the new economics professor, visited the Allens a few days ago. He asked Professor Allen a lot of questions about his foreign students. They had this conversation.

M: Some of your students know very little English. How do they get here by themselves?

A: Most of them come by plane as far as New York. They come from New York by bus.

M: How do they find places to live after they get here?

A: By inquiring at the Student Housing Bureau. Sometimes the Dean of Foreign Students helps them find rooms.

M: How do they respond when strangers speak to them?

A: By smiling, or nodding, or shaking their heads. Sometimes they get their friends to translate for them.

M: How do you speak to them at first? Do they understand you?

A: Oh, yes. They understand when I speak slowly and clearly.

M: How do you begin to teach them? What do you do first?

A: I begin with sentence patterns. First I make them repeat my sentences. Then I let them ask questions about the sentence patterns. Later I have them prepare questions and answers. For homework I get them to write short paragraphs.

M: How do they like American food?

A: Not very well at first, but they get used to it.

M: How long does it take them to get used to eating American food?

A: That depends on the student and where he is from. Latin Americans never get used to our coffee. They like their coffee very strong. Students from the Middle East usually like their meat well-done[1] and highly spiced; they never eat meat rare.[2] Most students are used to American food and American ways by the end of their first semester, but some of them never do get used to living here.

M: How often do you have students from many different countries in the same class?

A: I always do. There are always students from South America and I usually have some from China or Japan. I often have students from Iran and I sometimes have one or two from Afghanistan. I seldom have any from Africa, although I had two from Ghana in my class last semester. I used to teach Europeans but I rarely do now. I have had students from most of the countries of the world, but I have never had a student from Tibet.

[1] Well-done describes meat which has been cooked for a long time. It is sometimes written without the hyphen.
[2] Rare, in reference to meat, is the opposite of well-done.

How-questions are not so specific as questions beginning with *when* or *who*. *How* asks about the means or method by which something is done, or the manner in which it is done, or the instrument with which it is accomplished. *How* questions must be answered in many different ways.

2 **Answers for *how*-questions**

a. *By* + noun answers questions about transportation or communication. The noun is a simple form without any article or modifier.

QUESTION	RESPONSE	STATEMENT
How do they get here from New York?	By bus.	They come by bus.
How do they contact their parents?	By cable.	They contact their parents by cable.

b. *By* + *ing*-form answers questions about action.

QUESTION	RESPONSE	STATEMENT
How do they respond?	By smiling.	They respond by smiling.
How do you show them the way?	By pointing.	I show them by pointing.

c. *With* + noun answers questions about instrument, equipment, or method used. The noun after *with* is clearly singular or plural and it may be modified (cf. a above).

QUESTION	RESPONSE
How do they find their way around campus?	With a map.
How do you begin to teach them?	With sentence patterns.

d. Single adjectives answer *how*-questions when they ask about the description of something. When the response is made in the form of a complete statement, the adjective follows the noun it modifies (cf. VI, 11b).

QUESTION	RESPONSE	STATEMENT
How do you like coffee?	Black.	I like coffee black.
How do you eat steak?	Rare.	I eat steak rare.

Some possible responses to questions of this type are: hot, cold, chilled, sweet, sour, fresh, raw, cooked, fried, boiled, strong, weak, rare, well-done.

e. *-ly* adverbs answer *how*-questions about manner.

QUESTION	RESPONSE
How do you speak to your students?	Slowly and clearly.
How do they behave?	Politely.
How do they listen?	Carefully.

3 **Adverbs of manner** are regularly formed by adding *ly* to related adjectives.

a.

ADJ.	quick	careful	wise	clear
ADV.	quickly	carefully	wisely	clearly

b. Irregular manner adverbs do not end in *ly*. There are only a few of these. *Hard* and *fast* are identical with their related adjectives. *Slow* is also sometimes used as an adverb instead of *slowly*. *Well* [3] is the adverbial form of the adjective *good*.

DESCRIPTIVE ADJECTIVES	MANNER ADVERBS
Bill is a *fast* worker.	Bill works *fast*.
He isn't a *slow* worker.	He doesn't work *slow*.
He is a *hard* worker, too.	He works *hard*.
He is a *good* worker.	He works *well*.

[3] *Well* is an adjective when it refers to the state of a person's health. It is the opposite of *ill*.

c. *-ly* words which are not manner adverbs sometimes cause learners to write ungrammatical sentences. Some of the frequency adverbs end in *ly* (IV, 1). *Hardly* is an adverb of measure rather than manner (cf. *hard* above). A few *ly* words are adjectives which cannot be made into adverbs. They are best remembered in two groups.

| -LY ADJECTIVES ||
Positive Attributes	Negative Attributes
friendly lovely manly	homely [4] ugly lonely

d. Positions of manner adverbs vary according to style and emphasis (cf. VIII, 10). They are never placed between a verb and its object, however. Since that is the normal position for manner words in many languages, learners often put them there in error. Observe the position of manner words in the following sentences.

(MA)	S	(MA)	V + O	(MA)
Gradually	George		improved his English.	
	George	gradually	improved his English.	
	George		improved his English	gradually.

4 *Homely,* in American English, means very plain, lacking beauty. It has nothing to do with *home.*

4 **Question phrases with *how***

a. *How* is often followed by an adjective or by a term of quantity, time, manner, distance, or frequency. The complete phrase is a unit which fills the QW position in an information question pattern.

Q-PHRASE	AUX/*BE*	S	V	O	P	T
How old	is	George?				
How well	does	he	speak	English?		
How far	is	he			from home	now?
How long ago	did	he	come		here?	
How much	did	his trip	cost?			
How often	does	he	write		to his parents?	

b. Some question phrases also include nouns.

Q-PHRASE	AUX/*BE*	S/EXPLETIVE	V	P
How many foreign students	are	there		in this class?
How many brothers	does	George	have?	
How high an average	must	a scholarship student	maintain?	

c. Responses to *how often* may be frequency adverbs or time phrases of recurrence.

QUESTION	RESPONSE
How often does Jack go to the movies?	Quite often. Every Saturday. Once a week.
How often does Bill go?	Rarely. Maybe twice a year.

Question phrases with *what, which, whose*

These words are often followed by nouns, forming question phrases similar to those above.

a.

Q-PHRASE	V	C	
What time	is	it?	
Which professor	visited	the Allens?	
Whose students	come		from abroad?

b.

Q-PHRASE	V	C
What celebration	took place	last Sunday?
Which boy's parents	didn't attend?	
Whose father	is going to visit	next Sunday?

c.

Q-PHRASE	AUX	S	V	C
What day	did	the boys	decorate	the dorm?
Which room	did	they	do	first?
Whose committee	did	Jack	work	on?

6 ***What kind of*** introduces a very common question phrase. *Sort, style, make,* and *type* are also used in this way, with or without *of. Color, flavor,* and *size* are used without *of.*

Q-PHRASE	AUX	S	V	C
What color tie	did	Bill	buy?	
What flavor ice cream	did	the Allens	serve?	
What style (of) fiction	does	Professor Miller	read?	
What make (of) car	does	Professor Baker	drive?	
What type (of) exams	does	he	give?	
What kind of assignments	do	you	have	in English?

7 **Causative constructions** are special sentence patterns with two verbs. They explain that one person causes another person to do something. The three verbs which are used in this way are *have, make,* and *get.* The pattern for *have* and *make* is just slightly different from the one for *get.*

a. Note the difference in the following examples.

CAUSER	CAUSATIVE VERB	ACTOR	ACTION VERB	OBJECT
Professor Allen	makes	the students	repeat	his sentences.
He	has	them	prepare	questions.
He	gets	them	to write	paragraphs.
They	get	him	to correct	their mistakes.

b. Note the forms of words in the examples above. The causative verb is the one which is inflected; i.e., it changes form. The action verb slot is filled with a SIMPLE verb form when the causative is *make* or *have* but with an INFINITIVE when the causative is *get.* When the actor word is a pronoun, it is an object form.

c. Meanings of *have, make,* and *get* do not vary greatly, but they do suggest something about the relationship between the causer and the actor.

Have is often used for someone we engage or employ.

Mrs. Allen has the butcher slice her meat thin.

Make suggests the use of force or pressure, either physical or psychological.

Professor Miller makes his students write in ink.

Get usually suggests persuasion.

Sometimes they get their friends to translate for them.

8 Let and **help** pattern in the same way as the causatives. *Let* is like *have* and *make; help* patterns both ways. The infinitive is used when the actor slot contains a modifying clause.

SUBJECT	HELP/LET	ACTOR	VERB	OBJECT
Professor Allen	lets	his students	ask	questions.
He	helps	them	learn	English.
The dean	helps	the students who come from abroad	to find	rooms.

9 Get used to and **be used to** are idioms that have to do with becoming and being accustomed. When one is accustomed to a situation, it seems perfectly normal, not strange in any way. These are very common idioms which must be learned. Do not confuse them with *used to* + simple verb (VIII, 1–2), which is an entirely different construction. Observe the sentence patterns for these idioms.

S	V			C	
	Get/Be	Used To	(Ing-form)	Noun/Pronoun	Time
George	is	used to	eating	American food	now.
He	got	used to		it	quickly.
Miss Liu	isn't	used to		it	yet.

10 **Appositives** are grammatical constructions in which two words or phrases referring to the same object or person and serving the same function in a sentence are placed next to one another. The second usually identifies the first. The subject of the first sentence in the model paragraph contains an appositive.

Michael Miller, *the new economics professor,* visited the Allens a few days ago.

11 **By a certain time.** When we say that something was done or will be done by a certain time, we usually refer to an activity or a process which requires an indefinite but considerable length of time. *By* indicates that the activity or process is or will be finished at the time mentioned or before that time.

12 **Verb with preposition** in this lesson is *depend on* or *depend upon* (cf. III, 9). *Upon* is more formal than *on*.

13 **Punctuation**

a. Note the comma after *oh* in the model conversation. A comma is always placed after a mild exclamation such as *oh* or *well*.

b. Note the commas before and after the appositive in the first sentence and in § 10 above. Appositives are set off from the rest of the sentence by commas. Be sure to include both of them; one alone may cause misreading.

14 **Exercises**

a. Answer the following questions with short responses of *by* + noun (§ 2a).

> Instructor: How do you keep in touch with your friends?
> Student: By telephone.

1. How did you come to the United States?
2. How did you come to class today?
3. How can you travel to Europe? Another way?
4. How can you go to Chicago? Another way?
5. How can you get from one side of a city to the other?

6. How do you keep in touch with your friends?
7. How do you send messages to your family?
8. How can you send a message faster than by letter?
9. How does the president talk to the people?
10. How do we detect aircraft?

11.   How can you get upstairs quickly?
12.   How can you get around campus quickly?
13.   How can you get to a railroad station in a hurry?
14.   How can you get downtown quickly?
15.   How do ships communicate with each other?

b. Answer the following questions with short responses of *by* + *ing*-form (§ 2b).

> Instructor: How can I find out your name?
> Student: By asking me.

1.   How does one learn a foreign language?
2.   How does one build a large vocabulary?
3.   How can I find out how to spell a word?
4.   How can you improve your pronunciation?
5.   How can you be sure that your word order is correct?

6.   How can I find out what the temperature is?
7.   How can I keep up with current events?
8.   How can I find out where the nearest bus stop is?
9.   How can I find out if the library has a book that I want?
10.   How can I find out what's playing at the movies?

11.   How do parents educate their children?
12.   How do children learn about religion?
13.   How do some people become rich?
14.   How do some people become poor?
15.   How does Professor Miller earn his living?

c. To the following questions give short responses beginning with *with* (§ 2c).

> Instructor: How do you unlock a door?
> Student: With a key.

1.   How do you cut bread?
2.   How do you toast bread?
3.   How do you prepare orange juice?
4.   How do you open a can?
5.   How do you open a bottle?

6. How do you comb your hair?
7. How do you brush your teeth?
8. How do you shorten your fingernails?
9. How do you shave yourself?
10. How do you dry yourself after a bath?

11. How do you draw a straight line?
12. How do you type your papers?
13. How do you light your room?
14. How do you cool your drinking water?
15. How do you keep rain off your head?

d. Answer the following questions with complete sentences. Include an adjective in your answer (§ 2d).

> Instructor: How do Americans like tea in summer?
> Student: They like it iced.

1. How do Latin Americans like their coffee?
2. How do you like your coffee?
3. How do you like your tea?
4. How do Americans drink beer?
5. How should one serve white wine?

6. How do you like rice, boiled or fried?
7. How do you like to eat potatoes?
8. How do you prefer to eat carrots, raw or cooked?
9. How do you prefer fruit?
10. How do Americans like desserts?

11. Jane likes short dresses. How does she wear her dresses?
12. She likes long hair. How does she wear her hair?
13. She eats toasted muffins for breakfast. How does she like her muffins?
14. She eats soft-boiled eggs, too. How does she like her eggs?
15. She doesn't like coffee. She drinks very cold milk. How does she like her milk?

e. Answer each of the following questions with one word only, if possible. Be especially careful with the last six items (§§ 2e, 3).

> Instructor: How does a poor typist type?
> Student: Poorly.

1. How does an interesting lecturer lecture?
2. How does a careful student do his assignments?
3. How does a graceful person dance?
4. How does a kind person treat others?
5. How does an awkward person walk?
6. How does a happy child play?
7. How does an intelligent student answer questions?
8. How does a clever writer write?
9. How does a quick person move?
10. How does an old man walk?
11. How does a hard-working person work?
12. How does a fast plane fly?
13. How does a good swimmer swim?
14. How does an ugly person act?
15. How does a friendly person treat others?

f. Taking into consideration the given information, add an appropriate adverb of manner to each of the numbered items (§ 3d).

> Information: Jane is athletic and sociable.
> She is not very studious.

1. Jane swims.
2. She dances.
3. She entertains.
4. She dresses.
5. She does her assignments.

> Information: Betty is very intellectual and musical.
> She is not a homemaker.

6. Betty solves problems.
7. She learns languages.
8. She plays the piano.
9. She doesn't cook.
10. She doesn't sew.

Information: Jack decided to get a job for the summer.

11. He went to the college placement office.   (immediately)
12. He asked the clerk for an application form.   (politely)
13. He took the form home and filled it out.   (carefully)
14. He returned it to the office.   (promptly)
15. He is waiting to be called for an interview.   (patiently)

g. Student 1:   Make an information question beginning with *how* based on
               the instructor's statement.
    Student 2:   Answer the question (§ 4).

> Instructor: Bill's typewriter weighs eighteen pounds.
> Student 1:   How heavy is Bill's typewriter?
> Student 2:   Eighteen pounds.

1. The length of the swimming pool is sixty feet.
2. The width of the pool is twenty-four feet.
3. The height of the gymnasium building is fifty feet.
4. Trans-Atlantic planes fly 30,000 feet above sea level.
5. No one knows the depth of the ocean.

6. A semester usually lasts sixteen weeks.
7. We have to maintain an average of 80 percent.
8. A slide rule is accurate enough for most calculations.
9. New York is over three thousand miles from San Francisco.
10. It is 80°F in the sun.

11. The United Nations was established in 1945.
12. The buildings where it is housed cost several million dollars.
13. New nations join each year.
14. The budget for the U.N. is enormous.
15. We hope the U.N. will last forever.

h. Student 1: Use the given words in a question beginning with *how much* or *how many*.

Student 2: Give a short response (§ 4).

> Instructor: post office – this town
> Student 1: How many post offices are there in this town?
> Student 2: Only one.

1. mail box – post office
2. mailman – post office
3. mail – handle per year
4. delivery – a day
5. time – sorting mail
6. package – mail
7. postage – put on
8. stamps – put on
9. insurance – buy
10. minutes – in line
11. airmail stamp – cost
12. money order – cost
13. registered letter – cost
14. special delivery – cost
15. postcard – cost

i. Answer each of the following questions with an adverb of frequency or a time phrase (§ 4c).

1. How often do we have class?
2. How often do we begin class on time?
3. How often do we finish early?
4. How often does someone arrive late?
5. How often is someone absent?

6. How often do you read a newspaper?
7. How often do you read the college paper?
8. How often do you listen to the radio?
9. How often do you watch TV?
10. How often do you go to the movies?

11. How often do you write to your parents?
12. How often do you telephone your friends?
13. How often do you oversleep?
14. How often do you eat in a cafeteria?
15. How often do you go to bed after midnight?

j. Make information questions from the following statements, substituting question phrases for the italicized words (§ 5).

1. It's *Wednesday.*
2. It's *half past two.*
3. Professor *Miller* drives a Ford.
4. The *three o'clock* bell just rang.
5. This is *Betty's* coat.

6. Jack gets up *at seven o'clock.*
7. Jane takes *the #4* bus to school every day.
8. *Mrs. Allen's* party was a success.
9. Of all his courses, Jack prefers *chemistry.*
10. He likes *Professor Baker's* lectures.

11. Bill usually takes *the 9:20* train to Westview.
12. He arrives in Westview *at 10:45.*
13. He returns to campus *on Sunday nights.*
14. Sometimes he rides back in *his friend's* car.
15. He came back on *the midnight* train last Sunday.

k. Make information questions from the following statements, substituting question phrases for the italicized words (§ 6).

1. Bill bought a *green* tie.
2. The girl in the library has *blond* hair.
3. The Allens' house is *white.*

4. Jack likes *chocolate* ice cream.
5. Jane prefers *strawberry.*
6. You can buy *vanilla* ice cream in the school cafeteria.

7. Professor Baker drives a *Mercedes.*
8. His lawn mower has a *Westinghouse* motor.
9. He uses a *Remington* typewriter.

10. We have to do our assignments on *8½-by-11-inch* paper.
11. Jack wears a *15½* shirt.
12. Professor Miller carries a *large* briefcase.

13. Jack wears *sport* shirts in summer.
14. Betty wears *tennis* shoes when she goes on picnics.
15. I bought a *loose-leaf* notebook today.

l. What kind of person do you have do these things for you? (§ 7)

> Instructor: cut your hair
> Student: I have a barber cut my hair.

1. wash your shirts
2. sew on your buttons
3. mend your socks
4. clean your room
5. serve your meals

What kind of person do you get to do the following things?

6. return a book to the library
7. drive you to the station
8. water your plants while you're away
9. take notes when you are absent
10. lend you some money

What do parents make their children do?

11. drink milk
12. eat vegetables
13. play in the sunshine
14. do their homework
15. go to bed early

m. Tell the class about something that someone lets you do or something that someone helps you do (§ 8). Here are two examples.

> My father lets me use his car.
> My sister helps me wash the dishes.

n. Tell the class about something you had to get used to. Also tell them how long it took (§ 9).

> I had to get used to eating potatoes.
> It took me six months to get used to it.

o. Tell which of the following things you can depend on and which you can't depend on. Answer with complete statements (§ 12).

1. a weather forecast
2. a bus schedule
3. an electric clock
4. a pocket dictionary
5. an official announcement

6. a politician
7. a banker
8. a drunken driver
9. a fortune-teller
10. a watchdog

11. a reliable person
12. an irresponsible person
13. a disreputable person
14. a corruptible person
15. a dependable person

15 **Assignments**

a. Write five sentences with appositives like the one in this lesson. Be sure to punctuate them correctly.

b. Write five interesting information questions beginning with *how* to ask your classmates. Ask about things you would really like to know.

c. Write a paragraph or two in which you tell how you came here, how you found a place to live, how you got registered and found your way around the first few days you were here. Tell also how you like American food and American customs and whether or not you are used to them yet. If you are used to them, tell how long it took you to get used to them. If you are not used to them, tell how long you think it will take to get used to them.

REVIEW X

a. Make one sentence from each of the following pairs, using *while* or *when* as a time clause marker in each sentence.

1. Mr. Jones waited. His wife dressed.
2. It was raining. They started toward College Town.
3. They arrived in College Town. It stopped raining.
4. Jack was waiting for them. They entered the dormitory.
5. He was reading a magazine. His father greeted him.

6. Jack and his parents were talking. Jack's roommate entered the lounge.
7. They waited for dinner. Jack showed his parents his room.
8. After dinner the boys provided entertainment. The parents watched.
9. One boy played a guitar. Two others sang.
10. The boys stopped singing. The audience clapped.

11. The entertainment was over. The Joneses started home.
12. They left. It was about six-thirty.
13. They were driving home. There was a lot of traffic.
14. They finally arrived home. It was very late.
15. Mrs. Jones prepared something to eat. Mr. Jones put the car in the garage.

b. Copy the following sentences, filling in each blank with some form of *used to, be used to,* or *get used to.*

1. Some people _____ changes more easily than others do.
2. I _____ the weather now, but I can't _____ the food.
3. My mother _____ cook special dishes for me.
4. I didn't _____ thank her; I was thoughtless.
5. She _____ my thoughtlessness; she didn't mind.

6. When Tom was a young boy he _____ go swimming every day.
7. When he got older he had to _____ going less often.
8. That was hard, but he _____ it now.
9. He didn't _____ spend much time on school work.
10. He (past) _____ having a good time all the time.

11. Professor Baker _____ drive a Volkswagen.
12. He _____ driving a small car.
13. It took him quite a while to _____ his Mercedes.
14. He _____ it now. He likes it very much.
15. But he _____ like his Volkswagen before he got his Mercedes.

PRESENT PERFECT: SIMPLE AND CONTINUOUS
AUXILIARY *HAVE*
FOR, SINCE, JUST, RECENTLY, ALREADY, YET

Miss Liu came here about six months ago. She has been here for about six months. She has already taken Professor Allen's course in remedial English for foreign students, but she hasn't mastered all the patterns yet. She still makes a lot of mistakes. She has been living in a furnished room since she arrived, but she has just decided to move into a dormitory next semester. She will have more opportunity to speak English in the dorm.

Professor Allen has been teaching English to foreign students for quite a long time. He has been working in this field for about six years, as a matter of fact. He has tried several different methods of teaching the verb tenses, but he has never found a way that is completely satisfactory. He has spoken to many of his students and they have assured him that his explanations are easy to understand, but he is still trying to make them better.

Simple present perfect tense is a verb phrase made from a present form of auxiliary *have* and a past participle.

 Auxiliary *have* has the same forms as verb *have*. The two are identical except that the auxiliary more readily joins with pronouns and with *not* to form contractions.

a. Present

PERSON	SINGULAR	PLURAL
1	I've	we've
2	◄——you've——►	
3	he's she's it's	they've

b. Past

PERSON	SINGULAR	PLURAL
1	I'd	we'd
2	◄——you'd——►	
3	he'd she'd it'd	they'd

c. These contractions are never used as the last word in a sentence or before *too* or *either* in a compound sentence (IX, 5).

d. The negative contractions are *haven't, hasn't, hadn't.*

 Past participles are regularly the same as past tense verb forms. About fifty irregular verbs have special past participle forms, most of which end in *en*. These are listed in VII, 4.

 Time expressions are not essential. Those used with simple present perfect indicate duration or unspecified past time. Specific past times are never stated with simple present perfect tense.

5 **Sentence patterns**

SUBJECT	VERB			COMPLEMENT		
	Aux	Mod	PP	O	P	T
a. Professor Allen	has		tried	different methods.		
b. Miss Liu	has	already	taken	Professor Allen's course.		
She	hasn't		mastered	the patterns		yet.
c. She	has		lived		here	for six months.
She	has		lived		here	since September.

6 **Uses.** Simple present perfect in the main clause of a sentence signals one of the following meanings:

a. An action or state which was repeated in the past and which may be repeated in the future.

b. An action or state completed at some unspecified past time. Sentences of this type may include words like *just, already, recently.* Negative statements of this type often include the word *yet.*

c. An action or state which began some time in the past and has continued to the moment of speaking. This kind of sentence usually includes a time expression introduced by *for* or *since.*

7 *For* and *since* expressions fit into the usual time positions.

a. *For* introduces phrases of duration as explained in VIII, 12. The actual length of time is stated: *for six months.*

b. *Since* phrases name the beginning of the time duration. The end is the moment of speaking. *Since September* means from September until now.

c. *Since* clauses name an action which occurred at the beginning of the time duration: *since she arrived.* The end of the duration is the moment of speaking or writing.

8 *Just, recently, already,* and *yet* often occur in the position of the frequency adverbs (IV, 2), between the auxiliary and the main verb. This is the only position for *just;* the others may occur at the end. *Yet,* which is used only in questions and negative statements, usually comes at the end.

a. *Just* means immediately before speaking.

b. *Recently* is within a short time past.

c. *Already* emphasizes the completion of an action at a time sooner than expected by the hearer.

d. *Yet,* with a negative, suggests a time later than expected.

9 | **Present perfect** | vs. | **Simple past**

	Miss Liu came here six months ago. (Simple statement of fact. No implication for the present.)
She has already taken Professor Allen's course. (Implication: Her present performance in English should reflect that recent past event.)	She took Professor Allen's course last semester. (Simple statement of fact. No implication for the present.)
Professor Allen has tried several different methods of teaching verb tenses. (Implication: He will continue to try new methods.)	Professor Allen tried several different methods of teaching verb tenses. (Implication: He is not going to try any more methods.)

Many facts may be stated in either tense, but the implications differ.

10 **Continuous present perfect** verb phrases have three parts: a present form of auxiliary *have* plus *been* plus *ing*-form.

11 **Time expressions are essential** with this tense as with the continuous past (IX, 2). They are phrases or clauses of duration introduced by *for* or *since* (§ 7) or less specific expressions of recent time such as *this week, today, recently.*

12 **Sentence patterns**

Q-PHRASE	AUX (NOT)	S	V			C		
			Aux	Been	ing	O	P	T
		Miss Liu	has	been	living		in a private room	since she arrived.
	Has	Miss Liu		been	living		in a private room	since she arrived?
How long	has	Miss Liu		been	living		in a private room?	
		Some students	have	been	helping	her	with her lessons	recently.

13 **Use.** The continuous tenses emphasize duration and this one is no exception. The continuous present perfect also often implies that the action or state will continue for some time in the future. Verbs not used in the other continuous tenses (III, 8) are not used in this one either.

14 **Simple present perfect**   vs.   **Continuous present perfect**

Professor Allen has taught in many foreign countries. (repeated, completed activity)

Professor Allen has been teaching foreign students for about six years. (uninterrupted activity)

It has rained every day this week. (repeated, completed occurrence)

It has been raining all morning. (continuous occurrence)

There is really not a great deal of difference in meaning between these two tenses. The continuous emphasizes duration, whereas the simple perfect focuses on repetition and/or completion. Many of the statements in this lesson could be expressed in either tense without anyone's noticing the difference.

15 **Pronunciation helps: a common error to avoid**

When sentences have verb constructions beginning with *has* or *have*, the subject is often joined to the auxiliary in the form of a contraction. Native speakers frequently speak quite fast and slur over certain sounds so that it is difficult for a learner to hear the *'ve* of *have* or the *'s* of *has* unless he is especially listening for it. In your own speech be careful to pronounce these sounds distinctly so that when you write you won't make the mistake of leaving them out. In other words, never say or write *we been working* for *we've been working* or *they been studying* for *they've been studying,* even though you may think you hear it.

16 **Exercises**

a. Find out where our classmates have been. Ask them about places where you have been (§ 5).

> Student 1: Have you ever been to London?
> Student 2: No, I haven't. Have you?
> Student 1: Yes, I was in London in 1970.

b. Student 1: Using your instructor's cue words, make a question in the present perfect tense.
Student 2: Answer the question and ask another (§ 5).

> Instructor: eat snails
> Student 1: Have you ever eaten snails?
> Student 2: Oh, yes, many times. Have you?
> Student 1: No, I've never tasted snails.

1. eat pancakes	7. fly a kite	13. tell a lie
2. drink buttermilk	8. sail a boat	14. make a mistake
3. smoke a cigar	9. play horseshoes	15. borrow money
4. catch a fish	10. oversleep	
5. shoot a duck	11. be late to class	
6. trap a rabbit	12. be absent	

c. Repeat the given sentence, substituting contractions wherever possible (§ 2).

> Instructor: It has been raining all morning.
> Student: It's been raining all morning.

1. I have written a long letter.
2. It has taken all morning.
3. It is to my parents.
4. They have been worried about me lately.
5. I have not written home as often as you have.

6. You have been sitting in the sun and Maria has too.
7. You are sunburned and so is she.
8. You are not burned as badly as she is.
9. You have tougher skin than she has.
10. She is going to be sore tomorrow and you are too.

11. Jack has had to do a lot of homework lately and so has Bill.
12. They have not had much time for social activities and I have not either.
13. They have been playing quite a little tennis, though, and I have too.
14. They have not lost a game this week but I have.
15. They are better players than I am.

d. Student 1: Ask your neighbor a question about his condition or customary activity. If the answer is *no*, ask another student. If the answer is *yes*, ask about the duration of that custom or condition.

Student 2: Answer the questions using *for* or *since* (§§ 5, 7, 13, 14).

> Instructor: drive a car
> Student 1: Do you drive a car?
> Student 2: Yes I do.
> Student 1: How long have you been driving?
> Student 2: Since I was eighteen.

1. live around here [1]
2. have your own apartment
3. buy from the drugstore on the corner
4. read an English newspaper
5. know your neighbors

6. married
7. play an instrument
8. own a TV set
9. use a tape recorder for language study
10. work late nights

11. wear glasses when you read
12. have trouble with your teeth
13. have hospitalization insurance
14. carry life insurance
15. pay taxes

[1] *Around here* is colloquial for *in this neighborhood.*

e. Find out what your classmates know about history or current events. Ask questions which you can answer or which you think your classmates can answer. Use simple or continous present perfect. Answer appropriately (§§ 5, 12).

> How long has India been independent?
> What has been happening in Uganda recently?

f. Change the verbs in the following statements to present perfect. Make any other changes which are necessary (§§ 4, 5).

> Instructor: I saw Jack a minute ago.
> Student: I have just seen Jack.
>
> Instructor: I mailed your letters last night.
> Student: I have mailed your letters.

1. We took a placement exam when we came here.
2. We didn't see our papers afterwards.
3. We had other exams during the semester.
4. We corrected the errors on them when we saw them.
5. We threw them away after we corrected them.

6. We studied irregular verbs a few weeks ago.
7. We didn't discuss the past perfect yet.
8. We practiced causatives at the last class meeting.
9. We didn't have any trouble with them while we were in class.
10. We will try to use them in the future.

11. George sent a cable to his father last month.
12. He asked for some money.
13. Until now, his father didn't answer.
14. George had to borrow some money last week.
15. He didn't pay it back up to now.

g. Add the given adverb of frequency to each of the following sentences (§ 8).

1. George has thought about getting a part-time job. (often)
2. He has been almost completely out of money. (frequently)
3. He has had to borrow from friends. (occasionally)
4. He has wanted to do that. (never)
5. He has been very prompt about repaying his debts. (always)

6. Jane has considered quitting school. (frequently)
7. She has thought that she would be happier working in an office. (often)
8. She has enjoyed her studies. (never)
9. She has enjoyed the social life at college very much though. (always)
10. Her father hasn't allowed her to quit, however. (ever)

11. The Allens have invited Professor Miller to visit them. (often)
12. He has accepted their invitations. (seldom)
13. He has wanted to. (usually)
14. But he has been too busy. (almost always)
15. The Allens have understood why he couldn't come. (always)

h. Answer the following questions with complete sentences including *already* or *yet* and appropriate pronouns (§ 8).

> Instructor: When is Pedro going to graduate?
> Student: He has already graduated.
> Instructor: When did he leave the university?
> Student: He hasn't left yet.

1. When does the paper come?
2. Why doesn't Jack buy some new ties?
3. Why doesn't George drop economics?
4. When is Professor Miller going to call on the Allens?
5. When is Jack going to meet Jane?

6. When did Nick hear from his father?
7. Is this library book due?
8. What time did you eat?
9. What kind of radio did you buy?
10. When did Miss Liu receive her check?

11. When do you have midterm exams?
12. Are the grades posted?
13. When will next semester's schedule be out?
14. Have you decided on courses for next semester?
15. Do you have enough money for next term's fees?

i. Read the following sentences, supplying the most appropriate tense of the verb in parentheses.

> Book: This (be) an easy exercise.
> Student: This is an easy exercise.
> Book: We (neg. do) one like this before.
> Student: We haven't done one like this before.

1. Tom (be) a successful young artist.
2. He (paint) landscapes in modern designs.
3. He (receive) several awards for his paintings.
4. He (sell) his first picture just one year ago.
5. He (sell) over fifty pictures since then.

6. Dick (work) in a bank, but he doesn't any more.
7. He (leave) his job at the bank two years ago.
8. He (have) several different jobs since then.
9. He (neg. work) for the past three months.
10. He (look for) a job for three months.

11. Harry (write) short stories.
12. He (write) several good ones.
13. He (neg. have) any of them published yet.
14. He (write) one right now.
15. He (work) on it for the past ten days.

17 **Assignments**

a. Write a paragraph in which you tell some of the things you did just before you came here and some of the things you have done since you arrived.

b. Write a paragraph in which you tell what you and your family or your friends have been doing lately.

REVIEW XI

a. Read or write the following sentences, supplying the appropriate tense of each verb in parentheses. Make verbs preceded by *n.* negative.

1. We (have) an English lesson right now.
2. We (have) one at this time last week, too.
3. We (have) classes at this hour since the beginning of the term.
4. The bell (n. ring) right now.
5. The bell (ring) when the teacher entered the room.
6. The bell (n. ring) on time lately.
7. Miss Liu (try) to get used to American food ever since she came here.
8. Jane (get) poor marks in chemistry lately.
9. Professor Miller (give) free lectures for over a year.
10. He (give) one while we were attending the concert last night.
11. Mrs. Allen (work) ever since she graduated from college.
12. Mrs. Baker (n. teach) for a long time now.
13. She used to teach before she was married. She (take) a vacation when she met Mr. Baker.
14. They (travel) to Europe on the same ship.
15. They moved to College Town shortly after they were married, and they (live) there ever since.

b. Combine each of the following pairs of sentences to express the indicated relationship, making only necessary changes. Be very careful to use the appropriate articles in your sentences.

> Instructor: Gail is a typist. She types my letters.
> Student: Gail is the typist who types my letters.

> Instructor: Bob is a computer programmer. He works in Chicago.
> Student: Bob is a computer programmer who works in Chicago.

1. Dr. Smith is a dentist.
   He always repairs my teeth.
2. Dr. Brown is an optometrist.
   His office is in this city.

3. Dr. Baker is a chemistry professor.
   His class had a test last week.
   (None of the other chemistry professors gave a test last week.)
4. Dr. Jones is a veterinary.
   He takes care of the Allens' dog when they go on vacation.
5. Dr. Green is a biology teacher.
   He used to teach in this university.

6. Mary is a college girl.
   She likes to go to dances.
7. Bill is a boy in the story.
   His mother lives in Westview.
8. Tom is an American student.
   He is majoring in accounting.
9. John is a twelve-year-old boy.
   He takes music lessons on Saturdays.
10. Jane is a girl in the story.
    She has red hair.

11. The U.S.A. is an industrial country.
    It produces the most automobiles.
12. New York is a large city.
    It has the tallest buildings in the world.
13. Alaska is a state.
    It is larger than any other state in the United States.
14. Australia is a continent.
    It is also an island.
15. This is a difficult exercise.
    Our teacher warned us about this one.

LESSON

XII

PAST PERFECT: SIMPLE AND CONTINUOUS
INDIRECT OBJECTS, NOUN CLAUSES

The students in Professor Baker's afternoon class had been waiting for almost ten minutes this afternoon when the professor finally showed up. He said that he was very sorry. He told them he had lost his watch. He asked one of the students the time and the student replied that it was ten after two. After that, Professor Baker explained oxidation to his students, and he asked them some questions which he had prepared for them. When he had finished, he announced an exam for next week. Then he dismissed the class.

George had been living in College Town for almost six months when his cousin Nick arrived from Greece. He had been boarding with an American family since his arrival, and he had learned a great deal about American habits and customs. He had gained considerable facility in English, and he had gotten used to eating American food. He hadn't had many letters from home, however, and he was anxious for news of his family. Nick told him that his father had been quite ill for several weeks during the summer. "But he got over his illness before I left," Nick added.

Bill had been working on the same problem for two hours when Jack called him up and asked if he had solved it. Bill said that he hadn't but that he was still trying to. Jack said that he had spent from four o'clock until six o'clock trying to solve it, but that he hadn't been able to. He told Bill that he had given up at six o'clock and gone to dinner.

Simple past perfect tense is a verb phrase made from the past form of the auxiliary *have* and a past participle. *Had* is often joined to pronoun subjects and to *not* as illustrated in XI, 2.

 Uses. The simple past perfect is used chiefly in three situations.

a. To express the time relationship between two events in the past, particularly when the clause marker does not indicate this relationship.

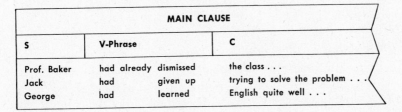

MAIN CLAUSE		
S	**V-Phrase**	**C**
Prof. Baker	had already dismissed	the class . . .
Jack	had given up	trying to solve the problem . . .
George	had learned	English quite well . . .

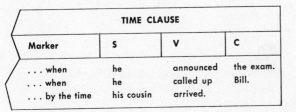

TIME CLAUSE			
Marker	**S**	**V**	**C**
. . . when	he	announced	the exam.
. . . when	he	called up	Bill.
. . . by the time	his cousin	arrived.	

b. To report statements made in the simple past tense or the present perfect.

Direct speech	vs. **Reported speech**
Professor Baker said, "I have lost my watch."	Professor Baker said that he had lost his watch.
Jack said, "I gave up at six o'clock."	Jack said that he had given up at six o'clock.
Nick told George, "Your father got over his illness."	Nick told George that his father had gotten over his illness.

c. To express wishes and unreal conditions about the past. These uses are discussed in Lesson XIX.

Professor Baker wishes that he *had* not *lost* his watch.
If he *had* not *lost* it, he would not have been late.

3 | **Past perfect** | vs. | **Simple past**

Jack had spent two hours on the problem when he gave up. (The sequence of events is reflected in the verb tenses. The first event is expressed in the past perfect.)

Jack spent two hours on the problem before he gave up. (The sequence of events is expressed by the use of the time-word *before*.)

George had lived here for six months when his cousin Nick arrived from Greece. (The sequence of events is reflected in the verb tenses. The first event is expressed in the past perfect.)

George lived here six months. Then his cousin Nick arrived from Greece. (The sequence is expressed by the use of *then* [VI, 5b].)

Professor Baker had already dismissed the class when he announced the exam. (The past perfect tense shows that the dismissing occurred first. The *already* indicates that the order is unusual or unexpected.)

Professor Baker announced an exam after he dismissed the class. (The time relationship of the two events is shown by the time-word *after*.)

As you can see from the above examples, the same facts can be expressed in either tense. The past perfect is used more in formal written language than in speaking.

4 **Continuous past perfect** is a verb phrase made from *had* plus *been* plus *ing*-form.

5 **Use.** This tense is concerned with expressing the duration of an event or activity of the past which was interrupted or concluded by another past activity or event.

6 **Two time expressions** or their equivalents are required in the environment of a past perfect tense—either in the same sentence or in one just before or after it.

a. T$_1$ must express the duration of the activity. Expressions of this type begin with *for* or *since* (XI, 7).

b. T$_2$ states the time or the event which interrupted or concluded the activity.

Sentence pattern

S	V	P	T₁	T₂
The students	had been waiting		for almost ten minutes	when Prof. Baker showed up.
Bill	had been working		for two hours	when Jack called.
George	had been living	in College Town	for almost six months	when Nick came from Greece.

Past perfect	vs. **Continuous past perfect**
a. George had lived with an American family for six months when Nick arrived. (This sentence may suggest to some speakers that he changed his living arrangements after Nick arrived, but it does not specifically say so.)	George had been living with an American family for six months when Nick arrived. (This sentence may suggest to some speakers that he will continue the same living arrangements, but it does not actually say so.)

Both sentences can be used to express the same situation.

b. Professor Baker had already dismissed the class when he announced the exam. (The past perfect verb phrase expresses a one-time completed act. It cannot be expressed in a continuous tense.)

Most statements in the continuous can also be stated in the simple past perfect with little or no difference in meaning. Past perfect statements which refer to completed punctual acts cannot be expressed in the continuous, however. Verbs of mental state, condition, and perception (III, 8) are not used in continuous tenses.

9 | **Indirect objects.** We have already discussed the fact that some verbs never take objects and that some others always do (IV, 10). There are also some verbs that frequently have two objects, one direct and one indirect. An indirect object is usually a person to whom or for whom something is done.

a. Ø,[1] to, or for. Some indirect objects occur without an introductory preposition. Others are introduced by *to* or *for*. The pattern is controlled by the verb. Some verbs allow two patterns. Here is a list of some of the most common ones.

TO	TO or Ø	Ø	Ø or FOR	FOR
admit	bring	ask	build	answer
announce	give	charge	buy	cash
describe	lend	cost	draw	change
explain	offer		find	design
introduce	owe		get	do
mention	pay		make	prepare
recommend	sell			prescribe
say	send			pronounce
speak	show			
suggest	teach			
	tell			
	write			

[1] Verbs marked ø take indirect objects without prepositions.

b. Position of an **indirect object** in a sentence varies according to whether or not it is introduced by a preposition, and also according to the nature of the direct object.

1. If no preposition introduces the indirect object, it precedes the direct object.

S	V	I.O.	D.O.
Professor Baker	asked	a student	the time.
The student	told	him	that it was ten after two.

2. If the indirect object is introduced by *to* or *for,* and if the direct object is a simple noun phrase, the indirect object follows the direct object.

S	V	D.O.	I.O.
Professor Baker	explained	oxidation	to his students.
He	had prepared	some questions	for them.

3. If the direct object is a clause, or if it contains a clause, the indirect object precedes it.

S	V	I.O.	D.O.
Professor Baker	told	his students	that he had lost his watch.
He	mentioned	to them	that he was sorry he was late.
He	had prepared	for them	some questions which would help them understand the lesson.

10 *Say/tell/talk/speak.* Students frequently have difficulty deciding which of these words to use, and that is not surprising because they all refer to the same activity. The difference is that they are used in different patterns.

a. *Say* is most frequently used to introduce direct or indirect quotation.

S	V	D.O.
Professor Baker	said,	"I have lost my watch."
Professor Baker	said	that he had lost his watch.

b. *Tell* is rarely used for direct quotation. It requires an indirect object except in certain idioms.

S	V	I.O.	D.O.
Professor Baker	told	his students	that he had lost his watch.

Tell is also used in the following idioms, with or without an indirect object.

tell a story	tell the truth	tell the time
tell a secret	tell a lie	tell (all) about

c. *Talk* usually refers to a conversation between two (or more) people. It is not followed by a direct object (except in a few idioms; e.g., *talk business*). It sometimes has an indirect object after *to*.

S	V	I.O.	T
The students	talked		until the professor arrived.
Students	do not talk	to one another	during an examination.

d. *Speak* sometimes means to greet. In this case it is followed by an indirect object introduced by *to*.

Professor Baker always speaks to his students when he meets them on campus.

Speak is also used in reference to more formal situations.

Professor Miller spoke at the Rotary Club. (He gave a lecture.)
The dean spoke to Jack about his attendance record. (He reprimanded him.)

Speak is always used with the names of languages.

George speaks Greek with his cousin and English with his classmates.

11 **Noun clauses** are frequently used as direct objects after certain verbs (see examples in 10a and b above).

a. *That* is the connective most often used to introduce a noun-clause object after *say* or *tell*. It is often omitted in speech and in informal writing.

S	V	I.O.	D.O.			
			CM	S	V	C
Professor Baker	said		(that)	he	was	sorry.
He	told	his students	(that)	he	had lost	his watch.
Nick	said		(that)	George's father	had been	ill.

b. *Ask,* when it means to place a question, is never followed by a *that*-clause. It may have a clause object introduced by *if*.[2]

S	V	I.O.	D.O.			
			CM	S	V	C
Jack	asked	Bill	if	he	had solved	the problem.
Bill	asked	Jack	if	he	had eaten	dinner.

[2] For other patterns, see Lesson XV.

12 **Two-word verbs** in this lesson are:

> show up: appear
> give up: surrender, stop trying
> get over (an illness): recover from

13 **Verb with preposition** in this lesson is *work on.*

14 **Pronunciation helps**

a. Be careful to pronounce the *'d* of *I'd, you'd, he'd, she'd, we'd, they'd* when speaking in the past perfect tense.

b. *It'd* has two syllables. The second (unwritten) vowel sound is the same as the first or slightly lower and more centralized. It is not stressed but it must be pronounced.

15 **Exercises**

a. Change the following sentences in such a way that one of the verbs is in the past perfect (§ 2a).

> Instructor: I read the book. Then I saw the movie.
> Student: I had read the book when I saw the movie.

1. John finished his assignment.
   Then he wrote his father a letter.
2. After he wrote to his father he went to the library.
3. He waited for fifteen minutes before the librarian brought him the book he wanted.
4. He read part of the book.
   Then he returned it to the librarian.
5. He had a cup of coffee.
   Then he went to bed.
   He didn't sleep well.

6. Helen came here in 1972.
   She was in Turkey for three years before that.
7. She was here for six months.
   Then I met her.
8. I knew her for a long time.
   One day she told me about her family.
9. She said, "My father died when I was very young."
10. She said, "I started to work when I was sixteen."

11. Betty finished playing a game of tennis with Bill.
    Then Jane asked Betty to play with her.
12. Betty said she was too tired.
    Then she changed her mind and decided to play.
13. She played one game with Jane.
    Then she went home.
14. She took a shower and dressed.
    A friend called her and invited her to dinner.
15. She did her homework before she played tennis.
    Therefore, she was able to accept the invitation.

b. Change the following quotations to reported speech (§ 2b).

Instructor: Professor Baker said, "I have lost my watch."
Student: Professor Baker said that he had lost his watch.

1. One of the students said, "We waited for ten minutes."
2. Another student said, "Professor Baker was ten minutes late."
3. Jack said, "Professor Baker arrived at ten after two."
4. Betty said, "Professor Baker announced an exam for next week."
5. Bill said, "He dismissed the class before he announced the exam."

6. Jack said, "I spent two hours working on one problem."
7. He added, "I didn't solve it. I gave up."
8. Bill said, "I have been working on that problem for two hours."
9. He added, "I haven't given up yet."
10. He said, "I have just thought of a new approach."

11. George asked Nick, "Did you see my father before you left Athens?"
12. Nick replied, "I saw him the day before I left."
13. Then George asked, "Did you enjoy your trip?"
14. Nick replied, "Not very much."
15. Then he added, "The plane was very crowded."

c. Complete the given sentence beginnings, keeping in mind that continuous past perfect statements require the expression of two times: a duration or inception, and an end point. Use the information in the model paragraphs (§§ 5, 6, 7).

1. The students had been waiting . . .
2. Bill had been working . . .
3. George had been living . . .
4. Betty had been playing tennis . . .
5. Miss Liu had been studying . . .

6. Professor Allen had been teaching . . .
7. Professor Miller had been talking . . .
8. Professor Baker had been lecturing . . .
9. Mrs. Allen had been shopping . . .
10. Mrs. Baker had been cooking . . .

11. The boys in Jack's dorm had been planning . . .
12. The foreign students in this university had been traveling . . .
13. Mrs. Allen had been preparing refreshments . . .
14. Bill had been talking to his mother on the telephone . . .
15. George had been attending Professor Miller's economics course . . .

d. Add an appropriate indirect object to each of the following sentences. Follow the pattern that does not require a preposition (§ 9b, 1).[3]

> Instructor: Nick brought good news.
> Student: Nick brought his cousin good news.

About Professor Allen and his wife

1. Professor Allen bought a car.
2. The car cost $3,000.
3. The bank lent $2,000.
4. He paid $2,000.
5. He still owes $1,000.

About Bill and Jack

1. Jack showed his new ties.
2. Bill asked a question.
3. He asked how much the salesman had charged for the ties.
4. Jack told the amount.
5. He gave one of the ties for a present.

[3] Instructor: This exercise will work best if you read each group of five items aloud before asking a student to answer.

About Miss Liu herself

1. Miss Liu found a room.
2. She got some furniture.
3. It cost $300.
4. She made some curtains.
5. Her friends brought some gifts.

e. Add appropriate indirect objects to each of the following sentences. Introduce each one by *to* or *for*,[3] whichever is appropriate (§ 9b, 2).

> Instructor: My teacher answered the question.
> Student: My teacher answered the question for me.

About me and my house

1. My architect designed a house.
2. He drew the plans.
3. Then he recommended a contractor.
4. The contractor built the house.
5. Would you like me to describe the house?

About my friend and the money

6. I mentioned that I needed some change.
7. He offered to cash a check.
8. I explained that I had a large bill.
9. Then he offered to change the bill.
10. It was kind of him to do that.

About my medicine

11. My doctor prescribed some medicine.
12. My pharmacist prepared the capsules.
13. His delivery boy brought them.
14. I gave a small tip.
15. I sent the money for the medicine.

f. The following sentences all include the word *tell*. In most cases *tell* can be changed to *say* if the indirect object is omitted. When *tell* is part of an idiom, it cannot be changed. Change *tell* to *say* wherever possible. If not possible, repeat the sentence (§ 10).

> Instructor: George told his adviser that he was having trouble.
> Student: George said that he was having trouble.
> Instructor: Jane told Betty a secret.
> Student: Jane told Betty a secret.

1. Professor Baker told his students that he had lost his watch.
2. He told them that he was sorry to be late.
3. One boy told the professor the time.
4. The professor told the students all about oxidation.
5. Then he told them that they would have an exam.

6. Bill told Jack that he was working on a difficult problem.
7. Jack told Bill that he had worked on that same problem for two hours.
8. He told Bill that he hadn't solved it.
9. He also told a white lie, however.
10. He told Bill that he had given up, but he really hadn't.

11. Nick told George that his father had been very ill.
12. He also told George that his father had completely recovered.
13. George said, "I hope you are telling the truth."
14. Nick told him that he was.
15. He also told George that his father was better than ever.

g. Change the following direct questions to reported speech. Include an *if*-clause in each (§ 11b).

1. Jane asked, "Was the lecture interesting?"
2. She asked, "Did the professor assign any reading?"
3. She asked, "Did the professor announce an exam?"
4. She asked, "Did Dr. Baker tell the students what to study?"
5. She asked, "Has Dr. Baker found his watch yet?"

6. The math teacher asked, "Did anyone solve the problem?"
7. Then he asked Bill, "Did you solve the problem all by yourself?"
8. Then he asked Jack, "Did you spend more than one hour on this problem?"
9. He asked the other students, "Would you like to see the solution?"
10. He asked Bill, "Would you put the solution on the board?"

11. George asked Nick, "Did you come on Air France?"
12. He also asked him, "Did you stop over in Paris?"
13. Then he asked, "Did you bring a message from my brother?"
14. Nick asked George, "Did you have trouble getting used to American customs?"
15. He asked him, "Didn't the food taste strange at first?"

h. Complete the following questions and answers by supplying *if*-clauses and *that*-clauses. Be sure that each answer fits the question made (§ 11).

Instructor: The registrar asked Jack . . .
Student: The registrar asked Jack if he had paid his laboratory fee.
Instructor: Jack said . . .
Student: Jack said that he hadn't.

1. The librarian asked me . . .
2. I said . . .
3. The dean asked George's adviser . . .
4. George's adviser said . . .
5. Nick asked the post office clerk . . .
6. The clerk said . . .
7. Mrs. Brown asked Mrs. Jones . . .
8. Mrs. Jones said . . .
9. Mrs. Baker asked Mrs. Allen . . .
10. Mrs. Allen said . . .
11. Miss Liu asked the librarian . . .
12. The librarian said . . .
13. Bill asked Betty . . .
14. Betty said . . .
15. Professor Miller asked Professor Allen . . .
16. Professor Allen said . . .

i. Answer the following questions as well as you can. Use complete sentences (§ 12).

1. How long does it take to get over the mumps? (V, 2)
2. How long does it take to get over the measles?
3. How long does it take to get over a cold?
4. How long does it take to get over the flu?
5. How long does it take to get over a broken heart?

6. Did you ever have a date with someone who didn't show up?
7. Have you ever made an appointment with someone and not shown up?
8. What happens when a person who has an airplane reservation doesn't show up?
9. When two people are arguing, what must one do?
10. When you can't solve a problem, what must you do?

j. Read the following sentences, supplying the missing prepositions (§ 13 and review).

1. Bill likes to listen _____ good music.
2. He enjoys looking _____ a good painting.
3. He likes to talk _____ interesting people.
4. He always depends _____ his friends.
5. After dinner he always works _____ his assignments.

16 Assignments

a. Copy the following paragraphs, filling each blank with some form of *ask, answer, say, tell, speak,* or *talk.*

    I saw Mr. Smith on the street today. He _____ to me and we stopped and _____. I _____ him about his wife, and he _____ by saying that she was never better. However, he _____ that his son had a bad cold. He also _____ me that his son was learning to _____ German because he was going to go to Germany in June. "That's wonderful," I _____. "Do you think that John will _____ at a meeting of our International Club when he comes back? He always _____ such interesting stories about his trips."

    "To _____ the truth, I don't know," Mr. Smith replied. "I'll _____ him if he's interested. I think he'll _____ 'yes.'"

    Mr. Smith and I _____ some more and then we _____ "Good-bye."

b. Write a short paragraph in which you tell some of the places you had been and some of the things you had seen and done before you came to this country. In another short paragraph tell where you have been and what you have seen and done since you came to this country.

c. Report in detail a short conversation you had with someone recently about a past event. Write it entirely in the patterns of reported speech.

REVIEW XII

a. Choose the correct verb phrase for each sentence.

1. The weather (has been/was) getting colder since the end of November.
2. Many of the students in this class (haven't seen/hadn't seen) snow before they came to this country.
3. They (have been/had been) looking forward to seeing snow for a long time when we finally had a good storm.
4. When the snow started to fall they (have become/became/had become) very excited.
5. After it (fell/had fallen/had been falling) for half an hour, they went outside to make snowballs.

6. How long (are you living/have you lived) in the United States?
7. How long (has it taken/did it take) you to come here?
8. (Have/Had) you traveled much before you made that trip?
9. (Have/Had) you ever been in New York?
10. (Have/Had) your parents been living in the same city (town, village) all their lives?

11. How long (did the students wait/have the students waited/had the students been waiting) when Professor Baker finally arrived?
12. (Do/Have) students usually (wait/waited) that long for a professor?
13. (Did/Have) Professor Allen's students (wait/waited) that long the day his car wouldn't start?
14. We (didn't have/haven't had) a quiz yesterday.
15. We (didn't have/haven't had) a dictation exercise in a long time.

b. Instructor: Read each statement aloud, raising your hand while saying the italicized words.

Student 1: Make an information question from the instructor's statement.

Student 2: Answer the question with a complete statement.

> Instructor: Jane got Betty to *help her with her homework.*
> Student 1: What did Jane get Betty to do?
> Student 2: She got Betty to help her with her homework.

1. Nick's mother made him *visit all his relatives* before he left Greece.
2. His father had the village tailor *make him a suit.*
3. Nick got his favorite teacher to write *a recommendation* for him.
4. His sister helped him *pack.*
5. She let him use *her* suitcase.

6. Professor Miller had his students read chapter *six.*
7. He made them turn in *outlines of the chapter.*
8. He got them to report on *outside readings.*
9. He helped them do the problems *at the end of the chapter.*
10. He let them use *their notes* during the quiz.

11. Mrs. Allen let Betty's friends *have a party* in her basement.
12. She got Betty to promise *that they wouldn't make much noise.*
13. She had the repair man *fix the record player* for them.
14. She helped Betty *make refreshments.*
15. She made the young people *clean up* before they left.

XIII

FUTURE PERFECT: SIMPLE AND CONTINUOUS
TWO-WORD VERBS, TAG QUESTIONS

Professor and Mrs. Baker have known each other since they were children. They grew up in the same town, but they went to different colleges. They hadn't seen each other for four years when they met on a ship going to England. During the trip they made up their minds to get married the following September. When they got home, they talked over their plans with their parents. At first Emily Baker's mother asked her to put off the wedding until December, but she changed her mind. That was almost forty years ago. Next September second, Dr. and Mrs. Baker will have been married for forty years. Dr. Baker will have retired, and they will have taken off for a trip around the world.

The Allens bought a house when they first moved to College Town. That was almost six years ago. By June first they will have been living in that house for six years. When Professor Miller called on them last week, he asked them about their house.

Prof. Miller:	You've owned this house quite a while, haven't you?
Prof. Allen:	It will be six years soon, won't it?
Mrs. Allen:	It will be six years in June.
Prof. Miller:	Taxes are pretty high in College Town, aren't they?
Prof. Allen:	Yes, they are, but it is nice to own your own home. You live in an apartment, don't you?
Prof. Miller:	Yes, I do. I'd like to own a home, but I think I'll wait until I get married. A house is a big responsibility for one person.
Prof. Allen:	That's right, isn't it, Ruth?
Mrs. Allen:	Yes, indeed. That's right.

1 **Simple future perfect tense** is a verb phrase made from *will* + *have* + past participle. It relates the completion of an act or condition before another action or time in the future. Sentences in this tense must include (or be in the environment of) a future time expression. These are usually in the form of *when*-clauses or phrases introduced by *in, next,* or *by.*

2 **Examples**

T	S	V			C
		Will	*Have*	*Part*	
Next September second	Dr. and Mrs. Baker	will	have	been	married for forty years.
By then	Dr. Baker	will	have	retired.	
	They	will	have	taken off	for a trip around the world.
By the time they get back	they	will	have	seen	many interesting sights.

3 **Continuous future perfect** is a verb phrase made from *will* + *have* + *been* + *ing*-form. It emphasizes the duration of a future event or a present situation which reaches into the future. Two time expressions are essential with this tense: (1) a specific future time or event, and (2) the duration.

4 **Examples**

T_1	S	V				P	T_2
		Will	*Have*	*Been*	*-ing*		
By June first	the Allens	will	have	been	living	in that house	for six years.
In September	George	will	have	been	studying	in this university	for two years.
When he gets his degree	he	will	have	been	living	abroad	for a long time.

5 **Choice of tense.** The future perfects are used less often than other tenses, probably because what they express can be stated in other less elegant ways. Probably every continuous future perfect statement could be expressed in the simple future perfect. The *ing*-form is used to emphasize duration; the past participle is used to emphasize completion. Though the verb phrases are long and cumbersome, they seldom cause learners much trouble.

6 | **Two-word verbs** in this lesson are:

call on: visit
hand in: submit
make up one's mind: decide
put off: postpone
take off: leave
talk over: discuss

7 | **Multiple meanings/multiple patterns.**   Many two-word verbs express different meanings in different contexts, and thus the grammatical patterns they follow differ also. One example is the unit *take off*, which is listed below as transitive and as intransitive but not as both. In the context of clothes, *take off* means to remove and it is transitive; in the context of travel, it means to leave and it is intransitive. The comments about particular two-word verbs below apply to them as they are used in these lessons.

8 | **Transitive/intransitive** (cf. IV, 10). The two-word verbs we have practiced so far may be classified as follows:

TRANSITIVE		BOTH	INTRANSITIVE
call on	put off	call up	get up
get over (illness)	put on	give up	make out
hand in	take off	hang up	show up
look up	talk over		take off
make up (mind)	try on		
pick out	wear out		
pick up			

9 **Separable/inseparable.** Transitive two-word verbs may be further classified as follows:

a. Inseparable two-word verbs are those whose objects never occur between the two parts of the verb.

> Professor Miller *called on* the Allens last week.
> George's father *got over* his illness by spring.

Call on and *get over* are the only two verbs in the list in § 8 which are inseparable.

b. Separable two-word verbs permit the object between the two parts in certain cases and require it there in others. Here are the rules:

1. *Short noun objects* which are not modified by a phrase or a clause may occur between the two parts of the verb or after the second part.

> Professor Baker *called* his secretary *up*.
> Professor Baker *called up* his secretary.

2. *Long noun objects* including phrases or clauses never split the two-word verb. They occur after it.

> Professor Baker *called up* the lady who works in his office.

3. *Pronoun objects* always occur between the two parts of a separable two-word verb.

> Professor Baker *called* her *up*.

10 **Scope of two-word verbs.** No one knows how many two-word verbs there are in English, but the number is very large. They are more common in speech than in writing, but some of them occur regularly in writing as there is no other natural way of expressing the same meanings. British and American two-word verbs differ rather more than other vocabulary items, and this fact sometimes leads to some very amusing misinterpretations. The meanings given in this book are all American.

11 **Some additional two-word verbs.** Here are twenty more common two-word verbs to memorize if you can. We shall have some practice with them in the exercises.

TRANSITIVE		INTRANSITIVE
Separable	**Inseparable**	
call off (cancel)	call on (ask to recite)	break down (stop functioning)
do over (repeat)	go over (review)	come back (return)
fill out (complete)	keep on (continue)	come over (visit)
find out (discover)	look into (investigate)	come to (regain consciousness)
leave out (omit)	run across (discover by chance)	get along (progress)
look over (examine)	run into (meet by chance)	pass out (faint)
pass out (distribute)		
take up (discuss)		

12 **Modification of two-word verbs.** Not many adverbs are used with two-word verbs. The most often used one is the word *right,* which in this context means something like immediately. It comes between the parts of the verb, even with inseparables and intransitives. When a separable verb is separated by an object and a modifier, the object precedes and the modifier follows.

> When the alarm clock rings, Bill *gets* right *up.*
> When a problem seems hard, Jack *gives* right *up.*
> When you don't know a word, you should *look* it right *up.*

13 **Tag questions** are short yes/no questions added to statements. They are conversation forms and seldom occur in writing except in reported speech. Sometimes tag questions are used just to keep the conversation going; other times the speaker is not absolutely sure of his statement and he is asking for confirmation. The two different situations are reflected in the intonation.[1]

Many languages have just one tag which is added to all statements: *n'est-ce pas? nicht wahr? değil mi?* هيأ مش؟ مـش؟ *μΕμΕἠ ɣ΄* ? है ना ?

English is more complicated. There is a separate tag for each sentence pattern. Observe the following facts about conversation questions:

[1] See Pronunciation helps.

a. When the statement is affirmative, the question is negative; when the statement is negative, the question is affirmative.

b. When the verb in the statement is a single form of *be*, the verb in the question is the same form.

Taxes are high in College Town, aren't they?
That's right, isn't it?

c. When the verb in the statement is a single form of any verb except *be*, the verb in the question is that same form (simple, *-s*, or past) of *do*.

You live in an apartment, don't you?
Professor Miller lives in an apartment, doesn't he?
Six years ago the Allens lived in an apartment, didn't they?

d. In most other cases, the verb in the question is the first auxiliary of the verb phrase.

You've owned this house quite a while, haven't you?
It will be six years soon, won't it?
You're not going to sell it, are you?
We hadn't thought of selling it, had we?

e. When the verb phrase in the statement is made with *used to* or *have to*, the verb in the question is *do*.

The Allens used to live in an apartment, didn't they?
They didn't have to pay property taxes then, did they?
They have to pay taxes now, don't they?

f. The second word of a tag question is always the subject form of a personal pronoun (I, 6), or one of the expletives *it* (VIII, 6), or *there* (III, 11). It is never a noun or any other noun substitute.

> This is a hard lesson, isn't it?
> There are many tag questions in English, aren't there?
> Learning all of them takes a long time, doesn't it?
> You have only one tag in your language, don't you? [2]

g. Statements made about one's self with the verb *be* are generally made in the negative, due to the lack of a contraction of *am + not* (I, 8). If the statement is affirmative, the full form must be used in the question. Though it sounds a bit pedantic, it is certainly quite acceptable.

> I'm not late, am I?
> I'm not going to see you again, am I?
> I'm going to see you again, am I not?

h. Responses to tag questions are the same as responses to any other yes/no questions. They vary according to facts and opinions.

14 **Verb with preposition** in this lesson is *grow up*—to change from an infant to an adult.

---

[2] In British English the tag for this question is *haven't you* (see II, 20a).

Pronunciation helps

a. When a speaker is quite sure that his statement is true, and he adds a tag question just to make conversation, the intonation of the question is the same as that of a statement.

You live in an a‾part‾ment, ‾don't‾ you?

b. When the speaker is not quite sure of his statement and he asks for confirmation, the intonation of the question is rising as for any yes/no question.

You live in an a‾part‾ment, don't‾ you?

Most learners find pattern a more difficult than pattern b. When you do the oral exercises, practice pattern a.

16 **Punctuation**

Taxes are high here⊙ aren't they?
That's right ⊙ isn't it?

Note the punctuation of a sentence containing a tag question. A comma (not a period or a semicolon) precedes the question. The first word of the question begins with a small letter, not a capital. A question mark is placed at the end.

221

17 Exercises

a. Use the future perfect tense to express the given information (§§ 1, 2).

> Instructor: Our professor will return from Mexico on June first.
> We will have our final exam on June third.
> Student: Our professor will have returned from Mexico by
> the time we have our final exam.

1. The Bakers are going to do many things before they start on their trip around the world. Tell what they will have done by the time they leave.

   (*a*)   sell their house
   (*b*)   buy a smaller house
   (*c*)   give their piano to their daughter
   (*d*)   put their Mercedes in storage
   (*e*)   purchase an expensive movie camera

2. Their travel agent will do many things for them before they leave. Tell what he will have done for them before they leave.

   (*a*)   arrange everything
   (*b*)   check all their plane connections
   (*c*)   confirm all their plane reservations
   (*d*)   reserve their hotel rooms
   (*e*)   hire cars and guides for them

3. While they are away, they will see and do many things. Tell what they will have seen and done by the time they come back.

   (*a*)   the famous art works in the Louvre
   (*b*)   the romantic canals of Venice
   (*c*)   the famous opera house in Milan
   (*d*)   St. Peter's Basilica in Rome
   (*e*)   the Acropolis in Athens
   (*f*)   the famous Blue Mosque of Istanbul
   (*g*)   the pyramids of Egypt
   (*h*)   Lenin's tomb in Red Square
   (*i*)   the floating market in Bangkok
   (*j*)   the Temple of the Thousand Lanterns

b. Combine the following pairs of sentences into one sentence in the future perfect tense. It is not necessary to include all the information in both sentences [3] (§§ 1, 2).

> Instructor: The play starts at eight forty.
> We won't get to the theater until nine.
> Student: The play will have started by the time we get to the theater.

1. The Allens eat at six thirty.
   Professor Miller is going to call on them at seven thirty.

2. Bill is going to leave for Westview at four next Friday.
   His mother is planning to call him up at five.

3. Bill is writing up his lab report now.
   The next lab session is tomorrow morning.

4. Jack is not going to write up his lab report tonight.
   The next lab session is tomorrow morning.

5. Betty will hand in her English term paper today.
   The due date is next Thursday.

6. Jane hasn't started her term paper yet.
   It is due tomorrow.

7. Mrs. Baker has not finished reading her library book.
   She has to return it to the library today.

8. George wants to move on the first of the month.
   He will find an apartment before then.

9. Nick is at Niagara Falls now.
   He will return before George moves.

10. Miss Liu has lived in College Town for six months.
    Three months from now she is going to move into a dorm.

11. The new chemistry professor is coming in June.
    Professor Baker leaves in August.

12. The dean is leaving for Mexico in May.
    The new chemistry professor is coming in June.

13. Professor Miller will finish his first book in May.
    He is going to start his second one in April.

[3] Instructor: Many of these items may be combined in two or more ways.

14. Betty is learning to play the piano.
    She will have her tenth lesson next Saturday.

15. Jane is learning to play bridge.
    She will have her eighth lesson this afternoon.

c. Change the following statements to information questions. Substitute question words or phrases for the italicized words (§§ 3, 4).

1. The Allens will have been living in their house *for six* years by June first.
2. Betty will have been living with them for two years *soon*.
3. *Professor Baker* will have been teaching chemistry for forty years when he retires.
4. Mrs. Baker will have been *keeping house* for forty years soon.
5. Professor *Miller* will have been working on his book for several years when it is published.
6. George will have been studying for *four* years when he gets his degree.
7. Bill will have been traveling for three hours when he reaches *Westview*.
8. By tomorrow Jane will have been taking *bridge* lessons for two months.
9. By next Saturday *Betty* will have been taking piano lessons for ten weeks.
10. By next month Mrs. Allen will have been working at the library *for two years*.
11. The pool will have been open for three months on *Labor Day*.
12. Summer School will have been over *for two weeks* by registration day.
13. *We* will have been practicing grammar for four months when we finish this course.
14. We will have been practicing *grammar* for four months when we finish this course.
15. We will have been *practicing grammar* for four months when we finish this course.

d. Substitute two-word verbs for the italicized verbs (§ 6).

> Instructor: The students are *discussing* the exam.
> Student: The students are *talking* over the exam.

1. Betty has *submitted* all her term papers.
2. Bill has *submitted* all his lab reports.
3. Jack is going to *submit* his on the last day.

4. Professor Miller *visited* the Allens last week.
5. The Allens *visited* the Bakers.
6. Who [4] did the Bakers *visit*?

7. Betty *postponed* her piano lesson this week.
8. Jane *postponed* her bridge lesson.
9. Will Professor Baker *postpone* the chemistry exam?

10. On June 30th the Allens will be *leaving* for the beach.
11. The Bakers will be *leaving* for Europe.
12. Where will Professor Miller be *leaving* for?

13. Jane *decided* to quit school.
14. George *decided* to look for a job.
15. The Bakers *decided* to travel around the world.

e. Student 1: Change the position of the object in the given sentence to another acceptable position, when possible.

Student 2: Repeat your neighbor's sentence, changing the object to a pronoun, when possible (§ 9b).
When it is not possible to move the object or to change it, simply repeat the sentence.

> Instructor: The Bakers didn't put off the wedding.
> Student 1: They didn't put the wedding off.
> Student 2: They didn't put it off.

1. The Bakers had made up their minds to be married.
2. To find the marriage license bureau, they looked up the address in the telephone directory.
3. They went there, and they filled out some forms.
4. Emily went shopping for the wedding. She picked out a beautiful dress.

[4] or *whom*

5. She tried on the dress.
6. She took off the dress.
7. She bought it and took it home. She hung up the dress carefully.
8. She talked over the wedding arrangements with her mother.
9. She looked over the invitations.
10. They hadn't left out anyone.

11. Jane handed in her term paper.
12. Her professor looked over her paper. She had misspelled many words.
13. He told her to look up those words.
14. When she copied her paper, she left out two paragraphs.
15. Her professor advised her to do over the paper.

f. Repeat the given sentence, substituting a pronoun for the italicized words. Make any necessary change in word order (§§ 9b, 11).

> Instructor: I had a bad cold last week. I just got over *the cold*.
> Student: I had a bad cold last week. I just got over it.

> Instructor: Jack wanted to speak to Bill. He called up *Bill*.
> Student: Jack wanted to speak to Bill. He called him up.

1. The freshmen hadn't studied oxidation. They took up *oxidation* last week.
2. Professor Baker wanted to find out if the students understood. He tried to find out *if they did*.
3. He decided to ask Joe. He called on *Joe*.
4. Joe didn't know part of the answer. He left out *part of it*.
5. Professor Baker repeated his explanation. He went over *the explanation* again.
6. George's adviser mentioned George's work. He asked George how he was getting along with *his work*.
7. George said that he wanted to talk over *his work* with his adviser.
8. His adviser mentioned his studies. He told George not to give up *his studies*.
9. He also mentioned assignments. He told George never to put off *assignments*.
10. He spoke about class notes. He told George he should go over *his class notes* every day.

11. I like my psychology professor. I ran into *my psychology professor* today.
12. He had some pamphlets. He was passing out *the pamphlets.*
13. I took one of his pamphlets. I looked over *the pamphlet.*
14. It was about a student complaint. The administration was looking into the *complaint.*
15. It concerned an evening activity. The administration had called off *the activity.*

g. Repeat the given statement and add a tag question. Pronounce the tag with falling intonation (§ 13b and f).

1. Mr. Allen is a professor.
2. His wife is attractive.
3. They are young.
4. They're not French.
5. They're American.

6. Mrs. Allen was in Greece once.
7. Mr. Allen never was.
8. Foreign students are often homesick.
9. George isn't homesick.
10. You aren't homesick.

11. This is an English class.
12. This exercise is easy.
13. The others are hard.
14. The last exam was difficult.
15. There were lots of hard questions on it.

h. Same as for exercise g (§ 13c).

1. Bill likes music.
2. He plays records at home.
3. He has a private room.
4. He introduced Jack to Jane.
5. Jack and Jane like each other.

6. Betty and her friends go on picnics.
7. They went on several last summer.
8. Betty didn't go swimming very often.
9. Her aunt and uncle had a good time when they went along.
10. Picnickers entertain themselves.

11. George came here a year ago.
12. He didn't like it here at first.
13. He likes it now though.
14. His parents write to him often.
15. They don't write in English.

i. Same as for exercise g (§ 13d).

1. We are practicing tag questions.
2. We aren't writing on the blackboard.
3. We're going to write on the blackboard later.
4. That will be in about half an hour.
5. We won't write on the blackboard until we finish the oral drills.

6. Professor Miller is going to give a lecture tonight.
7. There won't be any charge.
8. He is preparing his speech now.
9. His secretary will type it for him.
10. It will be a good speech.

11. The Allens have had their house for six years.
12. They aren't going to sell it.
13. They hadn't ever thought of it.
14. They will probably keep it until Professor Allen retires.
15. That's going to be a long time.

j. Same as for exercise g (§ 13e).

1. George used to live on a farm.
2. He and his brothers used to play together.
3. They used to chase rabbits.
4. George's uncle used to have a shoe store.
5. George used to help his uncle.

6. We have to come to class on time.
7. We have to do our homework every night.
8. Scholarship students have to keep up their grades.
9. Every foreign student has to take a placement exam.
10. Some don't have to take language classes.

11. You used to drink tea for breakfast.
12. You have to drink coffee now.
13. You aren't used to American food yet.
14. You have to eat it anyway.
15. You'll have to get used to it.

k. Same as for exercise g (§ 13a–g).

1. College Town is a small town.
2. There aren't many shops there.
3. Betty lives there with her aunt and uncle.
4. She used to live with her father and mother.
5. She's going to stay with her aunt and uncle until she graduates.

6. Studying a language is boring.
7. It requires a lot of time.
8. There are always more patterns.
9. They keep on getting more complicated.
10. I'm not going to give up, though.

11. You didn't use to have many tests.
12. You had to get used to taking tests.
13. You don't like it.
14. It helps you learn, though.
15. You'll be glad some day.

l. Tell the class where you grew up.

18 **Assignments**

a. Fill in the blanks with appropriate forms of two-word verbs (§§ 8, 11).

Jack _____ later than usual today. He didn't
          arise

_____ very well. He started off to school and his
          succeed

car _____. He _____ to get
      (stop functioning)   (return)

his bicycle. He ran so fast in the hot sun that he _____
                                                          (faint)

He _____ quickly, however, and rushed to class.
      (regain consciousness)

He was hoping to see Jane but she didn't _____.
                                                  (appear)

After class he went over to her house and _____
                                                    (discover)

that she had _____ for the mountains. Let's hope
                    (leave)

he _____ better tomorrow.
        (progress)

b. Write a paragraph in which you tell how long you will have been in this country when you go home. Tell some of the things that you think you will have done by that time. Tell some of the things that you hope you will have had an opportunity to do.

c. Write some statements about your classmates which you think are true but you're not sure. Add a tag question to each.

Mr. Lee, you grew up in Taiwan, didn't you?

REVIEW XIII

a. Make information questions from the following statements. Substitute question words or phrases for the italicized words.

1. Jack is *sick*.
2. Jane has *red* hair.
3. Bill has a *large* room.
4. Professor Baker *teaches chemistry*.
5. Mr. Allen teaches *foreign* students.

6. Thin people usually eat *salads*.
7. Bill usually calls his mother from *a public telephone in a drugstore near his house*.
8. There are *several thousand* books in the reference room.
9. Lake-of-the-Woods is about *fifteen miles* from College Town.
10. When people go there on picnics, they entertain themselves *by singing*.

11. People usually say *"How do you do"* when they are introduced.
12. The foreign students went on a trip to the TVA *six months* ago.
13. They visited *experimental* farms.
14. George used to live on *his grandfather's* farm.
15. He went to live with *his uncle* when he got old enough to go to school.

b. Read the following sentences aloud, supplying the appropriate tense of each verb in parentheses.

1. George (come) here two years ago.
2. He (live) in College Town since he arrived.
3. He (board) with an American family at first.
4. Then he (move) to a private room.
5. He (live) in a private room for several months now.

6. Betty (learn) to play tennis when she was fourteen.
7. She (play) every summer since that time.
8. She (play–neg.) very much last summer because she (have–neg.) a good partner.
9. She (like) to play tennis.
10. She (think) that it is good exercise.

11. Mrs. Allen (give) many parties.
12. She (give) one last Sunday.
13. She is going to have another one next Sunday and she (invite–already) the Bakers.
14. Mrs. Baker (answer–neg.) her invitation yet.
15. She (plan) to answer it tomorrow after she (has) an opportunity to discuss it with Professor Baker.

c. Punctuate the following dialogue without using quotation marks (V, 22 and VI, 13b).

mary where are you going john
john im going fishing i just bought a new fishing pole
mary what do you expect to catch
john nothing
mary why are you going fishing if you dont expect to catch anything
john mary why do you go shopping when you dont expect to buy anything

MODAL AUXILIARIES AND RELATED IDIOMS
TENSE SEQUENCE, REPORTED SPEECH

Miss Liu can't read for very long without getting a headache. One of the girls in her class told her that she should go to the Health Service and see a doctor. "You ought to see a doctor as soon as possible," she said. "You might need glasses."

As soon as Miss Liu had some free time, she went to the Health Service and asked for an appointment with an eye doctor. "I'd like an eye examination," she said.

The appointment clerk said that the doctor could see her at 3:15. "The doctor can see you at 3:15 this afternoon," she said.

Miss Liu replied that she would not be able to be there at 3:15 because she had a three o'clock class.

"The doctor might take you at about ten to four," the appointment clerk suggested, "but I'm not sure. Sometimes he goes home at four o'clock. Shall I put you down for ten to four, or would you rather come tomorrow?"

"I'll come at ten to four," Miss Liu replied. "I should have come last week. I may be straining my eyes."

When Miss Liu went to her three o'clock class, she asked her instructor for permission to leave a little early. "May I leave at 3:45 today?" she asked. "I have to have an eye examination. I get terrible headaches when I read. I must need glasses."

The instructor said that she might leave at 3:45, and then he added, "You had better take down the assignment for next time."

Miss Liu went back to the Health Service at 3:45. The doctor was busy and she had to wait about half an hour. She could have read her assignment in that time but she didn't. She would have done it if she hadn't had a headache. She couldn't help thinking, "I should be reading my assignment."

When she saw the doctor, he put drops in her eyes and then she couldn't read at all. "The effect of these drops will have worn off by midnight," the doctor told her. "You had better not try to read tonight."

1 **The ten modal auxiliaries** are: *can/could, will/would, shall/should–ought, may/might,* and *must.* They differ from the other auxiliaries (*do, be, have*) in that they have no *s*-forms, *ing*-forms, or participles. Furthermore, the so-called past forms of modals sometimes express the same meaning as the present or simple forms. They also occur in statements which refer to future time. Thus we must remember that the form of a modal does not necessarily indicate the time reference of the sentence in which it is used.

In addition, verb phrases with negated modals do not always express the opposite of affirmative ones; questions asked with one modal sometimes require answers expressed with another. All in all, the meanings of modals are very complex indeed.

Most of these words form contractions with *not,* the common ones being *can't,*[1] *couldn't, won't, wouldn't, shouldn't, mightn't, mustn't.* May, ought, and shall are seldom contracted in American English. *Will* and *would* also form contractions with subject pronouns. Contractions with *will* are listed in VI, 6a. Those with *would* are *I'd, you'd, he'd, she'd, it'd, we'd, they'd.* Contractions with pronouns are never used in sentence final position.

The best way to master the use of modals is to observe how they are used in situations and to practice making sentences like the ones you hear, always making absolutely sure of the meaning of what you are saying. The sentences in the model paragraphs and the explanations on the next few pages should help you understand some of the complexities of these unusual words.

a. *Can/could* (ability, possibility, opportunity, permission)

1. Present ability, affirmative and negative (*can*)

> George can read English quite well now.
> Miss Liu can't read without getting a headache.

2. Past ability with suggestion of changed condition (*could*)

> Until a short time ago, Miss Liu could read without getting a headache.
> George couldn't read English very well when he first came to America.

---

[1] Note that *can't* has only one *n*, not two.

3. Future possibility (*can* or *could*)

> The clerk said, "The doctor can see you at 3:15."
> The clerk said, "The doctor could see you at 3:15."

4. Present or future impossibility, contrary-to-fact(*could*). See XIX.

> Miss Liu could be reading her assignment now if she didn't have
>   drops in her eyes.
> Miss Liu could read her assignment tomorrow morning if she didn't
>   have a class.

5. Past impossibility inferred (*couldn't have* + past participle)

> Bill couldn't have gone home this weekend.
> I saw him at the ball game on Saturday and in the library on
>   Sunday.

6. Past opportunity not realized (*could have* + past participle)

> Miss Liu could have read her assignment while she waited for the
>   doctor. (She didn't.)

7. Past opportunity realized can not be expressed with a modal.

> Miss Liu was able to get an appointment with the doctor this
>   afternoon.

8. Present or future permission (*can/may*)

> Miss Liu's instructor said, "You can leave now."
> Miss Liu's instructor said, "You can leave at 3:45."

Can is widely used; *may* is preferred.

9. Past permission with suggestion of changed condition (*could/might*)

> When Mrs. Allen was a student, anyone could borrow books from
>   the library.

Could is widely used; *might* is the older form, still preferred by some
people.

b. *Will/would* (promise, agreement, request, contrary-to-fact)

1.   Future plan, promise, or agreement (VI, 1b) (*will*)

I will come at ten to four. (This is a definite appointment.)
"I will do whatever you advise," Miss Liu said to the doctor.

2.   Continuing future activity (VI, 3) (*will* + *be* + *ing*)

At midnight Miss Liu will be reading her assignment.

3.   Completion of future activity (XIII, 1) (*will* + *have* + past participle)

By midnight the effect of the drops will have worn off.

4.   Polite request for action in the immediate or distant future (*will* or *would*)

Will you please close the door?
Would you please close the door?

Will you please lock the door when you come in?
Would you please lock the door when you come in?

Some people consider *would* more polite than *will* in this pattern.

5.   Present and past contrary-to-fact statements (*would*)

If Miss Liu didn't have a headache now, she would be reading her assignment.
If Miss Liu didn't have a headache, she would read her assignment.
If Miss Liu hadn't had a headache, she would have read her assignment.

This type of sentence is called a conditional because a condition is set forth in the *if*-clause. Conditionals are more fully explained and practiced in Lesson XIX.

c. *Shall/should/ought* (advisability, obligation, expectation, chance)

1.   Affirmative questions of advisability, first person, immediate or distant future (*shall* or *should*)

Shall I put you down for ten to four?
Should I put you down for ten to four?
Shall we go to Europe next year?
Should we go to Europe next summer?

2. Negative questions of advisability, present or past (*should*)

>Shouldn't we be doing our homework? (We aren't.)
>Shouldn't Jack have done all the problems? (He didn't.)

3. Statements of advisability, all-time and future (*should* or *ought*)

>We should be careful crossing streets. (all time)
>We ought to be careful crossing streets.

>Miss Liu should see a doctor as soon as possible. (future)
>Miss Liu ought to see a doctor as soon as possible.

4. Unfulfilled obligation, present and past (*should* or *ought*)

>I should be reading my assignment. (I am not.)
>I ought to be reading my assignment. (I am not.)
>Miss Liu should have been reading her assignment while she was
>   waiting to see the doctor.

>I should have read my assignment yesterday. (I didn't.)
>I ought to have read my assignment yesterday. (I didn't.)

5. Fulfilled obligation, recurrent and past, can not be expressed with a modal.

>Bill is obliged to visit his mother every other weekend. (He does.)
>Professor Allen was obliged to entertain the new professor, Mr.
>   Miller. (He did.)

6. Expectation or likelihood (*should* or *ought*)

>It is eight o'clock. The guests should be arriving soon.
>George is bright and he works hard. He ought to do well.

7. Chance happening as a condition (*should*)

>Should you see Mr. Allen, give him my regards.
>If you should see Mr. Allen, give him my regards.

d. *May/might* (permission, conjecture)

1. Permission, present or future (*may*)

> Miss Liu asked, "May I leave at 3:45?"
> Her instructor said, "You may leave at 3:45."
> At 3:45 her instructor said, "You may leave now."

2. Past permission can not be expressed with a modal.

> Miss Liu had permission to leave class early.
> Miss Liu was permitted to leave class early.
> Miss Liu was allowed to leave class early.

3. Conjecture [2] about a present situation (*may* or *might*)

> Miss Liu may need glasses.
> Miss Liu might need glasses.

4. Conjecture about a present activity (*may* or *might* + *ing*)

> George may be writing to his father.
> Bill may be calling up his mother.

5. Conjecture about the future (*may* or *might*)

> Miss Liu may be absent tomorrow.
> Miss Liu might be absent tomorrow.
> She may not come to school.
> She might not feel well.

6. Conjecture about the past (*may* or *might* + *have* + past participle)

> Professor Baker may have lost his watch at the Golf Club.
> Professor Baker might have lost his watch at the Golf Club.

e. *Must* (necessity, abstention, deduction)

1. Necessity: present, future, and all-time

> The lecture must begin right now.
> Miss Liu must leave at 3:45.
> Students must read their assignments.

[2] A conjecture is a reasonable guess.

2. Abstention is signaled by the negative.

> We must not neglect our eyes.
> We must not break the law.

3. Lack of necessity can not be expressed with a modal (VIII, 4). *Have to* is used instead.

> Jane doesn't have to have an eye exam.
> She doesn't have to wear glasses.

4. Past necessity is also expressed with *have to*, since *must* has no past form.

> Miss Liu had to leave class early yesterday.

5. Deduction about a present situation or action (*must* + simple) or (*must* + *be* + *ing*)

> Miss Liu is frowning. Her head must be aching.
> She gets terrible headaches. She must need glasses.

6. Deduction about a future event includes *must* plus the future marker *going to*.

> It is getting very dark out. It must be going to rain.

7. Deduction about the past, simple and continuous (*must* + *have* + *been* . . .)

> The doctor wasn't free when Miss Liu arrived at the Health
>   Service.
> He must have been seeing [3] another patient.
> He kept her waiting for half an hour.
> He must have been very busy.

---

[3] *See* is one of the verbs of perception, not usually used in a continuous tense (III, 8). In the sentence above, however, *see* is a synonym for *examine* or *consult*. When *see* has this meaning, it is used in the continuous.

2 **Sentence patterns with modals**

a. All modals except *ought* are followed by simple-form verbs. Negatives are made by adding *not* to or after the modal. Questions are made by moving the modal before the subject as with any other auxiliary. Auxiliary *do* is never used with a modal.

QW	MODAL	S	V			C	
			Modal	Simple	Other	O	T
		Miss Liu	should	have	read	her assignment	this afternoon.
	Should	Miss Liu		have	read	her assignment	this afternoon?
Who	should	——		have	read	her assignment	this afternoon?
When	should	Miss Liu	——	have	read	her assignment?	

b. *Ought* is followed by an infinitive instead of by a simple form. In all other respects it is the same as the other modals.

QW	MODAL	S	V			C	
			Modal	Infinitive	Other	O	T
		Miss Liu	ought	to have	read	her assignment	this afternoon.
	Ought	Miss Liu	——	to have	read	her assignment	this afternoon?
Who	ought	——	——	to have	read	her assignment	this afternoon?
What	ought	Miss Liu	——	to have	done	——	this afternoon?

3 **Related words and idioms**

a. *Can't help* (past: *couldn't help*) is an idiom expressing inability to avoid or prevent. It is followed by an *ing*-form or *it*.

The doctor can't help keeping people waiting.
He doesn't like it, but he can't help it.

Miss Liu couldn't help thinking that she should be reading her assignment.

b. *Would like* is a polite synonym for *want*. It is frequently followed by an infinitive.

1. A question with *would like* is a kind of invitation.

> The doctor said, "Would you like to come in now?"
> Jack asked Jane if she would like to go to a movie.

2. A statement with *would like* is a kind of order.

> I would like a menu, please.
> I would like to see a menu, please.

Be very careful not to confuse *like* (enjoy) with *would like* (want). When the *would* is contracted, they sound almost the same, but the meanings differ.

> I like chocolate cake. (I enjoy eating it.)
> I'd like a piece of chocolate cake. (Bring me a piece now.)
> I'd like to have a piece of chocolate cake.

c. *Would rather* is an idiom which means *prefer*. It is followed by the simple form of a verb.

> Would you rather come tomorrow?
> Miss Liu said that she would rather come at ten to four.

d. *Had better* is an idiom which expresses advisability (see 1c). It is followed by a simple verb form. Although *had* is a past form, it does not refer to the past in this idiom. It is usually joined to a pronoun subject in the form of a contraction (XI, 2b).

> You had better take down the assignment for next time.
> You'd better take it down.

e. *Maybe* is one word, an adverb, a synonym for *perhaps*. It should not be confused with *may + be*, aux. plus verb. The two are similar in meaning but the sentence patterns are different.

> Maybe it is raining in London now.
> It may be raining in London.

f. *Willing* is an adjective denoting cheerful readiness.

> Professor Allen is always willing to help his students.

Sentence patterns with idioms

a. Each idiom is followed by a different verb form. Note particularly the forms following each idiom. Questions are made by moving the auxiliary in the idiom as in other sentence patterns.

S	V		C
	Idiom	(Note Form)	
The doctor	can't help	keeping	people waiting.
Miss Liu	would like	to see	an eye doctor.
We	had better	read	the assignment.

b. *Would rather* is a kind of comparative (see XVIII). It is followed by a simple-form verb which may or may not have an object. The complete form (not in the model paragraphs) then requires *than* followed by another simple verb or by another object of the same verb. Note the variations of the pattern in the following chart.

S	V		C			
	Idiom	Simple	O	Than	V	O
Betty	would rather	study		than	work.	
Betty	would rather	study	literature	than		chemistry.
Betty	would rather	study	chemistry	than	do	housework.

 Tense sequence. When the object of a verb is a noun clause (XII, 11), the verb in the clause usually agrees in tense with the main verb, or it is farther in the past than the main verb.

Professor Allen *knows* that his students *don't* always *understand*.
    (present)   (present)

Professor Allen *knew* that his students *didn't* always *understand*.
    (past)   (past)

Professor Allen *knew* that his students *hadn't* always *understood*.
    (past)   (past perfect)

This generalization is particularly true in the case of reporting speech (cf. XII, 2b, 11a and b).

6 **Reported speech and modals.** When changing sentences with modals from direct to indirect quotation, if the main verb is past, . . .

a. *Can →⁴ could*

> The clerk said, "The doctor can see you at 3:15."
> The clerk said that the doctor could see Miss Liu at 3:15.

b. *Will → would*

> Miss Liu said, "I will come at ten to four."
> Miss Liu said that she would come at ten to four.

c. *Shall → should*

> The clerk asked, "Shall I put you down for ten to four?"
> The clerk asked if she should put Miss Liu down for ten to four.

d. *Should* remains *should*

> Miss Liu kept thinking, "I should be reading my assignment."
> Miss Liu kept thinking that she should be reading her assignment.

e. *Ought* remains *ought*

> Miss Liu's friend said, "You ought to have your eyes examined."
> Miss Liu's friend said that she ought to have her eyes examined.

f. *May → might*

> Miss Liu's instructor said, "You may leave at 3:45."
> Miss Liu's instructor said that she might leave at 3:45.

g. *Must* remains *must* or *→ had to*

> Miss Liu said, "I must have my eyes examined."
> Miss Liu said that she must have her eyes examined.
> Miss Liu said that she had to have her eyes examined.

---

⁴ Read the arrow to mean *becomes.*

7 **Pronouns in reported speech.** Note particularly the difference in pronouns between direct quotation and reported speech in the sentences above. When reporting speech, be careful to use the appropriate pronouns.

8 **Pronunciation helps**

a. Contrast of *can* and *can't*. Very often when a student says that he can do something, the listener thinks he says that he can't do it. The trouble lies not with the pronunciation of the *t*, but with the vowel sound. *Can* is almost always unstressed [5] and, as a result, the vowel is shortened and centralized. The vowel in *can't* is usually given its full value and this provides a very noticeable contrast of the two words in the speech of a native speaker. Listen while your instructor pronounces the following sentence and note the contrast. Practice making the contrast in sentences of your own.

Mr. Allen can read French but he can't speak it.

b. Silent *l*. Do not pronounce the *l* in *could, should,* or *would. Would* sounds like *wood* and the other two words rhyme with it.

c. Silent *gh.* Do not pronounce the *gh* in *ought* or *might.*

d. The negatives. *Couldn't, mightn't, shouldn't,* and *wouldn't* all have two syllables, and the second syllable of each contains a syllabic *n* (see VII, 12c). The first *t* in *mustn't* is not pronounced.

---

[5] It is stressed only when it is emphasized, as in a contradiction: *You think I can't read Spanish but I cán.*

9 **Questions students sometimes ask**

a. How do we know whether the *'d* of contractions like *he'd* means *had* or *would*?

You can usually tell from what follows. *Would* is always followed by a simple form, *had* by a past participle. When the main verb of a sentence is one of those which has no special past forms (see list in VII, 3a), you will know from the context (what is said before and after).

b. In cases where there are two or three ways of expressing the same idea, how do you choose which one to use?

It is a matter of habit more than anything else. Different native speakers choose different forms. You should understand all of the verb phrases in this lesson, but you probably won't need to use all of them.

10 Exercises

a. Tell the class about some skill you have developed. Use *couldn't* and *can* as in the given example (§ 1a, 1 and 2).

> I *couldn't* play bridge last year but I *can* now.

b. Tell the class about some skill you have lost. Use *could* and *can't* as in the given example (§ 1a, 1 and 2).

> I *could* swim two miles when I was eighteen, but I *can't* any more.

c. Following are some statements about things that didn't happen. Assuming they are lost opportunities, tell what could have happened [6] (§ 1a, 6).

> Instructor: Miss Liu didn't read her assignment while she waited for the doctor.
>
> Student: Miss Liu could have read her assignment while she waited for the doctor.

1. The Allens didn't go to Hawaii on their vacation.
2. Mr. Allen didn't buy Professor Baker's Mercedes.
3. Mrs. Allen didn't take a full-time job in the library.
4. The Bakers didn't sell their house at a huge profit.
5. Professor Miller didn't require a term paper this semester.

6. Jack didn't enter the bridge tournament.
7. Jane didn't write up her lab reports on time.
8. Bill didn't get a ride to Westview last Saturday.
9. Betty didn't win the tennis championship last summer.
10. George didn't go on the trip to the TVA.

11. You didn't write a very good paragraph.
12. You didn't solve all the assigned problems.
13. You didn't attend all of the lectures.
14. You didn't consult with your professors.
15. You didn't ask your classmates for help.

---

[6] Instructor: In a few of the items (e.g., 3, 8), changing the main verb makes a better response.

---

d. Tell the class something you believe to be advisable for all of us. Use *should* or *ought,* affirmative or negative (§ 1c, 3).

> We should eat a balanced diet.
> We ought not to be rude to anyone.

e. Following are some statements about some things that didn't happen. Assuming they are unfulfilled past obligations, tell what should have happened (§ 1c, 4).

> Instructor: Jack didn't do all the problems.
> Student: Jack should have done all the problems.

1. Professor Baker didn't arrive at two o'clock.
2. He didn't make a homework assignment.
3. He didn't announce the exam before he dismissed the class.
4. He didn't tell the class what the exam would cover.
5. He didn't keep his four o'clock appointment with the dean.

6. Mrs. Brown forgot to give Bill his check last Sunday.
7. Mr. Jones forgot to pay the electricity bill.
8. Mrs. Jones forgot to go to the hairdresser.
9. Professor Miller forgot to call up his publisher.
10. Mrs. Baker forgot to inquire at the Golf Club about Professor Baker's watch.

11. George failed to renew his visa.
12. Nick failed to make up his mind about his major.
13. Jane failed to review her notes before the exam.
14. Betty failed to tell her aunt that she wouldn't be home for supper.
15. Miss Liu failed to notify her landlady that she was going to move.

f. Student 1: Try to get a confession from one of your classmates by asking him the two questions below. You may ask about any time of the day or night.

Student 2: Answer in a humorous way. Don't worry about the truth this time (§ 1c, 4).

> Student 1: What were you doing at 2 a.m.?
> Student 2: I was watching the late-late show.
> Student 1: What should you have been doing?
> Student 2: I should have been cutting my toenails.

g. Tell what is permitted and what is not permitted to some particular group in your country. Follow the pattern of the given sentence (§ 1d, 1).

In the United States a foreigner may discuss politics but he may not vote.

h. Make a conjecture about the present-moment activity of some famous or infamous world figure. Mention that person by name. Use *may* or *might* (§ 1d, 4).

Queen Elizabeth II may be making a speech.
Liza Minelli might be making a movie.

i. There are many things we do not know about the past. Make a conjecture about some past event, using the cue words (§ 1d, 6).

Instructor: The first people
Student: The first people may have lived in Africa.

1. The first birds	6. The Phoenicians	11. The first cultivated crop
2. The first fish	7. The Egyptians	12. The first domesticated animal
3. The first plants	8. The Persians	13. The first pet
4. The first insects	9. The Greeks	14. The first musical instrument
5. The first animals	10. The Romans	15. The first religion

j. Following is a list of activities. Some of them we *must* do, some we *must not* do, and others we *don't have to* do. Make the appropriate sentence for each item (§ 1e, 1–3).

Instructor: buy expensive clothes
Student: We don't have to buy expensive clothes.

1. improve our English	11. go to the movies
2. disturb our neighbors	12. do our assignments
3. eat spinach	13. carry a gun without a license
4. stand up when the professor enters	14. take exams
5. pay tuition	15. play tennis
6. drive on the left side of the street	
7. take other people's belongings	
8. obey the law	
9. go swimming	
10. cross the street against a red light	

k. Tell what you deduce from the following. Use the cue word (§ 1e, 5).

> Instructor: Miss Liu is holding her hand on her head. (headache)
> Student: She must have a headache.

1. Your pen won't write. (ink)
2. You can't open your door. (lock)
3. It is getting dark. (late)
4. Your room is cold. (heat)
5. Jack drinks milk with every meal. (like)

6. I smell smoke. (burn)
7. I feel a draft. (window)
8. I hear footsteps. (come)
9. I see a student running. (late)
10. Bill is absent today. (sick)

11. Jack didn't eat any breakfast this morning. (hungry)
12. You just called your friend up but no one answered the telephone. (out)
13. Jane won the girls' swimming contest. (good)
14. Mrs. Allen goes to the library every week. (read)
15. Professor Baker drives a new Mercedes. (money)

l. Tell what you deduce about the past from the following statements (§ 1e, 7).

> Instructor: Jack was early to class today.
> Student: He must have gotten up early.

1. Mr. Park was late to class today. (get up)
2. He seemed very tired. (bed)
3. He was carrying an umbrella when he arrived. (rain)
4. He knew that we were going to have a test. (tell)
5. He answered all the questions in twenty minutes. (study)

6. Professor Miller found a ticket on his car this afternoon. (park)
7. Then he couldn't find his car keys. (lose)
8. After he found them, he couldn't start his car. (gas)
9. He phoned his garage but no one answered for a long time. (busy)
10. Professor Miller had to take a taxi home to dinner. (angry)

11. Mrs. Allen had dinner at a friend's house last night. (invited)
12. Her husband ate at home, alone. (invited)
13. Betty stayed on campus and ate in the cafeteria. (work)
14. Mrs. Allen went right to bed when she got home. (tired)
15. She woke up early this morning. (sleep)

m. Tell the class about something you can't help or something you couldn't help at some time in the past. Make your own sentence or, if you prefer, ask the instructor for a suggestion (§ 2a).

> I can't help feeling homesick.
> I can't help missing my family.

1. worry about	6. wake up	11. be honest
2. think about	7. fall asleep	12. be undiplomatic
3. talk about	8. be late	13. hurt people's feelings
4. laugh at	9. get sick	14. say what I think
5. cry over	10. lose weight	15. make people angry

n. Student 1: Ask your neighbor if he likes something.
Student 2: Answer yes or no. If yes, . . .
Student 1: Ask him if he would like to have it or do it now.[7]
Student 2: Answer (§ 2b).

> Instructor: tennis
> Student 1: Do you like tennis?
> Student 2: Yes.
> Student 1: Would you like a game of tennis?
> (or) Would you like to play tennis?
> Student 2: Not now, thank you. I am busy just now.

1. cigars	6. sailing	11. chess
2. candy	7. skiing	12. bridge
3. beer	8. picnics	13. parties
4. ice cream	9. hiking	14. dancing
5. peanuts	10. fishing	15. movies

[7] Instructor: Listen carefully for appropriate quantifiers, e.g., *a, some, a glass of, a dish of*, etc.

o. Change the following sentences to include the idiom *would rather*. Be very careful of your sentence structure (§ 4b).

> Instructor: For swimming, Mrs. Brown prefers fresh water to salt water.
> Student: Mrs. Brown would rather swim in fresh water than in salt water.
> Instructor: She prefers sewing to shopping for clothes.
> Student: She would rather sew than go shopping.
> (or) She would rather make her clothes than buy them.

1. Betty prefers tennis to swimming.
2. Jack prefers rock to classical music.
3. He also prefers chemistry to English.
4. Bill prefers concerts to movies.
5. Jane prefers parties to studies.

6. Mr. Jones prefers steak to chicken.
7. Mrs. Jones prefers tea to coffee.
8. Mrs. Allen prefers library work to housework.
9. Mr. Allen prefers a pipe to cigarettes.
10. Professor Miller prefers lecturing to writing.

11. Jack prefers chocolate ice cream to vanilla.
12. Bill prefers green ties to brown ones.
13. Professor Baker prefers a Mercedes to a Jaguar.
14. Professor Miller prefers being single to being married.
15. For marriage, George prefers Greek girls to American girls.

p. Tell what the person mentioned had better do in the situation. Use a contracted form (§§ 1, 3d).

> Instructor: Mrs. Jones is tired.
> Student: She'd better go to bed.

1. Miss Liu is sick.
2. Mr. Lee is late.
3. We are late.
4. Mr. Baker's phone is ringing.
5. My phone is ringing.

6. Mrs. Baker has a toothache.
7. Mr. Miller needs a new pair of shoes.
8. Jack's hair is too long.
9. Jane's pen doesn't write.
10. You haven't any writing paper.

11. I have to go out and it's raining.
12. Bill is very hungry.
13. He is cold.
14. Jack and Bill both have tests tomorrow.
15. You have a test today.

11 Assignments

a. Change the following sentences in such a way that one of the modal auxiliaries appears in each. Chose the modal which best expresses the meaning in each case.

> Example: Miss Liu has permission to leave class early.
> Change: Miss Liu may leave class early.

1. It is advisable for Miss Liu to go to a doctor.
2. She promises to go this afternoon.
3. She is not able to go at 3:15.
4. I guess she will go at 3:50.
5. She has permission to leave her three o'clock class early.

6. Teachers are obligated to help their students.
7. George's adviser promised to help George.
8. He told George that it was possible for him to have an appointment on Friday.
9. George asked, "Do you want me to come at eight o'clock?"
10. His adviser answered, "Yes, if you are able."

11. It is necessary for all students to have ID cards.
12. They are obligated to do their best work.
13. If they do their best, they are going to pass.
14. George had the ability to pass economics if he had tried.
15. Perhaps students don't always know how to study.

b. Write one sentence to express each of the following.

1. Something that you have the ability to do
2. Something that you don't have the ability to do
3. An act that you had an opportunity to perform but didn't
4. Something that you had an opportunity to do and you did
5. A conjecture about some time in the future
6. A conjecture about the present, another place
7. A conjecture about the past
8. Something that you mustn't do and something that you don't have to do
9. Something that you are not able to prevent
10. A question of advisability

11. A situation which is known to be impossible
12. A past obligation which you did not discharge
13. Something that you like
14. Something that you would like
15. An invitation

c. Change the following sentences from direct quotation to reported speech (§§ 5, 6). Pay particular attention to the sequence of tenses and to the pronoun forms. Be sure that your statements are complete sentences.

> Professor Miller often says, "I like giving public lectures."
> Professor Miller often says that he likes giving public lectures.
> He said, "I am going to talk about price controls next week."
> He said that he was going to talk about price controls next week.

1. Betty said, "I can't do the third problem."
2. Bill said, "I will explain it to you."
3. Professor Allen said to Betty, "You shouldn't have Bill do your problems. You should do them yourself."
4. Bill said, "I'm not going to do the problem for her; I'm just going to explain it to her."
5. Professor Allen added, "Betty, you'd better be sure that you understand it."

6. Miss Liu often says, "I can't help thinking of home."
7. Her roommate always answers, "You should try not to think of home so often."
8. Miss Liu replies, "I can't seem to get used to American food."
9. Then her roommate asks her, "Why don't you learn to cook?"
10. Miss Liu always answers, "I don't like to cook."

11. George: How many more credits do I need for graduation?
12. Adviser: Twenty-six.
13. George: Must I take a qualifying examination in English?
14. Adviser: No.
15. George: Why not?
16. Adviser: Because you have a grade of A in English.

REVIEW XIV

a. Choose the appropriate verb phrase from those in parentheses; then read the sentence aloud.

1. Mr. Smith is absent today. He (has to be, could have been, might be, must have been) sick.

2. If you walk down the hall to your left you (can find, will meet, will see, can come to) a stairway.

3. Miss Lee (could have gone, wasn't able to go) to Lake-of-the-Woods last Sunday. She (must, had to) attend a reception in College Town.

4. (Do, Would, Will) you like to go on a picnic?

5. If wishes were horses, beggars (can, could, would have to) ride.

6. (Shall, Will) these papers be graded by tomorrow?

7. (Should, Ought) we to stop writing when the bell rings?

8. George (was going to go, could have gone, was able to go) to the YMCA program last Sunday, but he changed his mind.

9. Jim (used to, had to) travel by bus, but now he travels by plane.

10. I can't find my key. I (must lose, must have lost, might lose) it.

11. If I had a bathing suit I (could have gone, could go, will go) swimming.

12. I haven't written to my father lately, but I (should, ought, must) to.

13. Joe wants to make a good grade. He (can, should, have to) study hard.

14. When you use a ruler, you (must, can, have to) draw a straight line.

15. If the weather gets colder, the flowers (will, can, should) die.

b. Add a tag question to each of the following statements.

1. Jane can dance.
2. Betty likes to play tennis.
3. George might go home this summer.
4. People can't help making mistakes.
5. We shouldn't cross streets without looking both ways.

6. Students must take good care of their eyes.
7. They should have them examined.
8. Miss Liu had better have hers examined.
9. She will do it.
10. She promised her roommate that she would.

11. Mrs. Allen would like to have another party.
12. She might have one at Christmas time.
13. Jack and Jane would be invited.
14. They'd go.
15. Jane would rather go to a party than study.

LESSON

XV

DIRECTIONS, INSTRUCTIONS, SUGGESTIONS
ORDER OF MODIFIERS, MORE NOUN CLAUSES

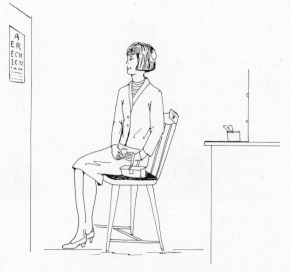

The doctor in the Health Service who examined Miss Liu's eyes told her that she needed glasses but he did not prescribe any for her. "I do not prescribe lenses," he said. "You will have to go to someone else for that. You will have to go to an optometrist." He gave her a small white card with a name and address on it. "Don't put it off," he warned. "Make an appointment today."

Miss Liu called the telephone number on the card and made an appointment to see the optometrist. She asked the appointment clerk how to get to the office. "Take a #2 bus to Main and Elm," the clerk said. "Get off there and walk two blocks east on Elm. Go as far as Beech Street. Cross Beech Street and then turn left and walk about half a block along Beech until you come to 457. It's across the street from the Town Building. Take the elevator; the doctor's office is on the third floor, Room 323. Please get here on time. Please don't be late; the doctor is very busy."

Miss Liu was very interested in what she saw in the optometrist's office. There was a large upright leather chair in the middle of the room with a metal cabinet full of lenses beside it. On the wall opposite the chair was a chart with letters of all sizes on it. In back of the chair there was a mirror on the wall which had a small electric light bulb above it. Before Miss Liu finished looking around, the doctor entered and asked her to sit down in the large chair. He asked her who had recommended him to her. She couldn't remember the doctor's name just then, but she remembered it afterwards.

1 **Directions and instructions** are most easily understood when they are given in the imperative pattern. This sentence type starts with the verb phrase and has no expressed subject. A negative verb phrase may be made in the usual way or with the frequency word *never*.

(DO + NOT)	VERB SIMPLE FORM	OBJECT	PLACE	TIME
	Take	a #2 bus	to Main and Elm.	
	Walk		along Beech	until you come to 457.
Don't	put off	seeing an optometrist.		
Never	neglect	your eyes.		

2 **Requests** are made in the same pattern (cf. XIV, 1b, 4) by the addition of the courtesy word *please*. It is most polite to place *please* first, though it may occur at the end. Never put *please* between a verb and its object.

PLEASE	VERB		COMPLEMENT	
	(Do + Not)	Simple	P	T
Please		get	here	on time.
Please	don't	be		late.

3 **Let's** introduces a suggestion which includes the speaker. It is a contraction of *let us* but the full form is seldom used. The direct object of *let* is always another verb, with or without a complement.

LET'S	(NOT)	VERB	COMPLEMENT	
Let's		go	to class.	
Let's		hurry.		
Let's	not	be	late.	
Let's		help	Professor Baker	look for his watch.

4 **Suggestions** of a more formal nature are expressed in sentences with noun-clause objects introduced by *that* (cf. XII, 11). The tense-sequence rule (XIV, 5) does not apply in these cases, since the verb in the noun clause refers to a condition which does not exist at the time of speaking. The verb in the noun-clause object is always a simple form (called subjunctive when thus used), regardless of the tense of the verb in the independent clause.

S	V	O			
		CM	S	V	C
The doctor	suggested	that	Miss Liu	see	an optometrist.
He	urged	that	she	make	an appointment at once.
The clerk	requested	that	she	be	on time.

5 **Verbs taking subjunctive noun-clause objects** [1]

advise	insist	request
ask [2]	prefer	require
demand	propose	suggest
forbid	recommend	urge

6 **Noun-clause objects made from questions**

a. Verb *be* questions have the verb before the subject (I, 4). When these are made into noun clauses, however, the verb follows the subject, as in statements.

Question:		Where is the office?	
Noun clause:	. . .	where	the office is
As object:	Who knows	where	the office is?
Question:		What street is it on?	
Noun clause:	. . .	what street it is on	
As object:	Do you know	what street it is on?	

---

[1] There are others, but these are probably the most frequent ones. These verbs are also used in other patterns.
[2] when it means *request*

b. Auxiliary *be, have,* and modal questions have the auxiliary before the subject (III, VI, XI, XIV). When these are made into noun clauses, the auxiliary follows the subject.

Question: Why is Miss Liu   going downtown?

Noun clause: . . . why   Miss Liu is going downtown
As object: Who knows why   Miss Liu is going downtown?

Question: What has she done about her headaches?

Noun clause: . . . what she has done about her headaches
As object: Do you know what she has done about her headaches?

Question: What time will she be back?

Noun clause: . . . what time she will be back
As object: No one knows what time she will be back.

c. Auxiliary *do* questions lose the auxiliary when they are transformed to noun-clause objects. The inflectional ending on *do,* when there is one, is transferred to the main verb.

Question: What does an eye examination cost?
Noun clause: . . . what   an eye examination costs
As object: I'm not sure what   an eye examination costs.

Question: How much did you pay for yours?
Noun clause: . . . how much   you paid for yours
As object: Can you remember how much   you paid for yours?

d. When the question word or phrase replaces the subject, however, the word order does not change.

Question: Who went to the optometrist?
Noun clause: . . . who went to the optometrist
As object: Someone asked who went to the optometrist.

7 **Expressions of place** are mentioned in several earlier lessons (II, 13–14; IV, 7b; VI, 9; VII, 11). They are mainly concerned with the fixed uses of *at, in,* and *on,* which are, by far, the most frequently used prepositions. Below are listed some other prepositions, some adverbs, and some phrases used in referring to place. Check your knowledge of these terms by seeing if you can use each one correctly.

a. Relative position indicators

by	in front of	above	around
near	in back of	below	opposite
next to	before	beneath	across (from)
against	behind	over	on top of
beside	between	under	in the middle of
along side of	among	underneath	at the bottom of

b. Direction indicators, used after verbs of motion

from	up	through	on	north	inside
to	down	past	off	south	outside
into³	across	as far as⁴	right	east	upstairs
out of	along	around	left	west	downstairs

8 **Words that sometimes get confused**

a. *Cross and across*

Cross is a verb; it indicates action.

Cross Beech Street.
Never cross a street without looking both ways.

Across is an indicator of position or direction.

The doctor's office is across the street from the Town Building.
Walk across Beech Street.

b. *Past and passed*

Past is an indicator of direction when used after a verb of motion.

Go past the drugstore on the corner.

Passed is the past form of the verb *pass.*

Miss Liu passed a drugstore on her way to the optometrist's office.

³ Note that *into* is written as one word but *out of* is written as two.
⁴ Do not confuse this expression with *until* (VIII, 12b).

c. *Remind* and *remember*

Remember means to think of something without any assistance. There is only one person involved.

> Miss Liu remembered the doctor's name after she left the optometrist's office.

Remind means to cause someone to think about something (cf. X, 7). There are usually two persons involved. The first person mentioned is the causer.

> Miss Liu's *roommate* reminded *her* to keep her appointment with the optometrist.

The causer may be a thing instead of a person.

> The *chair* in the optometrist's office reminded *Miss Liu* of a dentist's chair. (It caused her to think about a dentist's chair.)

d. *After* and *afterwards* [5]

After is usually used as a preposition, to introduce a time phrase or a time clause (VII, 7a). Note the following examples. The activity mentioned in the time clause happened first.

> Miss Liu went downtown after lunch.
> Miss Liu went downtown after she ate lunch.
> After Miss Liu ate lunch, she went downtown.

Afterwards is a time adverb. It is used alone in the *T* position of a sentence pattern. It is a synonym for *later* or for the sequence signal *then* (VI, 5b).
The sentences below express the same meaning as those above.

> Miss Liu ate lunch. She went downtown afterwards. (later)
> Miss Liu ate lunch, and afterwards she went downtown. (then)

---

[5] *Afterward* is another form of the same word. Neither is preferred. Be consistent in your usage.

9 **Order of nominal modifiers** is fixed. We have had many examples of this in previous lessons. Let's review what we have already learned and look at some additional patterns.

a. Modifiers which precede

1. Articles and possessives never modify the same noun. An article before a possessive modifies the possessive.

    the assignment   my assignment   the student's assignment

2. A possessive pronoun frequently modifies an apostrophe-form possessive.

    your roommate's assignment   your father's advice

3. Two or more apostrophe forms may follow one another in a sentence. Each modifies the word it precedes.

    Mrs. Baker's husband's students' exams

4. Numbers follow possessives; ordinals precede cardinals.

    the students' first three quizzes

5. Next come descriptive adjectives. Two or more may modify the same noun, though three is the normal limit. The usual order is:

OPINION	SIZE	SHAPE	CONDITION	AGE	COLOR	ORIGIN	NOUN
	small				white		card
	large	upright					chair
beautiful				old		oriental	carpet
	large		sunny				laboratory

6. Nouns which modify other nouns follow adjectives and immediately precede the head noun. When there are two or more, they follow a fixed order.

ADJECTIVES	NOUN MODIFIERS				NOUN
	Material	Operation	Power	Purpose	
large, upright	leather				chair
tidy	metal			lens	cabinet
small			electric	light	bulb
large, sunny				chemistry	laboratory
		automatic		traffic	signal

b. Modifiers which follow

1. Adjective phrases and clauses follow the nouns they modify. When a noun is modified by both a phrase and a clause, the phrase precedes.

the doctor   in the Health Service   who examined Miss Liu's eyes

the cabinet   beside the chair   which was full of lenses

the mirror   on the wall   which had a small light above it

2. *Else* is a modifier meaning *more* or *other*. It is used only with the indefinite compounds (IX, 10) and with question words. It follows the word it modifies.

someone else   what else?   no one else
everybody else   where else?   anybody else

3. Adjective modifiers of the indefinite compounds also follow:

something interesting   nothing important

10 **Exercises**

a. Give some instructions, both affirmative and negative, that you would expect to hear in the following places (§ 1).

> Instructor: in the classroom
> Student: Don't talk during tests.

1. in a doctor's office
2. in a dentist's office
3. at a dry cleaning establishment
4. at a gas station
5. in an elevator

6. in a bus
7. in an airplane
8. at a restaurant
9. at a cafeteria
10. on a public telephone

11. at a party
12. on a picnic
13. on a farm
14. in a laboratory
15. in a classroom

b. State a request, either affirmative or negative, that you might hear from each of the following people (§ 2).

> Instructor: someone who is not quite ready
> Student: Please wait for me.

1. Someone who has a cigarette but no match
2. Someone who has his hands full and wants to go through a door
3. Someone who didn't understand what you said
4. A student who hands in an assignment late
5. A clerk who must write down a name but doesn't know how to spell it
6. Someone who wants someone else to turn on a radio
7. Someone who wants a guest to stay longer
8. A person who wants a librarian to notify him when a certain book is available
9. A person who needs help with a problem
10. A person who needs to borrow some money

11. A person who is riding on a bus and wants to get off at Main and Elm
12. A person who is riding in an elevator and wants to get off at the third floor
13. Someone who doesn't want someone else to be late for an appointment
14. Someone who wants someone else to return a book which he borrowed
15. A teacher who wants his students to do well on their examinations

c. Make a suggestion, either affirmative or negative, to do something in which the whole class can participate (§ 3). Use the traditional *let's*.

Let's bring newspapers to class.

d. Complete the sentences below with noun clauses suggested by the context. Remember to use simple form verbs (§§ 4, 5).

> Instructor: George was having trouble with economics.
> His adviser suggested that . . .
> Student: His adviser suggested that he work hard.

1. Professor Baker was overweight. His doctor advised that . . .
2. Mrs. Baker's club needed money. Mrs. Baker proposed that . . .
3. Professor Allen's students sometimes forget their homework. He requires that . . .
4. Mrs. Allen's car was in the garage. She asked that . . .
5. Professor Miller overdrew his bank account. The bank demanded that . . .
6. Betty doesn't like unexpected visitors. She prefers that . . .
7. Jane wasn't doing well in chemistry. Her friends recommended that . . .
8. Bill's mother wasn't feeling well. Bill insisted that . . .
9. Jack had borrowed a lot of money. His father forbid that . . .
10. George likes to hear from his sister. He requested that . . .
11. Miss Liu was lonely in her private room. The Dean of Women suggested . . . (dorm)
12. She applied for a room in the dorm. The manager demanded . . . (deposit)
13. She didn't have enough money. He proposed . . . (borrow)
14. She doesn't like to borrow. She urged . . . (wait)
15. He agreed, but he insisted . . . (I.O.U.)

e. Answer each of the following questions with complete statements. Begin your answer with "I don't know . . ." (§ 6).

> Instructor: How old is John?
> Student: I don't know how old John is.

1. What time is it?
2. What day is it?
3. What month is it?
4. What lesson are we on?
5. What page are we on?
6. Where is Professor Allen going?
7. When will he be back?
8. How long is he going to stay?
9. Who is going with him?
10. Which plane is he going to take?

11. How old is Jack?
12. How many sisters does Betty have?
13. How much does Jane study?
14. Whose work is unsatisfactory?
15. Where did Professor Baker lose his watch?

f. From each of the following questions make another question beginning with "Does anybody know . . . ?" (§ 6).

> Instructor: Where is Lake-of-the-Woods?
> Student: Does anybody know where Lake-of-the-Woods is?

1. What's the date?
2. What's it like out?
3. What kind of weather are we going to have tomorrow?
4. When does the spring vacation begin?
5. What day do we have to be back?

6. How many foreign students are there in this university?
7. Where do most of them come from?
8. How long do they usually stay?
9. How much tuition do they have to pay?
10. What percentage of them remain in this country?

11. Why do we study grammar?
12. What does *subjunctive* mean?
13. When are we going to take up the conditional?
14. Which lessons will the final exam be on?
15. When do we get our final grades?

g. Describe the positions of people and things in your classroom. Use different words from the list of position indicators (§ 7a).[6]

> **The lights are *above* our heads.**
> **Mr. Tanaka is sitting *near* the door.**

h. Combine each of the following pairs of sentences in two different ways, once with *after* and once with *afterwards*. Make all the necessary changes in sentence structure (§ 8d).

> Instructor: Professor Allen read the newspaper.
> Then he watched television.
> Student 1: Professor Allen watched television after he read the newspaper.
> Student 2: Professor Allen read the newspaper and afterwards he watched television.

1. Mrs. Brown went shopping today.
   She paid her electric bill first.

2. She bought a tablecloth.
   Later, she bought some clothes.

3. She shopped until four o'clock.
   Then she went home and prepared dinner.

4. She put the potatoes on first.
   She put the meat on later.

5. She ate dinner.
   She washed the dishes.

6. Jack finished his assignments.
   Then he went to the Drivers' License Bureau.

7. He had read a book of traffic regulations.
   Then he took a written test.

8. He passed the written test.
   He took a road test.

9. He parked his car.
   He didn't put on the brakes.

10. Jack and the examiner walked back to the Bureau.
    Then the examiner told Jack that he had made a mistake.

[6] Instructor: If necessary, give the indicators as cues. Check that each one is understood. Avoid trying to find meaning differences for those which are synonymous.

11. Miss Liu left the Health Service.
    Then she telephoned the optometrist.

12. She asked the appointment clerk how to get to the optometrist's office.

    She made an appointment first, though.

13. The appointment clerk made an appointment for Miss Liu.
    Then she asked her not to be late.

14. Miss Liu got off the bus at the corner of Main and Elm.
    Then she walked two blocks east on Elm.

15. She didn't remember the doctor's name when the optometrist asked her.
    She remembered it later.

i. Add the given modifiers to the given sentences in their proper order and make any necessary deletions (§ 9).

	Example:	The watch is lost.
	Instructor:	gold
	Student:	The gold watch is lost.
	Instructor:	Prof. Baker's
	Student:	Prof. Baker's gold watch is lost.
	Instructor:	wrist
	Student:	Prof. Baker's gold wrist watch is lost.
	Instructor:	expensive
	Student:	Prof. Baker's expensive gold wrist watch is lost.
	Instructor:	self-winding
	Student:	Prof. Baker's expensive gold self-winding wrist watch is lost.

1. The suits are at the cleaner's.
   brown – Jack's – two – father's – old

2. Betty threw away the shoes.
   old – dirty – her – tennis – blue

3. The skirt shrank.
   linen – with the coffee stain on it – white – Jane's

4. The cups are on the table.
   coffee – our – dirty – three – china

5. The soup was nourishing.
   vegetable – delicious – which Betty had for lunch – from the cafeteria

6. The machines are in the basement.
   coin-operated – washing – electric – which the students use

7. The words are not English.
   on the blackboard – long – which the instructor is reading – three

8. Those covers will keep your books dry.
   plastic – cheap – book – on sale at the bookstore

9. The carrel is quiet.
   where I work – in the library – small – stuffy

10. The house is in Westview.
    brick – comfortable – red – mother's – Bill's

11. The farm is pleasant.
    where George's grandfather lives – tiny – in Greece – vegetable

12. The bank was held up.
    where Jack's father works – commercial – in Chicago – famous

13. The lifeguard is engaged.
    who works from four till seven – handsome – Swedish – new

14. The receptionist is out.
    from California – young – pretty – who works for the optometrist

15. The optometrist prescribed corrective lenses for Miss Liu.
    jolly – bald – recommended by the Health Service – whose office is
    on Beech Street

j. Modify the indefinite compounds in the following sentences (§ 9b, 2–3).

With single words: *valuable, exciting, important,* etc.

1. I wish I had something to do.
2. Nothing happened while you were away.
3. I haven't heard anything from my family.
4. Nothing was lost in the fire.
5. We need someone to do this work.
6. No one can do it.

With phrases: *in the class, from Alaska,* etc.

7. I met somebody in the drugstore.
8. No one speaks English very well.
9. We looked everywhere for the ball.

With unmarked clauses: *you see, you know,* etc.

10. Ask anybody where the bus stops.
11. Don't believe everything.
12. Jack invited everyone to his party.
13. You can go anywhere.
14. The doctor did everything to save the patient's life.
15. Some people can afford to buy everything.

11 Assignments

a. Read the second paragraph of the reading carefully. Draw a map showing the bus stop at the corner of Main and Elm, the Town Building, and #457 Beech Street. Let the top of your paper represent the north.

b. Copy the following sentences, filling each blank with an appropriate direction indicator.

1. Miss Liu asked the clerk how to get _____ campus _____ the optometrist's office.
2. The clerk told her to take a bus and get _____ at Main and Elm.
3. She told Miss Liu to walk _____ Elm.
4. She told her to go _____ Beech Street at the corner of Beech and Elm.
5. "Then," she said, "turn _____."
6. Walk _____ Beech Street _____ #457.
7. When Miss Liu reached the building she got _____ the elevator.
8. The operator wasn't listening when she said "Third floor please" and he went right _____ the third floor.
9. She got _____ the elevator on the fourth floor.
10. She had to walk _____ one flight.
11. She wandered _____ the hall for a while before she found Room 323.
12. When she found it, she opened the door and went _____ the reception room.
13. There was no one there, so she went _____ that room and entered the next one.
14. The optometrist entered _____ another door.
15. "I am sorry that there was no one in the reception room," he said. "My receptionist went _____ for some coffee a few minutes ago."

c. Word choice

   (1)   Fill in the blanks in the following sentences with a form of *cross* or *across*.

   1. You can't _____ a bridge until you come to it.
   2. The player kicked the ball _____ the field.
   3. Jack and Jane were sitting _____ the table from each other.
   4. Mrs. Allen _____ the room and sat down at the piano.
   5. Lindbergh was the first pilot to _____ the Atlantic in a plane.

   (2)   Fill in the blanks in the following sentences with *past* or *passed*.

   6. We drove _____ the United Nations Building.
   7. We _____ many other tall buildings on the way.
   8. Do you go _____ a drugstore on your way to school?
   9. The instructor _____ out the examinations and we began to write.
   10. An ambulance just drove _____.

   (3)   Fill in the blanks in the following sentences with *remind* or *remember*.

   11. Try to _____ to return your library books on time.
   12. Please _____ me to turn the radio on at 6:45.
   13. Do you always _____ to take your medicine?
   14. No, I don't always _____, but my roommate _____ me when I forget.
   15. George can't _____ how much his dictionary cost.

d. Write a paragraph in which you tell someone how to go from your English classroom to the place where you are now living. Give all details. Use the patterns in today's lesson.

e. Write a description of a room in the house or building where you live. Describe the furniture and tell where each piece is located. Remember that most rooms do not have a front or back. It is better to use expressions such as *on the south side, in the northwest corner.*

REVIEW XV

a. Include the given word or words in the appropriate place in each of the following sentences. Add any necessary function words.

1. The subject that we like best we study hardest. (usually)
2. Jack likes his chemistry class best. (inorganic)
3. He studies chemistry every day. (for at least two hours)
4. He gets good grades in the quizzes. (always)
5. The quizzes are hard. (that Professor Baker gives)

6. Bill wanted to buy a present for Mother's Day. (his mother)
7. He asked what he should get. (his sister)
8. His sister explained her idea about Mother's Day. (him)
9. She suggested, "Why don't you make something?" (her)
10. Then she added, "Or you could do some work, like cleaning out the basement." (her)

11. Jane went shopping today and she bought a handbag. (red)
12. She bought some gloves too. (made of leather)
13. She bought Jack some handkerchiefs for his birthday. (with his initials on them)
14. She didn't get him anything. (expensive)
15. She doesn't know him well. (enough)

b. Change the following sentences from direct quotation to reported speech.

1. Bob said, "It is very warm for May."
2. Bill added, "There is a nice breeze."
3. Jane announced, "I'm going swimming."
4. Bob said, "I will drive you to the lake."
5. Their friends said, "You had better take sweaters with you."

6. "I have a cold," said Tom.
7. "I am sorry," said Professor Miller. "I hope you will feel better tomorrow."
8. Tom answered, "I think I will."
9. Then Professor Miller said, "There is going to be a meeting of the Economics Club on Friday."
10. "I'll be there," Tom said.

11. George said, "I am having a little trouble."
12. His adviser asked, "What seems to be the matter?"
13. George said, "I am taking economics but I don't know much math."
14. His adviser replied, "You don't need much math for economics."
15. He added, "Work hard."

LESSON

XVI

INFINITIVES AND INFINITIVE PHRASES
MORE ADJECTIVE CLAUSES:
RESTRICTIVE vs. NONRESTRICTIVE

It is sometimes difficult for a teacher to persuade a student to work hard enough to pass. Most students who go abroad to study want to succeed; they try to understand the assignments that their teachers give them and do their work well. Unfortunately, many of them fail to realize their language handicap. They allow themselves to believe they will learn just by listening, and they pretend to understand everything anyone says to them. Really they need to study grammar, which is essential for communication, but they would rather spend their time on other things. Their teachers urge them to attend language classes, but they can't force them to.

To do your best in any field, you need to know the language of instruction well. Don't be afraid to ask questions about things you don't understand. If you can't find anyone to ask, bring your questions to class; if your teacher can't answer them, someone else will be able to. Your classmates, whose experiences are different from yours, are eager to help and be helped. It is not easy to study in a foreign language, but you will succeed if you are determined to.

1 *Infinitive* is the name of a two-word unit, *to* + simple verb, which serves a single function in a sentence pattern (cf. VIII, 8). Although it is made from a verb form, an infinitive can never be the main verb of a sentence. It does have certain verbal qualities, however, for it can have a subject and/or an object or other complement.

2 *Infinitive phrase* means simply an infinitive together with its subject and/or complement. Such phrases also function as units in a sentence pattern.

3 **Infinitives and infinitive phrases as subjects**

a. Normal subject position, before the main verb, may be filled by an infinitive, though this is not a very frequent pattern. When used, it is almost always as a statement, not as a question. Note that an infinitive subject is followed by an *s*-form verb. The subject of an infinitive phrase so used is introduced by *for*.

SUBJECT			V	C
S	Infinitive	C		
	To study		isn't	easy.
For anyone	to study	in a foreign language	isn't	easy.
	To succeed		requires	effort.
For anyone	to succeed	at college	requires	effort.

b. **Displaced subject** is the name sometimes given to an infinitive or an infinitive phrase which occurs after the verb in a sentence which begins with anticipatory *it* (VIII, 6b). Note that when the subject of an infinitive is a pronoun, it is an object form preceded by *for*.

QW	BE/DO	IT	V	C	DISPLACED SUBJECT		
					S	Infinitive	C
		It	is not	easy		to study.	
		It	is not	easy	for me	to study	in a foreign language.
		It	requires	effort		to succeed.	
	Is	it		easy		to study?	
	Is	it		easy	for you	to study	in a foreign language?
	Does	it	require	effort		to succeed?	
Why	is	it		hard		to study?	
Why	is	it		hard	for me	to study	in a foreign language?
Where	does	it	require	effort		to succeed?	

** 4 Infinitives and infinitive phrases as direct objects**

a. When the subject of the infinitive object is the same as the subject of the sentence, it is not repeated.

S	V	O	
		Infinitive	Object of Infinitive
Most students	want	to succeed.	
They	try	to understand	their assignments.
They	fail	to realize	their handicap.

b. When the subject of an infinitive is different from the subject of the sentence, it appears before the infinitive. If it is a pronoun, it is an object form.

S	V	O		
		S	Infinitive	O
Most fathers	want	their sons	to succeed.	
They	encourage	them	to study	science.
They	expect	them	to do	their best.

5 **Verbs which take infinitive objects.** Not all verbs may have infinitives as objects. Of those that do, some pattern as in 4a above, some as in 4b; a few, such as *want,* occur in both patterns. The lists below are minimal but they will serve as a guide for practicing the patterns.

PATTERN 4a Students try to succeed.		PATTERN 4b Their fathers encourage them to study.		BOTH PATTERNS
agree	learn	advise	permit	ask [2]
attempt	mean	allow	persuade	expect
begin	neglect	cause	remind	like
care	offer	convince	request	need
consent	plan	encourage	teach	prepare
continue	prefer	forbid	tell	want
decide	pretend	force	urge	would like
desire	promise	get [1]		
fail	refuse	hire		
forget	remember	instruct		
hesitate	start	invite		
hope	try	oblige		
intend		order		

6 **Infinitive and infinitive-phrase objects in compound sentences.** When a compound sentence has an infinitive or an infinitive phrase in the object position of the first independent clause, the sentence frequently ends in *to.* The *to* indicates that the second independent clause has the same object as the first one.

Simple sentences

Their teachers urge them to attend language classes.
Their teachers can't force them to attend language classes.

Compound sentence pattern

Their teachers urge them to attend language classes,
but they can't force them to.

---

[1] only when it means cause (X, 7).
[2] The meaning of *ask* is somewhat different in the different patterns.
Permission: Miss Liu asked to leave early. She said, "May I leave early?"
Request: The clerk asked Miss Liu to come early. She said, "Please come early."

Infinitives as modifiers

a. Of nouns. Infinitives often modify nouns. Observe the following pattern:

Betty has a term paper to write. She has a lab report to finish, too.

b. Of adjectives or adverbs. This use is illustrated and practiced in VIII, 8. Examples from this lesson are:

Don't be afraid to ask questions.

Some students don't work hard enough to pass.

c. Of verbs. Infinitives which express purpose may be considered modifiers of the verb phrases of the sentences in which they occur. They may optionally be preceded by the words *in order*.

Many young people go abroad to study.

They study (in order) to learn.

Some of them must work to earn money.

d. Of the compound indefinites

I don't have anything to do this afternoon.

I'd like something interesting to do.

e. Of question words and phrases. Objects consisting of question words or question phrases are often modified by infinitives.

S	V	C			
		QW/QP	Infinitive	Complement	(Connective)
Some students	don't know	how	to plan	their time.	
They	can't decide	which subject	to study	first	or
		how long	to spend	on each assignment.	

This pattern also occurs with some verbs which require indirect objects. The indirect objects are subjects of the infinitives.

S	V	C			
		I.O.	D.O.		(Conn)
			QW	Infinitive	
George's adviser	advised	him	what	to do.	
He	showed	him	where	to go.	
He	told	him	who [3]	to see	and
			what	to say.	

 8 **Infinitives in reported speech**

An imperative in direct quotation becomes an infinitive in reported speech.

George's adviser said, "Work hard."
George's adviser told him *to work* hard.

The clerk said to Miss Liu, "Don't be late."
The clerk said not *to be* late.
The clerk asked Miss Liu not *to be* late.

---

[3] or *whom,* if you prefer

9 **More adjective clauses** (cf. IX, 7 and 16). There are six adjective clauses in the model paragraphs. They represent most of the kinds you will come across in your reading. Here they are listed in the order in which they occur. Let's look at them and discover in what ways they are similar and in what ways they differ.

NOUN/PRONOUN	ADJECTIVE CLAUSE				
	CM	CM = Subject	Subject	Verb	Complement
1. students		who		go	abroad to study
2. assignments	that		their teachers	give	them
3. everything			anyone	says	to them
4. grammar,		which		is	essential for communication,
5. things			you	don't understand	
6. classmates,	whose		experiences	are	different from yours,

a. **Similarities.** Each clause has a subject and a verb and it modifies the word which precedes it.

b. **Differences.** The clauses differ from one another in several ways.

1. *Marked* versus *unmarked*. Note that items 3 and 5 do not have any clause markers. Clauses of this type are sometimes called unmarked. They frequently cause difficulty in reading for learners who are not familiar with this construction. These clauses could be marked with a *which* or *that* in clause marker position, but in actual speech and informal writing they very often aren't (cf. XII, 11).

2. *Clause marker = subject* versus *clause marker + subject*. When the modified word is also the logical subject of the verb in the clause, as in items 1 and 4 (*students go abroad, grammar is essential*), one word serves both functions, clause marker and subject.
   When the modified word is the logical direct object of the verb in the clause, as in 2 (teachers give them *assignments*) and 5 (you don't understand *things*), a separate clause marker (*that, which,* or *whom*) or no clause marker is used.
   When the subject of the clause refers to something owned or experienced by the referent of the modified word, the clause marker is the possessive word *whose*, as in item 6.

3. *Restrictive* versus *non-restrictive*.   Most adjective clauses in speech and in informal writing are essential to the meaning of the sentences in which they occur. They serve to identify, to specify, to limit the referents of the words they modify. These are the ones we call restrictive and we do not punctuate.

Occasionally we add a clause which is not essential to the main message of the sentence. The information could just as well be put into another sentence or left out altogether. These we pronounce in a special way,[4] and we place commas before and after them. These are the ones we call non-restrictive or non-essential.

Find the two non-restrictive adjective clauses in the model paragraphs and underline them. Then read the sentences without the clauses and note that the information you leave out does not affect the main message of the sentence.

They need to study grammar, but they would rather do other things.
Your classmates are eager to help and be helped.

Pronunciation helps

a. The final *to* of a shortened compound sentence (§ 6) is never stressed, but the vowel receives its full quality; i.e., it rhymes with *too*.

b. There is a drop in intonation and a short pause both before and after a non-restrictive clause. Listen while your teacher pronounces the following:

Grammar, which is essential for communication, is sometimes boring.

Your classmates, whose experiences are different from yours,

are eager to help and be helped.

---

[4] See Pronunciation helps.

11 Punctuation—avoid these common errors.

a. Do not place a comma before an essential clause; it causes misreading.

People who put commas in wrong places cause confusion.

If we put a comma before *who* and after *places,* the sentence would mean that all people put commas in wrong places, and that simply isn't true.

b. Do not forget the second comma, the one that marks the end of a non-essential clause, unless the clause comes at the end of the sentence.

Jack's father ⊙who lives in Chicago ⊙visited us last weekend.
We were visited by Jack's father ⊙ who lives in Chicago.

12 Exercises

a. Following are some sentences with infinitives or infinitive phrases as subjects. Change them to the more common pattern which begins with anticipatory *it* (§ 3b).

Instructor: To leave now would be impolite.
Student: It would be impolite to leave now.

1. To lie on the beach is relaxing.
2. To swim in the sea is invigorating.
3. To read a good book is rewarding.
4. To discuss philosophy is stimulating.
5. To drink cool water is refreshing.

6. To smoke cigarettes is bad for your health.
7. To drive fast is dangerous.
8. To gamble is risky.
9. To win all the time is impossible.
10. To lose money is disappointing.

11. To lose weight is difficult.
12. To eat sweets is enjoyable.
13. To exercise takes time.
14. To diet requires self-discipline.
15. To play tennis takes skill.

b. Substitute an appropriate form of the given verb for the main verb of the given sentence. Make any necessary changes in structure (§§ 4, 5).

Mr. Smith agreed to go to the meeting.

> Instructor: urge
> Student: Mr. Smith urged me to go to the meeting.
> Instructor: forget
> Student: Mr. Smith forgot to go to the meeting.

1. refuse	8. persuade	16. decide	24. intend
2. invite	9. ask	17. allow	25. force
3. want	10. promise	18. fail	26. neglect
4. plan	11. advise	19. remember	27. expect
5. tell	12. would like	20. convince	28. promise
6. expect	13. permit	21. offer	29. hope
7. hope	14. remind	22. hire	30. persuade
	15. encourage	23. agree	

c. Join each pair of sentences below with *and* or *but,* whichever is appropriate (see II, 11). Make the appropriate changes in the second clause. Watch your stress and intonation (§§ 6 and 10a).

> Instructor: Professor Miller invited Betty to join the Economics Club.
> Betty plans to join the Economics Club.
> Student: Professor Miller invited Betty to join the Economics Club and she plans to.

1. Mr. Allen would like to be able to speak French.
   He doesn't know how to speak French.

2. Mrs. Allen wants to make a cherry pie.
   She never learned how to make a cherry pie.

3. The Rotary Club asked Professor Miller to make a speech.
   Professor Miller plans to make a speech.

4. Professor Baker said that he would give his chemistry students an exam.
   Professor Baker is going to give his chemistry students an exam.

5. Mrs. Baker said that she would try to find her husband's wrist watch.
   Mrs. Baker forgot to try to find her husband's wrist watch.

6. Bill's father advised him to be careful with his money.
   Bill is trying to be careful with his money.

7. Jack doesn't know how to drive a car.
   Jack is learning to drive a car.

8. The examiner didn't remind Jack to put on his brakes.
   Jack failed to put on his brakes.

9. Jack tried to pass the driver's exam.
   Jack wasn't able to pass the driver's exam.

10. Jack doesn't know whether he can pass it now or not.
    He is going to try to pass it.

11. The appointment clerk asked Miss Liu to get to the optometrist's office on time.
    Miss Liu promised to get to the optometrist's office on time.

12. Miss Liu didn't know how to get to the optometrist's office.
    She asked the appointment clerk how to get to the optometrist's office.

13. Jane doesn't want to have her eyes examined.
    Jane ought to have her eyes examined.

14. She likes to go shopping every afternoon.
    She doesn't really need to go shopping every afternoon.

15. She should spend all of her afternoons studying.
    She doesn't like to spend all of her afternoons studying.

d. Here is a list of things which most people think they need. Tell what they are needed for by adding an infinitive modifier to each. Some of them will need a preposition as well (§ 7a).

> Instructor: a car
> Student: Everyone needs a car to drive.
> Instructor: a good road
> Student: Everyone needs a good road to drive on.

1. food	6. a chair	11. time
2. water	7. a bed	12. music
3. a house	8. pots	13. paper
4. clothes	9. soap	14. friends
5. money	10. fuel	15. books

e. Complete each of the following by adding an infinitive phrase. Make your completion fit the meaning of the beginning (§ 7b).

> Instructor: You were lucky
> Student: You were lucky to win the sweepstakes.

1. You are right
2. You are wise
3. You are kind
4. You are generous
5. You are smart

6. You were brave
7. You were strong
8. You were nice
9. We were eager
10. We were happy

11. You would have been foolish
12. You would have been wrong
13. You would have been unwise
14. It would have been dangerous
15. It would have been careless

f. Tell the purpose behind the following gestures by adding an infinitive or infinitive phrase to each (§ 7c).

> Instructor: wave our arms
> Student: We wave our arms to greet people.

1. clap our hands
2. snap our fingers
3. shake our heads up and down
4. shake our heads from side to side
5. stamp our feet
6. raise our eyebrows
7. shrug our shoulders
8. point our fingers
9. clench our fists
10. smile
11. laugh
12. wink
13. scowl
14. grunt
15. groan

g. Complete the following sentence beginnings with infinitives or infinitive phrases. Consider the context when preparing your sentences (§ 7d and e).

> Instructor: I want to get a bus. Can you tell me where . . .
> Student: Can you tell me where to wait?

George and Nick were planning a party.

1. Nick asked George who . . .
2. They had to decide when . . .
3. They discussed what . . .
4. They weren't sure where . . .
5. They agreed on how much . . .

Bill wanted to plant a garden in Westview.

6. He needed someone . . .
7. He couldn't find anyone . . .
8. He asked his mother . . .
9. She couldn't because she had something . . .
10. He decided not . . .

Jack was going to meet Jane's parents.

11. He wasn't sure how . . .
12. He asked his mother which suit . . .
13. He asked his sister what kind of flowers . . .
14. He asked his father what . . .
15. He asked his brother how long . . .

h. Change the following direct quotations to reported speech. Change *say* to *tell* (XII, 10 and § 8).

> Instructor: Our teacher said, "Ask questions."
> Student: Our teacher told us to ask questions.

1. The doctor said, "Take a deep breath and hold it."
2. The nurse said, "Make a fist."
3. The dentist said, "Rinse out your mouth."
4. The optometrist said, "Read the bottom line."
5. The receptionist said, "Come back tomorrow."

6. The captain said, "Fasten your seatbelts."
7. The hostess said, "Read the safety regulations."
8. The steward said, "Ring if you need service."
9. The man in the seat beside me said, "Look out the window."
10. I couldn't see anything, so he added, "Change seats with me."

11. The math teacher said, "Open your books to page fifty-four."
12. Then he said, "Do problem number six."
13. A few minutes later he said to me, "Put your solution on the blackboard."
14. He said to the class, "Watch for mistakes."
15. When I had finished he said to another student, "Correct the mistake on the blackboard."

i. From each pair of sentences below construct a single sentence containing an unmarked adjective clause (§ 9b1).

> Instructor: The lesson is about clauses.
> I studied it.
> Student: The lesson I studied is about clauses.

1. The book was interesting. My teacher lent it to me.
2. The art exhibition was canceled. Mr. Smith told me about it.
3. The concert lasted two hours. Bill went to it.
4. The movie was filmed in Japan. Jack saw it.
5. The evening dress cost fifty dollars. Jane bought it.

6. The apartment is small. Professor Miller lives in it.
7. The house is made of brick. Mrs. Brown owns it.
8. The office is in the Chemistry Building.
Professor Baker shares it with his assistant.
9. The bridge club is going to have a bake sale.
Mrs. Baker belongs to it.
10. The dorm is for women only.
Miss Liu is going to move into it.

11. The economics course was too advanced. George registered for it.
12. The chemistry course required a lot of laboratory work.
Jane failed it.
13. The math problem was very difficult. Bill solved it.
14. The tennis match was intramural. Betty won it.
15. The car used to belong to Mr. Smith. Jack bought it.

j. From each pair of sentences below construct a single sentence containing a marked adjective clause. Some markers will also be subjects and others will not (§ 9b2).

> Instructor: Some students go abroad to study.
> They want to succeed.
> Student: Students who go abroad to study want to succeed.

1. Some students want to succeed. They must do their assignments.
2. Some people work all the time. They don't enjoy life.
3. Some professors write books. They get promotions.
4. Some professors give public lectures. They serve the community.
5. Some people help foreign students. They enjoy the experience.

6. Some cars use a lot of gasoline. They are expensive to run.
7. It doesn't cost much to run some cars. They don't use much gas.
8. Some animals are quiet and gentle. They make good house pets.
9. People shouldn't make pets of some dogs. They are noisy and vicious.
10. Some dogs are especially trained to help blind people. They are very valuable.

11. We buy some books. We may write in them.
12. We borrow some books from the library. We must not write in them.
13. We can not borrow some books. They are in the reference collection.
14. Some books are on reserve. They do not circulate.
15. We sometimes lose library books. We must pay for them.

k. From the following pairs make single sentences containing restrictive clauses marked by *whose*.

> Instructor: The man called the police.
> His car was stolen.
> Student: The man whose car was stolen called the police.

1. There is the professor. I am taking his course.
2. The man is in China. We just met his wife.
3. The lady is a travel agent. I borrowed her car.
4. The boy put an advertisement in the newspaper. His dog was lost.
5. The girl is in my class. Her mother was elected to parliament.
6. I have a friend from Argentina. His father is a musician.
7. I know a girl. Her brother owns a sailboat.
8. Some students did not receive grades. Their papers were handed in late.

9. Here is a picture of a pilot. His plane crashed yesterday.
10. There are the people. Their son was in the plane.
11. Some novelists write stories that are not popular. They are usually poor.
12. Some novelists write stories that are very popular. They make a lot of money.
13. The designer won first prize. His work was most original.
14. The architect charged a high fee. We selected his plan.
15. The committee member resigned. His suggestion was rejected.

I. The following sentences, which lack internal punctuation, contain adjective clauses. Some are restrictive, some are non-restrictive, and others may be either, depending upon how they are pronounced and punctuated. Read the sentences aloud, indicating the kind of clause by your intonation. Tell where commas are needed.

1. Students who come late miss their assignments.
2. Students who don't hear well should sit in a front seat.
3. Foreign students who read slowly don't get enough sleep.
4. Miss Liu who wears glasses now doesn't get headaches any more.
5. George who came here from Greece two years ago is one of the best students in the college.
6. Trucks which weigh more than five tons are not permitted on the highway.
7. Passenger cars which are considerably lighter than trucks don't wear out the roads so fast.
8. Owners of passenger cars who have to pay high road taxes don't like the trucks to wear out the roads.
9. Pedestrians who don't look both ways before crossing a street are likely to get run over.
10. Bicycle riders who should not be permitted on busy streets cause many accidents.
11. The French language which is spoken in many parts of the world is a Romance language.
12. The French which one hears in Provence is quite different from the French which one hears in Paris.
13. People who live in glass houses shouldn't throw stones.
14. He who laughs last laughs best.
15. The Lord helps those who help themselves.

Assignments

a. Summarize in one paragraph a short article from today's news. Write it in a way which illustrates the different uses of infinitives. Underline the infinitives.

b. Choose five proverbs and/or superstitions from your own culture and translate them into English. State them in ways which illustrate the uses of adjective clauses.

REVIEW XVI

a. Substitute the given verbs into the second part of each of the following sentences. Change the connective or leave it out whenever it is appropriate to do so.

1. We don't like to work hard but we have to.
    plan   promise   will learn   refuse   persuade

2. Fathers don't like to study but they expect their sons to.
    tell   want   ask   teach   remind

3. Not all students who go to college pass, but most of them try to.
    hope   expect   want   would like   fail

b. Each of the following sentences contains a dependent clause. For each sentence tell which word is the clause marker and which word is the subject of the clause.

1. Students who want to succeed should budget their time.
2. Everyone agrees that students need some recreation.
3. No one thinks we should study all the time.
4. What we need is a balanced schedule.
5. When freshmen first come to college someone should help them plan their time.
6. Jack is the boy who likes rock music.
7. The records that Jack buys are cheap.
8. Bill doesn't like the records Jack buys.
9. He says that rock music is just a lot of noise.
10. Most young people who like music like rock.
11. Professor Baker told Mrs. Baker that he had lost his watch.
12. Mrs. Baker decided that she should buy him a new one.
13. She went to the shop of the man who had been her family's jeweler for many years.
14. She asked the jeweler about a watch which she saw in his shop.
15. He said that was a good watch.

XVII

USES OF *ING*-FORMS
PASSIVE VOICE

Taking a course in elementary science in a large university can be a very trying experience. Such courses are usually taught by groups of staff members instead of by individual professors. The lectures are given in huge auditoriums and may be attended by as many as five hundred students. Just finding a seat can be a problem. Interrupting a lecture to request an explanation is out of the question.[1]

Students do have a chance to ask questions, however, while meeting in the quiz sections they are required to attend. These are smaller groups supervised by teaching assistants. At these meetings, readings are assigned and problems discussed. Quizzes are given regularly; all grades are recorded and averaged at the end of a semester. Getting behind in one's assignments can be very upsetting.

Regular laboratory work is also a part of these courses. Certain prescribed experiments must be completed and written up. Some of these necessitate setting up complicated equipment. An inexperienced student either risks breaking the equipment or waits for the lab attendant to help him. In either case he probably will not have time to finish experimenting before the bell rings and another student comes to take over his place. It is indeed amazing that such experiences seem to produce many capable, enterprising scientists.

[1] To say something is *out of the question* means it is impossible.

1   **Ing-forms as verbs.**[2] We have seen how *ing*-forms are used with the auxiliary *be* to form the main verb phrases of sentences in continuous tenses (Lessons III, VI, IX, XI, XII, XIII). We must remember, though, that an *ing*-form alone can never be the main verb of a sentence.

2   **Ing-forms as nouns.**[3] Some *ing*-forms are so generally used as nouns that we tend to forget their verbal origin. They usually pattern as uncountables, though occasionally the plural ending is added, for instance, in *readings, writings, teachings, misspellings.*

As nouns, *ing*-forms can be subjects, objects or other complements of verbs, and objects of prepositions. In other words, they are found in all the noun positions in sentence patterns.

3   **Ing-form phrases.** The verbal nature of the *ing*-form is illustrated by the fact that it can have its own subject and complement (cf. XVI, 2–4).

a. In formal writing and speaking, the subject of an *ing*-form is usually a possessive.

S			V	C		
S	*Ing*-Form	C		S	*Ing*-Form	C
Jack's	forgetting	to read the assignment	resulted in	his	failing	a quiz.
Jane's	not handing in	lab reports	prevented	her	getting	a good grade.

b. In less formal language and after sense perception verbs (III, 8 and § 5 below), the subject of an *ing*-form may be a simple-form noun or an object-form pronoun.

S	V	C		
		S	*Ing*-Form	C
I	watched	Jack	doing	his assignment.
I	noticed	him	underlining	some sentences.
I	didn't see	him	taking	notes.

[2] These are traditionally called present participles.
[3] These are traditionally called gerunds.

4 **Verbs which take *ing*-form objects.**   Certain verbs frequently take *ing*-form objects but never infinitives. Other verbs may be followed by *ing*-forms or infinitives and express the same meaning. In a few cases an *ing*-form object expresses a meaning which is different from that of the infinitive object. This situation is very confusing for a learner and is the source of many mistakes.

The minimal lists below will serve as a guide for practicing the patterns. For more complete lists see a reference grammar.[4]

a. These verbs frequently have *ing*-form objects. They never have infinitive objects.		b. These verbs may be followed by *ing*-forms or infinitives. The meaning of the two patterns is the same.
Bill enjoys reading.		*Bill likes reading.* *Bill likes to read.*
admit	keep	attempt
appreciate	keep on	begin
avoid	postpone	continue
can't help	practice	intend
consider	recall	like
deny	regret	neglect
enjoy	risk	plan
finish	stop [5]	prefer
get through	suggest	start
give up	understand	try

[4] Such lists can be found in Marcella Frank, *Modern English: A Practical Reference Guide* (Englewood Cliffs, N.J.: Prentice-Hall, 1972).

[5] You may hear *stop* followed by an infinitive. The infinitive is not an object, however; it does not answer the question *who* or *what*. It answers the question *why*, and thus it is a modifier expressing purpose (see XVI, 7c).

5 **Sense perception verbs**[6] may have either simple or *ing*-form objects but not infinitives. The subject of the *ing*-form is usually expressed.

a. The verbs   notice   observe   see   watch

                hear   smell   feel

b. The patterns

S	V	C		
		S	Simple or *Ing*	O
We	watched	the lab assistant	set up	the equipment.
We	watched	the lab assistant	setting up	the equipment.
We	saw	him	heat	some glass tubes.
We	saw	him	heating	some glass tubes.

c. The difference is not really in meaning but rather in emphasis. The *ing*-form emphasizes the duration of the activity; the simple form suggests that it is completed.

6 **Forget and remember** are followed by both *ing*-forms and infinitives, but the different patterns express different meanings. The difference is in the time relationship between the main verb and its verbal object.

a. *Ing*-form objects express actions or situations which occur before the action of the main verb.

          ②   ①

Jack remembers talking with his instructor.

       ②   ①

He forgets making an appointment with him.

b. Infinitive objects express actions or situations which occur either after (in the case of *remember*) or not at all (in the case of *forget*).

           ①   ②

Jack remembered to make an appointment with his instructor.

      ①   ⓧ

He forgot to keep it.

---

[6] *Taste* is a sense perception verb which does not seem to fit this pattern.

7 ***Ing*-forms as noun modifiers.** *Ing*-forms are quite generally used to modify nouns. They occupy the same positions as ordinary adjectives.[7]

a. Before the noun to be modified: *teaching* assistants, *enterprising* scientists

b. After the verb *be* (I, 2): Getting behind is *upsetting*.

c. After the noun to be modified (X, 2d): I find my work *challenging*.

8 **Meanings of *ing*-form modifiers.** *Ing*-forms are so commonly used as adjectives that it would be impossible to explain all the different relationships between them and the nouns they modify. However, to help distinguish them from past participle modifiers (see § 15), we should note these two very frequent uses.

a. To describe the effect of one person or situation on another

> An interesting person is a person who interests you.
> A boring lecture is a lecture which bores you.
> A challenging lesson is a lesson which challenges you.
> A disappointing experience is an experience which disappoints you.

b. To indicate an action in process

> A growing boy is a boy who is in the process of growing.
> An aching tooth is a tooth which is in the process of aching.
> Boiling water is water which is in the process of boiling.

9 ***Ing*-forms in time phrases.** The only verb form ever used immediately after the time words *before, after, until, since, while,* and *when* is the *ing*-form.[8] Never place an infinitive immediately after one of these words.

> We finish our assignments before relaxing.
> We relax after finishing our assignments.
> Don't try to listen to the radio while studying.

---

[7] *Ing*-forms in modifying position are traditionally called present participles or verbal adjectives.
[8] All of these words may also be followed by clauses, as explained in earlier lessons.

10 ***Ing*-forms after other prepositions.** The only verb form which occurs immediately after a preposition (except *to*) is the *ing*-form.

a. Review the use of *ing*-forms after *by* (X, 2b).

b. Note the examples of *ing*-forms after prepositions in the following paragraph.

> If you are interested in *taking* a course in elementary science in a large university, plan on *reading* the assignments before *attending* the lectures so that you will understand what is being said. There is no opportunity for *asking* questions during lectures. Try to get some experience in *setting up* lab equipment; don't depend on your lab partner *doing* it for you. And don't be surprised at *having* to take unannounced quizzes. That's par for the course.[9]

11 **The passive voice.** Although in the usual order of the English sentence the subject is the performer of the action expressed by the verb, there are some sentences in which the performer occurs in a prepositional phrase at the end or not at all. The grammatical subject names the person or thing which would normally occur in object position. These sentences are said to be in the passive voice, as opposed to the usual active voice. Only transitive verbs can be used in the passive construction.

> Active: Teaching assistants assign readings.
> Passive: Readings are assigned by teaching assistants.

12 **Patterns of passive sentences**

a. A passive sentence always contains some form of the auxiliary *be* followed by a past participle. Other auxiliaries, if any, precede *be*.

b.

S	V			C	
	Aux	Be	PP	By	Performer
Courses		are	taught	by	groups of professors.
Lectures		are	attended	by	many students.
Quiz sections	have to	be	supervised.		
Experiments	must	be	completed.		

[9] The last sentence is a kind of joke. It means the situation is normal, to be expected.

13 **When to use the passive voice.** The verb construction called the passive voice is not used as much in English as it is in some other languages. It is sometimes used by a writer simply to vary the style of his sentence patterns, but that use is not important to students who are striving mainly for clarity. The active voice patterns, those in which the subject is the performer, are by far more common in English both in speaking and in writing. There are, however, specific situations in which the passive voice is used. They are the following:

a. When we don't know who performed the action

Bill's slide rule *was made* in Germany.
The second-hand book that he bought *had been written in.*

b. When it is preferable not to mention the performer

Miss Liu *was given* some bad advice when she first arrived here.
She *was told* that her English was satisfactory for university work.

c. When we wish to emphasize the active object

Quizzes *are given* regularly.
Grades *are averaged.*
Equipment *is set up* by lab attendants.

d. In situations of social and historical significance, when the work resulting from the action is as well or better known than the performer, as in the case of famous music, writing, paintings, and inventions.

Romeo and Juliet was written by Shakespeare.
The *Moonlight Sonata was composed* by Beethoven.
The *Mona Lisa was painted* by da Vinci.
The electric light bulb *was invented* by Edison.

In sentences of types a and b, the performer is never mentioned. In sentences of type c, the performer may be mentioned or omitted. In sentences of type d, the performer must be mentioned to complete the statement. The performer, or agent as it is sometimes called, follows the verb and is introduced by *by.*

14 **Passive-like causatives.**   In causative constructions with *have* (cf. X, 7) we often omit the performer of the caused action because it is either obvious or of no particular importance. Such constructions are not true passives because they do not contain the auxiliary *be*, but the action verb is a past participle. Compare the two patterns below.

Prof. Miller has his students write all papers   in ink.
Prof. Miller has   all papers written in ink.

As in true passives, the performer may be mentioned at the end in a *by*-phrase.

Miss Liu had her eyes examined by an optometrist.

15 **Past participles as modifiers**

  A pattern which is closely related to the passive construction is the use of past participles as noun modifiers.

Passive: Quiz sections are supervised by assistants.
Modifier: The students attend supervised quiz sections.

Passive: Readings are assigned.
Modifier: The course includes assigned readings.

b. Past participle modifiers refer to action already completed, in contrast to action in process (§ 8).

Boiled water is water which has been boiled.
Boiling water is water which is in the process of boiling.

16 Exercises

a. Rearrange the following sentences in such a way that a possessive form functions as the subject of the *ing*-form (§ 3a).

> Instructor: Tennis playing keeps Betty fit.
> Student: Betty's tennis playing keeps her fit.

1. Shopping takes Jane a lot of time.
2. Going to concerts costs Bill a lot of money.
3. Jack finds TV watching cheaper.
4. Changing his major made George lose a semester of work.
5. Wearing glasses has changed Miss Liu's appearance.

6. Good teaching, like that of Professor Allen, is the result of considerable experience.
7. Working in the library and keeping house keep Mrs. Allen busy.
8. Being without a watch caused Professor Baker to be late.
9. Cooking is Mrs. Baker's hobby.
10. Professor Miller provides a community service by giving free lectures on economics.

11. Taking part in too many social activities may cause a student to fail.
12. Budgeting his time as well as his money is essential for a student.
13. Success often results from seizing opportunities.
14. Speaking should reflect our thinking.
15. Reading should be carefully chosen by everyone.

b. Substitute the given verb for the main verb in the given sentence. If possible, change the object to an *ing*-form. If that is not possible, repeat the infinitive and make any necessary changes. Do not change the meaning (XVI, 5, and XVII, 4).

> Instructor: We decided to go. (start)
> Student 1: We started going. (agree)
> Student 2: We agreed to go. (invite)
> Student 3: We invited Bill to go.

1.	consider	6.	risk	11.	need	16.	promise	21.	remind
2.	stop	7.	advise	12.	see	17.	watch	22.	like
3.	want	8.	avoid	13.	begin	18.	start	23.	neglect
4.	tell	9.	keep on	14.	can't help	19.	hear	24.	finish
5.	refuse	10.	notice	15.	expect	20.	intend	25.	prefer

c. Make a sentence suggested by the given one. Include the verb *stop* followed by an infinitive or an *ing*-form. (See footnote 5.)

Instructor:	Bill used to play chess.
Student:	Bill stopped playing chess.
Instructor:	It was noon. Bill was hungry.
Student:	Bill stopped to eat lunch.

1. George finished his studies at midnight.
2. Betty interrupted her dinner when the phone rang.
3. Mrs. Baker was out walking. She met a friend.
4. Bill used to work in the school cafeteria.
5. While Jane was walking on Main Street, she saw a pretty dress in a shop window.
6. Mr. Allen used to smoke a pipe.
7. Professor Baker needed a new watch. Mrs. Baker saw a jeweler's shop.
8. Jack went to a movie every Sunday when he was a freshman.
9. While driving to the Allens', Professor Miller had to ask his way.
10. At seven o'clock every evening, Professor Miller stops whatever he is doing. He listens to the news.
11. Professor Baker grades test papers until five o'clock.
12. Jane often dreams. She should stop it and start to work.
13. Bill was driving. He put on his brakes. A little girl wanted to cross the street.
14. Mrs. Baker used to teach before she was married.
15. Let's stop and have a cup of coffee.

d. Make one good sentence from each of the following pairs. Be careful not to change the meaning (§ 6).

Instructor: Mrs. Allen intended to buy stamps. She forgot.
Student: Mrs. Allen forgot to buy stamps.
Instructor: Prof. Allen asked Betty to be home at eleven. He remembers.
Student: Prof. Allen remembers asking Betty to be home at eleven.

1. Jane made a mistake in her homework. She remembers it now.
2. Jack took Jane to a party six months ago. He remembers it.
3. Jack's father asked him to write home every week. He remembered and he did it.
4. Bill had an appointment to meet a friend in the library yesterday. He remembered and he did it.
5. George said good-bye to all his friends when he left for the United States. He often remembers it.
6. Miss Liu should wear her glasses when she reads. Sometimes she forgets.
7. Betty planned to go to a lecture last night. She forgot it.
8. Betty lived in California when she was three years old. She doesn't remember it.
9. Professor Miller met Dr. Jones several years ago. He forgets it.
10. Mrs. Smith was very ill for three months. She doesn't remember it.
11. Jane planned to buy some stamps this afternoon. She forgot.
12. I promised to remind my friend to buy cigarettes. I remembered and I reminded him.
13. Professor Baker asked Mrs. Baker to remind him to grade the test papers. She forgot.
14. Bill couldn't find his glasses when he got up this morning. Finally, he found them in his bureau drawer. He must have put them there but he doesn't remember doing it.
15. Our homework must be done before we go to bed. We mustn't forget.

e. Change the following statements to information questions. Substitute question words or phrases for the italicized words.

1. *Getting up* is the hardest thing I do all day.
2. Dressing takes *only five minutes*.
3. Sleeping is a luxury for *students*.
4. Dreaming is caused by *eating before going to bed*.
5. *Exercising* helps to keep us in condition.

6. Dancing is popular in *South America.*
7. *Skating* requires a good sense of balance.
8. Swimming exercises the *arm and leg* muscles.
9. *Gambling* is against the law.
10. Hurrying *tires* one *out.*

11. Reading influences *our thinking.*
12. *Traveling* takes less time than it used to.
13. Dining means *eating in a formal atmosphere.*
14. Entertaining gives one *pleasure.*
15. "Parting is such *sweet* sorrow."

f. Answer the following questions with short answers, not complete sentences. Be careful that you use the appropriate number, singular or plural (§ 8a).

> Instructor: If an experience excites you, what kind of an experience is it?
> Student: an exciting experience

1. If information reassures you, what kind of information is it?
2. If an ice-pack soothes your headache, how could you describe it?
3. If John's job exhausts him, what kind of job does he have?
4. If a book fascinates you, what kind of book is it?
5. If a noise disturbs you, what kind of noise is it?
6. If an incident upsets you, what kind of incident is it?
7. If entertainment diverts you, what kind of entertainment is it?
8. If a line of latitude divides two countries, what kind of line is it?
9. If a man works for a living, how can he be described?
10. If a companion travels with you, what kind of companion is he?
11. If you receive reward for your work, what kind of work is it?
12. If a problem irritates you, what kind of problem is it?
13. If a question puzzles you, what kind of question is it?
14. If a situation confuses you, what kind of situation is it?
15. If a meal satisfies you, what kind of meal is it?

g. Read the following sentences aloud, including in each the appropriate form of the verb in parentheses (§§ 9, 10).

1. We always review before (take) an exam.
2. After (take) an exam we always worry.
3. We don't have time to worry while (write).
4. Since (enter) the university we have made many friends.
5. We often meet friends while (walk) across campus.

6. Betty was thinking about (go) home for Christmas.
7. She was planning on (take) a plane.
8. She was looking forward to (see) her parents.
9. She depended on their (meet) her at the airport.
10. She didn't figure on the weather's (be) bad.
11. She didn't think there was any necessity for (check) the train schedule.

12. Bill is fond of (listen) to classical music.
13. He isn't interested in (hear) rock.
14. When (buy) records he always insists on (get) the best.
15. No salesman, however clever, is capable of (sell) him an inferior record.

h. State which of the following sentences are active and which are passive (§ 11).

1. Spring is the busiest season of the year for farmers.
2. The ground must be plowed and crops have to be planted.
3. In many farming communities, teen-aged boys are excused from school to help with the planting.
4. When the planting is finished, the boys return to school.
5. People feel that this practice contributes to the well-being of the community.

6. Summer is called the vacation season.
7. Schools are closed and working hours are shortened.
8. We push ahead our clocks in order to enjoy long, light evenings.
9. Many people go camping in the mountains or at the seaside.
10. Not much work is done.

11. Birds fly south in fall.
12. They are usually gone by the end of September.
13. The leaves change color at that time, too.
14. They are blown off the trees by the north wind.
15. The roots of the trees are covered with straw to protect them from the cold.

16. In the northernmost parts of the United States the winters are very cold.
17. Lakes and ponds freeze over and children go skating on them.
18. The children are taught to skate by their parents.
19. Many years ago sleighs were used for transportation in those areas.
20. They use snowmobiles now.

i. All of the verb constructions in the following sentences are active. A number of them should be passive. Find which ones should be passive and change them accordingly (§ 13).

1. Mr. Jones went to Minneapolis on a business trip last week.
2. He arrived at his hotel at 4:30 p.m.
3. He asked what time the waitresses would serve dinner.
4. The clerk told him that someone would open the dining room at 5:45.
5. He bought a newspaper and went to his room.

6. The furniture in his room was new.
7. Some manufacturers in Denmark had made it.
8. The appearance of the room pleased Mr. Jones.
9. Someone had designed it for comfort.
10. He sat down in a large leather chair and started to read his newspaper.

11. He read a news report about a woman whom somebody had run over.
12. According to the report, the impact of the car didn't injure her seriously.
13. An ambulance driver took her to a hospital.
14. A young intern treated her for minor bruises and scratches.
15. The hospital clerk released her half an hour after he admitted her.

j. Change the following sentences in such a way that the performer of the caused action is not mentioned (§ 14).

> Instructor: Sue had the librarian renew her book.
> Student: Sue had her book renewed.

1. George had his adviser check his schedule.
2. He had the dean approve his transfer.
3. He had the consul extend his visa.
4. He had his teacher correct his sentences.
5. He had the librarian renew his book.

6. Professor Baker has the janitor wash his windows.
7. He has a neighbor boy cut his lawn.
8. He has his secretary type his letters.
9. He has his wife prepare his meals.
10. He has an accountant figure his income tax.

11. Mrs. Allen has a hairdresser wash her hair.
12. She has a dressmaker make her dresses.
13. She has a cleaning woman clean her house.
14. She has a paper boy bring her paper.
15. She has a delivery boy deliver her meat.

k. Answer the following questions by giving the noun and its modifiers. Do not make complete sentences. Pay particular attention to number when giving your answer.

> Instructor: If equipment has been broken, what do we call it?
> Student: broken equipment
> Instructor: If a paper has been well written, what will the professor call it?
> Student: a well-written paper

1. If a house has just been freshly painted, how might it be described?
2. If a car has been completely repaired, how might it be described?
3. If a TV set has been broken, how would one refer to it?
4. If furniture has been used and a person wishes to sell it, how must he advertise it?
5. If a motor has been rebuilt, how could we refer to it?

6. What do we call orange juice which has been kept at very low temperature?
7. What do we call grapes that have been dried in the sun?
8. What do we call apples that are picked by hand?
9. What do we call apples after someone bakes them?
10. What do we call apples after someone has covered them with candy?

11. If certain facts are well known, what kind of facts are they?
12. If someone hides a treasure, what kind of treasure is it?
13. If money is taken by someone to whom it does not belong, what do we call it?
14. If an agreement has never been put into writing, how do we refer to it?
15. If someone cancels a reservation, how is that reservation described?

17 Assignments

a. Write a paragraph in which you use all of the sense perception verbs in § 5. Use the patterns from 5b. Remember that a paragraph is a series of sentences all on the same topic.

b. Write a paragraph modeled after the one in § 10b but on a different topic. Your paragraph should illustrate the use of *ing*-forms after prepositions.

c. Write four passive sentences, one for each of the types listed in § 13. Tell about things which interest you.

d. Americans do many things themselves which people in other countries have done for them. Tell about some things you used to have done for you. Use the following sentence as a pattern.

I used to have my car washed, but now I wash it myself.

REVIEW XVII

a. Student 1: Add a tag question to the given statement.
Student 2: Make a short response to the question in accordance with the facts.

1. Elementary science courses are often taught by groups of staff members.
2. Students who study science have to do lab experiments.
3. Trigonometry is a branch of mathematics.
4. Bill's calculator was made in Japan.
5. The second-hand book that he bought hadn't been written in.

6. Miss Liu was given some bad advice when she first arrived here.
7. She was told that her English was satisfactory for university work.
8. It wasn't.
9. She hadn't studied English very seriously in Taiwan.
10. She has been trying hard to improve it since she started classes.

11. We've been working hard lately.
12. You've done your assignment.
13. Jane would rather shop than study.
14. She'd better get to work.
15. She's already been warned.

b. Answer the following questions including either an *ing*-form or a past participle modifier in each answer.

1. If a story interests you, what kind of story is it?
2. If a person has been discouraged, what kind of person is he?
3. If eggs have been boiled, what kind of eggs are they?
4. Do we drink boiled milk or boiling milk?
5. If a person's personality pleases you, how do you describe it?
6. If a person has become tired from a long journey, how might he describe his journey? What might he say about himself?
7. When a team is in the process of winning a game, what do we call the team?
8. When a dog has been injured, how might we refer to it?
9. When vegetables have been steamed, how can we describe them?
10. When fruit has been ripened on a tree, how is it usually advertised?
11. When fruit has been ripened artificially (colored with chemicals), is that fact usually advertised? How might we describe such fruit?
12. If a movie disappoints us, how might we describe the movie? How might we describe ourselves?
13. If a lecture bores you, what kind of lecture is it? What kind of person delivers it? How could you describe yourself in this situation?
14. If a report was made in writing, what kind of report was it?
15. When acid is not diluted, what kind of acid is it?

XVIII

COMPARISON AND CONTRAST
LIKE, ALIKE, THE SAME AS, DIFFERENT FROM

Since we have to learn the patterns of comparison, let's compare the people we know in College Town. Let's compare the professors first. Professor Allen, who teaches English to foreign students, is about the same age as Professor Miller, the economics teacher. They are much younger than Professor Baker. (As a matter of fact, Professor Baker is the oldest member of the staff. He is going to retire next year.) Professor Allen's personality is quite different from Professor Miller's. They are both good teachers and in that respect they are alike, but Professor Miller is much more serious than Professor Allen. Professor Allen is livelier and friendlier than Professor Miller; he participates more in social activities than Professor Miller does, and he doesn't work as hard as Professor Miller does. Professor Miller works like a beaver. He's probably the most ambitious member of the faculty.

Mrs. Allen and Mrs. Baker differ from each other in many ways besides age. Ruth Allen is taller and slimmer than Emily Baker. She walks faster and she gets things done more quickly than Mrs. Baker does. Mrs. Baker, on the other hand, is less busy than Mrs. Allen because she only keeps house; she doesn't work in the library. She is much more interested in politics than Ruth Allen is. She's a member of the League of Women Voters.

Bill is probably the best student of those we know, and Jane is undoubtedly the poorest. Jack's social interests are the same as Jane's, but he gets better grades than she does. Betty is like Bill. She studies hard and she doesn't relax until her assignments are finished. George, the boy from Greece, is one of the most intelligent students in the college, but his grades aren't quite as good as Bill's because he still has a little trouble with the language. The least happy of all the students is Miss Liu. She came here just a few months ago and she isn't used to it here yet. She will be much happier when she has been here longer and knows the language better.

Comparison of two or more things, persons, groups, or conditions requires sentence patterns which are quite different from the ones we have learned in the previous lessons. The following sections illustrate the most common ones.

 Complete sameness is expressed in two ways.

a. *The same as.* Learn this expression as a unit. Do not substitute any other word for *as*.

ONE	VERB (be)	THE SAME AS	ANOTHER
Jack's social interests	are	the same as	Jane's (social interests).[1]
My book	is	the same as	yours.
The front window	is	the same as	the rear window.

b. *Alike.* Note that in this pattern all the things to be compared are stated before the verb.

THINGS BEING COMPARED	VERB	ALIKE
Jack's and Jane's social interests	are	alike.
Your book and mine	are	alike.
The two windows in this room	are	alike.

 Similarity in many respects: *like* [2]

ONE	VERB	LIKE	ANOTHER
Betty	is	like	Bill.
Jack	looks [3]	like	his father.
Professor Miller	works	like	a beaver.

[1] The words in parentheses are usually omitted. The reader or listener understands the statement without them.
[2] Do not confuse this word with the verb *like*, which means *derive pleasure from*.
[3] *Look* in this pattern means *appear*.

Similarity in one respect is expressed in several ways.

a. *The same + (noun)*

THINGS BEING COMPARED	VERB	*THE SAME* + NOUN
Professor Allen and Professor Miller	are	the same age.
Jack and Jane	have	the same interests.
My book and yours	contain	the same information.

b. *The same (noun) as*

ONE	VERB	*THE SAME (NOUN) AS*	ANOTHER
Professor Allen	is	the same age as	Professor Miller (is).
Jack	has	the same interests as	Jane (has).
Betty's hair	is	the same color as	her mother's.
My book	contains	the same information as	yours.

c. *As (adj./adv./many + noun) as*

ONE	VERB	AS (ADJ/ADV/MANY + NOUN) AS	ANOTHER
Professor Allen	doesn't work	as [4] hard as	Professor Miller.
George's grades	aren't	as good as	Bill's.
Jane	dances	as well as	I [5] do.
I	can swim	as fast as	she [5] does.
Miss Liu	doesn't have	as many friends as	George has.

---

[4] British English has *so* in this position when the verb is negative. *So* is sometimes used in American English, but *as* is more frequent.

[5] Notice that the pronouns after the comparative phrase are subject forms, not object forms. The verb is usually expressed after a subject form pronoun.

4 **Set phrases with** *as . . . as.* Every language has certain figures of speech which are so frequently used that they become almost like single words. English is particularly rich in comparative phrases of the *as . . . as* pattern. Here is a short list of some you will hear. They are not usually used in formal writing.

as blind as a bat	as old as the hills
as brown as a berry	as pale as a ghost
as busy as a bee	as proud as a peacock
as cool as a cucumber	as quiet as a mouse
as dead as a doornail	as right as rain
as deaf as a post	as stubborn as a mule
as easy as ABC	as sure as fate
as good as gold	as thick as thieves
as hard as nails	as warm as toast
as large as life	as white as a sheet

5 **Modification of similarity terms.** All of the above expressions may be modified.

a. *Almost, nearly, about* suggest less similarity than an unqualified statement.

Professor Allen is almost the same age as Professor Miller.
George's grades are nearly as good as Bill's.

b. *Just* and *exactly* emphasize the similarity.

My book is just like yours.
They are exactly alike.

6 **General statements of difference** are expressed in two ways.

a. *Differ(s) from* [6]

ONE	DIFFER(S) FROM	ANOTHER	
Ruth Allen	differs from	Emily Baker	in many ways.
Bill's personality	differs from	Jack's.	
Children (often)	differ from	their parents.	

b. *Different from*

ONE	V	DIFFERENT FROM	ANOTHER
Professor Allen's personality	is	different from	Professor Miller's.
Mrs. Baker's interests	are	different from	Mrs. Allen's.
The British pattern	is	different from	the American.

 7 **Modification of terms of general difference**

a. *Somewhat* and *a little* suggest less difference than the unqualified patterns do. Note the positions of the qualifiers in the following illustrations.

The British pattern differs somewhat from the American one.
The British pattern is a little different from the American one.

b. *Quite, very,* and *entirely* emphasize the difference. An expression of quantity (V, 12–15) must also be included to qualify pattern 6a. Note the following patterns:

Bill's personality differs quite a lot from Jack's.
Bill's personality is entirely different from Jack's.

8 **Comparison of two things or groups which differ.**   Comparative forms of adjectives and adverbs end in *er* and are usually followed by *than.*[7]

---

[6] Note that *differ* is a verb. When this pattern is used, it is necessary to choose the appropriate verb form.
[7] When writing, be careful not to confuse this word with *then.* In rapid speech they sometimes sound alike.

a. One-syllable adjectives and adverbs have comparative forms made by adding *er* to the simple forms.

young	younger than	fast	faster than
tall	taller than	hard	harder than
slim	slimmer [8] than		

b. Two-syllable adjectives ending in *y* have comparative forms made by changing the *y* to *i* and adding *er*.

busy	busier than	happy	happier than
friendly	friendlier than	lively	livelier than

c. Adjectives and adverbs of two or more syllables (except as above) do not usually have comparative forms.[9] Comparison is expressed by placing *more* before the simple forms and *than* after them.

careful	more careful than	carefully	more carefully than
serious	more serious than	seriously	more seriously than

d. *Less* is the opposite of *more*. It is used in the same pattern and also with two-syllable adjectives which end in *y*.

less studious than	less carefully than
less ambitious than	less seriously than
less busy than	

9

The double comparative structure. When we wish to express that the degree of one quality or characteristic is dependent upon the degree of another, we use the following sentence pattern.

THE + { -ER / MORE / LESS	S	V	C	THE + { -ER / MORE / LESS	S	V	C
The ... farther	we	live	from campus	the ... earlier	we	have to get up.	
The ... more	we	study	during the semester	the ... less	we	have to cram	later.
The ... less	we	spend		the ... more	we	save.	

---

[8] A single final consonant preceded by a single vowel is doubled before adding *er* or *est*.

[9] A few of the more common ones do. You will hear *oftener* and *more often* used interchangeably.

10 **Comparison of three or more things or groups which differ.** Superlative forms of adjectives and adverbs end in *est* and are usually preceded by *the*.

a. One-syllable adjectives and adverbs have superlative forms made by adding *est* to the simple forms.

old	the oldest	fast	the fastest
poor	the poorest	hard	the hardest
slim	the slimmest		

b. Two-syllable adjectives ending in *y* have superlative forms made by changing the *y* to *i* and adding *est*.

pretty	the prettiest
happy	the happiest
lucky	the luckiest
angry	the angriest

c. Adjectives and adverbs of two or more syllables (except as above) do not have superlative forms. Comparison of three or more items is expressed by placing *the most* before the simple forms.

serious	the most serious	seriously	the most seriously
careful	the most careful	carefully	the most carefully

d. *Least* is the opposite of *most*. It is used in the same pattern and also with two-syllable adjectives which end in *y*.

the least serious	the least carefully
the least ambitious	the least happily
the least happy	

11 **Irregular comparative and superlative forms.** A few of the most common adjectives and adverbs have irregular forms.

good	better than	the best
well	better than	the best
bad	worse than	the worst
badly	worse than	the worst

little	less than	the least
much	more than	the most
many	more than	the most
far	farther than	the farthest

12 **Absolutes.** A person is either asleep or awake, either present or absent, either dead or alive. A statement is usually true or false; an answer is right or wrong. Words describing such absolute situations are not used in comparative and superlative patterns, except figuratively; for example, *deader than a doornail.*

13 **Common errors to avoid**

a. **Incomplete comparisons.** Advertisers frequently state that a certain product is *better* or *more durable* or *less costly*—without telling us what the product is being compared with. *Finer quality at greater savings* is a popular slogan. Such incomplete comparisons are not acceptable except for advertising.

There are some times, however, when it is not necessary to state the complete comparison because it is obvious. The final sentence of the model paragraphs is an illustration. The complete comparison would be *She will be much happier than she is* when she has been here longer *than she has* and knows the language better *than she does.*

b. **Ambiguity.** Although we may omit obvious information, we must be very careful not to make statements which can be interpreted in more than one way. For instance, the sentence *Betty is more like Bill than Jane* could mean (1) *Betty is more like Bill than Jane is* (*like Bill*) or (2) *Betty is more like Bill than she is like Jane.* In such cases it is necessary to include the whole pattern to make the meaning clear.

c. **Comparing the incomparable.** Only things of the same category can be compared: people with people, buildings with buildings, rooms with rooms. Note the corrections inserted in the following student-written sentences.

                                     those in
The rooms in the Hilton are more comfortable than⌃the Intercontinental.

             the one in
Our pool is bigger than⌃the YMCA.

                     that of
The history of China is longer than⌃America.

Exercises

a. Tell about the general sameness or difference of things which can be seen in the classroom or through a window. Use the expressions *the same as, alike, differ from,* and *different from.* Make complete sentences (§§ 1, 6).

> Instructor: two books
> Student: Mr. Lee's book is the same as mine.
> Instructor: two pens
> Student: My pen is different from Mr. Lee's.

1. two notebooks	6. doors	11. trees
2. two briefcases	7. windows	12. buildings
3. two seats	8. walls	13. streets
4. the blackboards	9. desks	14. signs
5. the lights	10. chairs	15. gardens

b. Modify the expressions of similarity and difference in the following sentences (§§ 5, 7).

1. No two people look alike.
2. Sometimes twins look alike.
3. They are usually the same size.
4. They often have the same coloring.
5. They frequently wear the same style clothes.

6. Professor Miller has been teaching as long as Professor Allen.
7. George's grades are as good as Bill's.
8. The Allens' house is different from the Bakers'.
9. Betty's taste in clothes differs from Jane's.
10. Bill doesn't make as many dates as Jack does.

11. My apartment is not like yours.
12. Our apartments are different.
13. Yours is twice as large as mine.
14. Mine is as hard to clean as yours.
15. However, yours is as convenient for you as mine is for me.

c. Do you look like any of your relatives? Tell the class who you look like. Do any of your children look like you (§ 2)?

d. Compare the appearance of two students in your class with respect to the following characteristics (§§ 3, 8).

1. height	6. length of arms	11. color of hair
2. body build	7. length of legs	12. length of hair
3. weight	8. length of nose	13. type of hair
4. complexion	9. size of hands	14. size of eyes
5. age	10. size of feet	15. color of eyes

e. Compare any two people you know in respect to the given qualities. Include yourself if you wish (§§ 3, 8).

1. kindness	6. carefulness	11. honesty
2. friendliness	7. neatness	12. strength
3. gregariousness	8. seriousness	13. concentration
4. fairness	9. punctuality	14. clarity of expression
5. consideration	10. determination	15. organization

f. Compare the following items in any way you think appropriate (§ 8).

> Instructor: a tractor and a donkey
> Student: A tractor can pull a plow faster than a donkey can.

1. an airplane and a ship
2. a train and a bus
3. a bicycle and a motorcycle
4. a horse and a pony
5. a sailboat and a motorboat

6. telephone and telegraph
7. radio and TV
8. TV and movies
9. movies and theater
10. records and cassettes

11. poetry and prose
12. novels and short stories
13. fiction and non-fiction
14. detective stories and science fiction
15. reading and writing

g. Of all the means of transportation that you know, tell which is:

1. the cheapest
2. the most expensive
3. the most comfortable
4. the most enjoyable
5. the least comfortable

6. the most popular
7. the oldest
8. the least dangerous
9. the most widely used
10. the most reliable

11. the safest
12. the most modern
13. the best in a jungle
14. the best in mountains
15. the best for shipping perishables

h. Which country of the world . . .

1. is the largest?
2. is the most densely populated?
3. is the smallest?
4. is the most highly industrialized?
5. grows the most coffee?

6. has the longest history?
7. exports the most oil?
8. has the most famous art collection?
9. has the longest sea coast?
10. has the largest city?

11. has the longest river?
12. has the least crime?
13. changes government most often?
14. has the largest desert?
15. has the tallest buildings?

i. Substitute the appropriate form of the given word into the question and ask your neighbor to answer it. The answer may be drawn from history, myth, or folklore, or perhaps you may simply have to say, "I don't know who . . ."

> Instructor: Who was the oldest person in the world?
> Student 1: I don't know who the oldest person in the world was.
> Student 2: Methuselah was the oldest person in the world.

1.	rich	6.	brave	11.	funny
2.	wise	7.	courageous	12.	kind
3.	powerful	8.	ambitious	13.	cruel
4.	strong	9.	miserly	14.	treacherous
5.	beautiful	10.	innocent	15.	charitable

j. Correct the following sentences by inserting the necessary words in the appropriate places (§ 13c). The asterisks indicate that the sentences are incorrect.

1. *Our library is better for research than State College.
2. *Trains in Europe are more reliable than America.
3. *Most highways in the United States are wider than Europe.
4. *The ideas of educated people are different from uneducated people.
5. *The automobiles of today are more powerful than ten years ago.
6. *Modern music is louder than a few years ago.
7. *The newspaper here has more advertisements than my city.
8. *The clock in the gym is faster than the office.
9. *Clothes that you make yourself fit better than in the store.
10. *Taking an exam is easier than a thesis.
11. *The students from abroad are more interested in their work than this country.
12. *The staple foods of North Americans are different from Latin Americans.
13. *The airport in New York is bigger than Chicago.
14. *Fishing for trout is more difficult than flounder.
15. *Swimming in the sea is harder than a lake.

15 **Assignments**

This white house belongs
to the Smiths.

This brown house belongs
to the Clarks.

This white house belongs
to the Walkers.

a. Write as many perfect sentences as you can comparing these houses. Try to use all the different patterns we have practiced and any others that you know. Number your sentences.

b. Write a paragraph in which you compare the members of your family. If you don't have sisters and brothers, write about your cousins or about a few of your friends or your children.

c. Write a paragraph in which you compare the place where you live now with some place where you used to live.

d. Write three statements which you believe to be true and which have the sentence pattern illustrated in § 9. They may be proverbs translated from your language if you know any appropriate ones.

REVIEW XVIII

a. Using the given patterns, tell the class about your preferences. You may consider yourself a spectator or a participant.

Instructor: football, baseball, cricket
Student 1: Which do you prefer, football, baseball, or cricket?
Student 2: Football. I would rather play (watch) football than baseball or cricket.

1. tennis, golf, badminton
2. wrestling, boxing, karate
3. track, high-jump, broad-jump
4. swimming, diving, boating
5. roller-skating, ice-skating, skiing
6. pool, ping-pong, bowling
7. bridge, poker, solitaire
8. chess, checkers, backgammon
9. boat races, horse races, auto races
10. movies, TV, radio
11. piano, violin, flute
12. news, sports, drama
13. ocean, lake, mountains
14. fishing, hunting, trapping
15. square dancing, folk dancing, modern dancing

b. Complete each of the following with a simple verb form, an infinitive, or an *ing*-form, whichever is grammatically correct. Use the given verb phrase. Make any changes which are necessary to make good sentences.

Given: play tennis
Instructor: Betty likes . . .
Student: Betty likes to play tennis.
Instructor: I don't enjoy . . .
Student: I don't enjoy playing tennis.

1. dance

(*a*) Bill can't . . .
(*b*) He doesn't know how . . .
(*c*) He wishes he could . . .
(*d*) He thinks he might enjoy . . .
(*e*) He plans to learn . . .

2. make a speech

   (*a*) The Young Democrats asked Professor Miller . . .
   (*b*) He said that he would . . .
   (*c*) He likes . . .
   (*d*) Have you ever tried . . .
   (*e*) It isn't easy . . .

3. take a part-time job

   (*a*) Have you ever considered . . .
   (*b*) When George came here, he intended . . .
   (*c*) His adviser suggested (negative) . . .
   (*d*) He said, "A foreign student shouldn't . . .
   (*e*) "I advise you (negative) . . .

4. budget your time

   (*a*) Every student must . . .
   (*b*) Professors encourage . . .
   (*c*) Jane didn't . . .
   (*d*) She neglected . . .
   (*e*) Now she regrets (negative) . . .

5. help other people

   (*a*) Most adults like . . .
   (*b*) They hate to refuse . . .
   (*c*) Little children aren't interested in . . .
   (*d*) Their parents have to persuade . . .
   (*e*) They say, "We should . . .

CONDITIONS AND RESULTS: *IF, WHETHER, UNLESS* **XIX** WISHES AND HOPES

Betty likes Jane even though she isn't a very good student. Betty worries about the poor marks that Jane gets in chemistry quizzes. She wishes that Jane worked harder. "What will you do if you don't pass chemistry?" she once asked her friend.

"If I don't pass it, I'll take it again," Jane answered. "It's a required course in my field. I'm in home economics." After a while she added, "Professor Baker says that my work is improving and that I can still pass if I do well on the final exam. I didn't understand the lectures at all at first, but I understand them better now." Betty said that she hoped that Jane would pass, and that she would help her review.

If Betty didn't have an aunt and uncle living in College Town, she would probably have to live in a dormitory. One day Jane asked her where she would live if her uncle went to teach in another college. "I don't know what I'd do if Uncle Bill moved away," Betty answered. "I suppose I would move to a dorm unless I went with him. I hope he won't leave until I finish my courses. I don't want to transfer to another school if I can help it." [1]

Miss Liu told George that she wouldn't have come to this country if she had known how difficult it was to study in a foreign language. "I wish I had studied English in high school," she said. "I had an opportunity to, but I didn't know whether I'd ever have a chance to use the language or not."

George told her to do her best and not to worry. "Give yourself a little more time," he said. "You'll begin to understand everything soon."

"I hope so," she sighed.

[1] *Help* here means *avoid*. See XIV, 3a.

1 **Conditionals:** *if.*   The principal (independent) clause of a sentence may express the imagined result of one or more conditions. The conditions are usually stated in clauses introduced by *if*, which may come before or after the result clause. *If* suggests something unreal, nonexistent, contrary-to-fact (cf. XIV, 1a4, 1b5) or future. The verb in an *if*-clause is never the same form as that in the result clause of the same sentence.[2]

2 **Future conditions** are stated in present tense (simple or *s*-form verbs).

RESULT CLAUSE (future time)	CONDITIONAL CLAUSE (present tense)
What will you do	if you don't pass chemistry?
Jane can pass	if she does well on her final exam.
Betty will help Jane	if Jane needs help.

3 **Present conditions** are stated in past tense (past-form verbs). The result clause includes one of the modal auxiliaries *would, could,* or *might.*

CONDITIONAL CLAUSE (past tense)	RESULT CLAUSE (present time)
If Professor Allen were [3] not in College Town,	Betty might live in a dorm.
If Professor Allen left College Town,	Betty would move to a dorm.

[2] The verb phrases in contrary-to-fact statements are traditionally called subjunctives.
[3] Note the use of *were* instead of *was. Were* is the traditional form for subjunctives, both singular and plural. Since *be* is the only verb with two past forms, the problem of choosing the correct form does not arise with other verbs.

4 *Past conditions* are stated in the past perfect tense (*had* + past participle; see Lesson XII). The result clause includes *would, could,* or *might* and is expressed in the present perfect tense (*have* + past participle; see Lesson XI).

RESULT CLAUSE (past time)	CONDITIONAL CLAUSE (past perfect tense)
Miss Liu wouldn't have come here She would have studied English	if she had known how difficult it would be. if she had been sure of coming.

5 **Modal auxiliaries in *if*-clauses** (see Lesson XIV). The patterns illustrated above are fairly easy to learn and to follow so long as the *if*-clause does not include a modal auxiliary. When it does, the learner is often at a loss to choose the correct form because modal auxiliaries do not have the same forms that other verbs have. One way to acquaint yourself with the appropriate forms is to memorize a group of typical sentences and use them as patterns. The following sentences should prove helpful.

If I can help you, I will. (I may be able to help. I am not sure.)
If I could help you, I would. (Unfortunately, I am not able to.)
If I could have helped you, I would have. (I did not because I wasn't able.)

6 **Whether . . . or not**

a. Meaning.   Conditional clauses introduced by *whether* might be considered the opposite of *if*-clauses. *Whether* indicates that the condition described has no effect on the fact mentioned in the independent clause.

b. Form.   Grammatically, conditional clauses introduced by *if* and those introduced by *whether* are very similar. The verb forms and tenses used in them are the same. The only difference is that a condition after *whether* is followed by *or not*. If the clause is very long, the *or not* immediately follows *whether*.

c. Illustration.   Note particularly the verb phrases in the following sentences.

Bill *will go* home on Saturday whether he *gets* a ride or not.
Jane *would have* trouble with chemistry whether she *studied* or not.
Miss Liu *should have studied* English in high school *whether or not* her father *had promised* to send her abroad.

d. Emphasis.   To emphasize the indifference to the stated condition, the *whether*-clause is placed before the independent clause.

Whether we like it or not, we must take examinations.

7 ***Unless*** also introduces conditional clauses. It means *if not*. The verb forms are the same as those in *if*-clauses except that negatives become affirmative and affirmatives become negative. Like other conditionals, *unless*-clauses may precede or follow independent clauses.

Betty *won't transfer* to another school unless she *has to.*
Betty *would move* to a dorm unless she *went* with her uncle.
Unless Professor Miller *had been promised* a promotion, he *would not have taken* the position here.

8 | **Wish** does not state a condition, but it often refers to the unreal, the contrary-to-fact. We wish for things we do not have, for events which can not happen. The verb forms in object clauses after *wish* bear the same relationship to time as those in conditional clauses: a wish about the present time is expressed in past tense, a wish about the past is expressed in the past perfect.

> Betty wishes that Jane *worked* harder.
> Jack wishes he *had* a car.
> Everyone occasionally wishes he *were* someone else.
> Miss Liu wishes that she *had studied* English in high school.

9 | **Possible wishes** are about the future. There are two patterns.

a. Wish + I.O. + D.O. expresses a desire for something to happen—usually something pleasant.

> We wish you a happy New Year.
> Everyone wished the graduates successful careers.

b. Wish + infinitive is a synonym for *want*. It is felt by some people to be slightly more elegant or more polite than *want*.

> Betty does not wish to transfer to another school.

10 *Hope* refers to the unknown of any time: present, past, or future. We hope only for the possible.

a. When a person expresses a hope for something related to himself, he may use an infinitive or a *that*-clause. The meaning is the same.

> Jane hopes to pass chemistry.
> Jane hopes that she will pass chemistry.
>
> Miss Liu hopes to understand everything soon.
> Miss Liu hopes that she will understand everything soon.

b. When expressing a hope not related to one's self, only a *that*-clause may be used. The word *that* may be omitted (XII, 11a).

> Betty hopes that Jane will pass.
> She hopes her uncle won't leave College Town.
> George hopes that Sue Liu will understand everything soon.

c. When a hope is about the present unknown, the verb in the clause is one of the present tenses.

> I hope my parents *are* well.
> I hope they *are enjoying* their holiday.
> I hope they *have received* my letter.

d. When a hope is about the past unknown, the verb in the clause is a past.

> We hope we *didn't disturb* the neighbors last night.

11 *Whether* **this or that.** In addition to the pattern explained above (§ 6), *whether* is used to introduce alternatives which are not conditions.

a. In object clauses: note especially the verb forms.

> I don't know whether the Allens have a Plymouth or a Ford.
> Do you know whether Bill is a sophomore or a junior?
> Jane didn't say whether she was alone or with friends.
> I don't know whether it's still raining or not.[4]

b. In infinitive phrases

> Jane can't decide whether to study or to go shopping.
> Bill didn't know whether to go home by train or by bus.
> When Sue Liu was in high school, her father hadn't decided whether or
> not to send her abroad to study.

12 **Pronunciation**

For many speakers of American English *whether* is pronounced exactly the same as *weather*. We must be careful not to confuse the two when writing.

13 **Punctuation**

> If Betty didn't have an aunt and uncle in College Town ⊙ she would
> probably have to live in a dormitory.

> If George calls I want to talk to him.

For clarity and ease of reading, we place a comma after any subordinate clause which precedes a main clause. In actual practice we often neglect to do so, particularly when the introductory clause is short, as in the second sentence above. It is quite proper to place a comma after *calls*, but not all writers would do so.

---

[4] You will hear this pattern without the *or not*. The complete pattern is preferred.

Exercises

a. Complete the following sentence beginnings, being careful to choose the correct verb forms (§ 2).

1. I will stay here for three years if . . .
2. I will work next summer if . . .
3. I will take another English course if . . .
4. I will move to a better apartment if . . .
5. I will buy a new record player if . . .

6. You won't get to your next class on time if . . .
7. You won't get good grades in your exams if . . .
8. You can't get the right answer to a problem if . . .
9. You won't get any letters if . . .
10. You won't make any new friends if . . .

11. Mrs. Allen will invite Jack and Bill if . . .
12. Jane will fail chemistry if . . .
13. George will go back to Greece in two years if . . .
14. Betty will go to summer school if . . .
15. Jack will buy some new records this week if . . .

b. When completing the following sentence beginnings, include the information from the previous sentence when possible (§ 3).

Instructor: We would go to the campus movie tonight if . . .
Student: We would go to the campus movie tonight if we had time.
Instructor: We would see an Italian film if . . .
Student: We would see an Italian film if we went to the campus movie.

1. Professor Baker would lose weight if . . .
2. Mrs. Baker would be happy if . . .
3. He would go on a diet if . . .
4. Mrs. Baker would prepare special food for him if . . .
5. He would eat the special food if . . .

6. Jane would study harder if . . .
7. Jack would take Jane out more often if . . .
8. Jane would have to buy some more new clothes if . . .
9. She would need more money than she gets if . . .
10. She would have to get a job if . . .

11. Bill wouldn't go home so often if . . .
12. Bill wouldn't be able to train his dog if . . .
13. He wouldn't be able to go hunting if . . .
14. He wouldn't catch any rabbits if . . .
15. His mother couldn't make him rabbit pie if . . .

c. Complete the following beginnings with *if*-clauses in the context of the model paragraphs (§ 4).

1. George might not have changed his major . . .
2. Miss Liu wouldn't have had her eyes examined . . .
3. Betty couldn't have won the tennis championship . . .
4. Jack might not have bought a car . . .
5. Bill wouldn't have phoned his mother in the morning . . .
6. Jane couldn't have passed math . . .
7. Mrs. Brown might have sold her house in Westview . . .
8. Mr. and Mrs. Jones would have sent Jack to a different college . . .
9. Betty's parents couldn't have sent her to college at all . . .
10. Mrs. Allen might have been a better cook . . .
11. Mrs. Baker would have become a teacher . . .
12. Professor Allen could have given up smoking . . .
13. Professor Baker might have remained a bachelor . . .
14. Professor Miller would have finished his book last month . . .
15. We could have learned the conditional sooner . . .

d. Tell the class about your own ideas by adding a result clause to each of the following (§§ 2, 3, 4).

1. If it rains tomorrow . . .
2. If I don't receive a letter today . . .
3. If I don't pass this course . . .
4. If I run out of money . . .
5. If I don't get my visa extended . . .

6. If I didn't get along with my roommate . . .
7. If I were late to class . . .
8. If my parents were here . . .
9. If I had a good job . . .
10. If I didn't have to study so much . . .

11. If I hadn't known any English . . .
12. If my friends hadn't helped me . . .
13. If I hadn't been invited . . .
14. If I hadn't had a vacation . . .
15. If I had had a longer vacation . . .

e. Make a conditional sentence about some person now in the news or some character from history. Tell what you think he will do if he can, what he would do if he could, or what he would have done if he could have (§ 5).

f. Answer the following questions with complete statements including the condition (cf. Lessons XII and XIV).

1. If George hadn't come to the United States, where might he have gone to study?
2. If he had gone to Paris, what language would he have had to learn?
3. What language would you have learned if you had gone to Moscow?
4. If you had gone to London, what famous chimes would you have heard?
5. What tower might you have climbed if you had gone to Paris?

6. What game might Jack be watching if he were in England?
7. Whose music might Bill be listening to if he were in Berlin?
8. What art museum might Betty be visiting if she were in France?
9. Which mountains might Jane be climbing if she were in Switzerland?
10. If Miss Liu were in Hong Kong, would she be having trouble with language?

11. If you had been born in 1910, how old would you be today?
12. If you were that old, how might you feel about work?
13. If you were tired of working, how would you pass the time?
14. Where would you be living if you had already retired?
15. Do you think old people are happy if they have nothing to do?

g. Give affirmative answers to the following questions. Include the expression *whether . . . or not* (§ 6).

> Instructor: Will we have class if several people are absent?
> Student: We will have class whether several people are absent or not.

1. Will Jane go shopping if it rains?
2. Would you go to a dentist regularly if you never had a toothache?
3. Will Betty neglect her homework if she gets home very late?

4. Would you play tennis if you didn't have a good racket?
5. Will Jack buy a car if his father lends him the money?
6. Would you come to class if you hadn't done your assignment?
7. Would Bill type his term papers if he didn't have to?
8. Will you type your papers if you buy a typewriter?
9. Will we have an exam if we finish this book?
10. Will we have a vacation if we finish this book?
11. Will George go home next year if he finishes his studies?
12. Will Professor Miller buy a house if he gets married?
13. Will Professor Baker sell his house if he goes abroad?
14. Will Professor Allen get a promotion if he writes another book?
15. Will we remember *whether* if we don't practice it any more?

h. Change the structure of the following sentences to include the word *unless*. Be careful not to change the meaning (§ 7).

> Instructor: Don't buy a watch if it isn't guaranteed.
> Student: Don't buy a watch unless it is guaranteed.
> Instructor: Jack will come if he is well.
> Student: Jack will come unless he isn't well.

1. Don't apply for a job if you are not qualified.
2. Don't study veterinary science if you don't love animals.
3. Don't rock the boat if you don't know how to swim.
4. Don't buy a second-hand car if you aren't a mechanic.
5. Don't try to take a picture indoors if you don't have a flash bulb.

We'll have a party.

6. Jill will bake a cake if her oven isn't out of order.
7. John will get the Cokes if he isn't broke.[5]
8. Tom will play his guitar if it doesn't have a broken string.
9. Mary will sing if she doesn't have a cold.
10. We'll have a good party if the neighbors don't complain.

11. You must not drive without a license.
12. You can't get on a plane without a reservation.
13. You shouldn't buy things you don't want.
14. When you aren't hungry, you shouldn't eat.
15. A student shouldn't be absent without a good reason.

---

[5] *To be broke* is a slang expression which means to be short of money.

i. Make a wish that is contrary to the fact mentioned by your instructor. Pay particular attention to the verb forms in your sentences. You may include *that* or leave it out (§ 8).

> Instructor: Today is Monday.
> Student: I wish that it were Friday.

1. I don't understand the lectures.
2. I can't do the problems.
3. I've broken my glasses.
4. John is coming over.
5. I haven't anything to eat.

6. I don't own a car.
7. I bought a bicycle.
8. It got a flat tire.
9. I put it in the basement.
10. It was stolen.

11. We went to an expensive restaurant last night.
12. We ran into some people we knew.
13. We ate too much.
14. We stayed too long.
15. We got home very late.

j. Tell something that you wish about the present and something that you hope for the future (§§ 8, 10).

> I wish money grew on trees.
> I hope I will earn some money soon.

k. Student 1: Make a *whether* question with the given alternatives.
Student 2: State that you don't know the answer (§ 11).

> Instructor: cigarettes or a pipe
> Student 1: Can you tell me whether Professor Allen smokes cigarettes or a pipe?
> Student 2: I can't remember whether he smokes cigarettes or a pipe.

1. a jet plane or a propeller plane
2. first class or economy class
3. a steward or a stewardess

4. fish or chicken
5. wine or beer
6. a student visa or a tourist visa
7. for a few weeks or for a year
8. buy textbooks or use library copies
9. the early show or the late show
10. at three o'clock or at three thirty
11. Jack or Bill
12. Jane or Betty
13. Mrs. Baker or Mrs. Brown
14. Professor Miller or Professor Allen
15. George's sister or his brother

15 Assignments

When writing these assignments, include as many of the patterns from this lesson as you can.

a. Write a paragraph about yourself which begins, "If I become a successful . . . (engineer, agronomist, doctor)." Tell what you will do. It is sufficient to include the *if*-clause in the first sentence only.

b. Write a paragraph about yourself which begins, "If I were. . . ." Mention some important person in the world today. Tell what you would do if you were that person.

c. Write a paragraph which begins, "If I had been. . . ." Mention some famous or infamous person from history. Tell what you would have done if you had been that person.

REVIEW XIX

a. Complete the following:

1. I'm not sure whether we have a test on Saturday or not, but I hope . . .
2. We always seem to have tests on Saturdays, but I wish . . .
3. I would prefer . . .

4. Jack doesn't study very much. His father wishes . . .
5. He suggests . . .
6. Jack realizes . . .

7. The Bakers have agreed to sell their house, but Mrs. Baker can't help . . .
8. She remembers . . .
9. She regrets . . .

10. George intends . . .
11. He hopes . . .
12. He expects . . .

13. Professor Miller wanted . . .
14. He asked . . .
15. The dean suggested . . .

b. Following are some situations. Tell what the results would be if the situations were reversed.

> Instructor: It's raining rather hard.
> Student: If it weren't raining so hard, I'd go for a walk.

1. Fruit is very expensive in this country.
2. Developing photographs requires a lot of equipment.
3. Pets are not permitted in dorms.
4. Parking fines are not very high.
5. The magazines in the barber shop aren't interesting.
6. There weren't any good movies in town last week.
7. The basketball games have all been in the evening.
8. The lakes near here are polluted.
9. There are too many advertisements on television.
10. Tape recorders were on sale last week, but I didn't have any money.
11. When I was in the post office, the mail had not been sorted.
12. The book I requested hasn't been returned to the library yet.
13. The best Broadway plays are made into movies.
14. Most good novels are published in paperback editions.
15. Symphony orchestras travel throughout the country.

XX

WHY? REASONS AND PURPOSES: *BECAUSE,*
SO THAT, IN ORDER TO
CONCESSION: *ALTHOUGH, EVEN THOUGH,*
IN SPITE OF, BUT . . . ANYWAY
CONSEQUENCE: *THUS, THEREFORE, CONSEQUENTLY,*
AS A RESULT

Although we have almost completed our review of English sentence patterns, we still haven't asked or answered any questions beginning with *why*. The reason we haven't is that there are many different ways to talk and write about causes and results. Some of the patterns are quite complex, and therefore we have left them until last. Let's look at a few paragraphs about causes and results to see if we can recognize the patterns.

Professor Allen spends a lot of time with his students because of the pleasure he gets from helping people. He particularly enjoys working with foreign students because he learns so much from them. He always says, "A teacher needs to keep on learning in order to improve his teaching." Mrs. Allen agrees, and thus she helps out by arranging social evenings, even though she is very busy with her work at the library.

Professor Baker is fond of his students, too, but he hasn't spent much time with them lately. He has been teaching for such a long time that he is a little tired of classrooms and laboratories and offices. Besides, his doctor told him to take it easy.[1] Consequently, he is looking forward to his retirement and to his trip around the world. Mrs. Baker is making all the arrangements for the trip so that there won't be any problems about the reservations. "Bruce is a very kind and generous man," she says, "but he is so forgetful that I have to take care of all the details myself."

One reason why Bill Brown goes to Westview to see his mother so[2] often is that his father died last year. Another reason is that he likes the beautiful countryside around Westview. He hopes to live there after he graduates. He will have to stay at college for several years, however, because he wants to be an engineer.

The other students may not have to stay so long. Miss Liu came here to learn to be a librarian. In spite of the difficulties she is having right now, she will probably do quite well. George was going to study history, but he became interested in sociology so he changed his program. His father says he isn't quite sure what a sociologist does, but he is proud of his son anyway. Jane is in home economics. Her parents want her to have a college degree even though she isn't interested in a career. Jack is still trying to find something he is interested in besides having a good time, and Betty is so interested in everything that she hasn't been able to make up her mind about a career yet.

[1] *Take it easy* means not to exert one's self.
[2] *So* here is a substitute for *as . . . as* (see XVIII, 3c).

1 **Why-**questions ask about causes. A cause may be something which has already happened—a reason; or it may be something we want to happen— a purpose.

Lady:	Why are you giving me a ticket?
Policeman:	Because you crossed the street against the traffic signal. [reason]
	Why did you do that?
Lady:	To get to the other side. [purpose]

2 **Oral responses** to *why*-questions usually consist of *because* plus a state- ment of reason or *so, to,* or *in order to* plus a statement of purpose. Since these words are all connectives of one sort or another, the responses are not considered complete sentences (cf. Lesson X).

3 **Complete statements** about reasons or purposes usually include informa- tion about the results as well. There are several different patterns. The most common ones are illustrated in the rest of this lesson.

4 **Result (independent clause) + reason (dependent clause)**

a. *Because, as, since,*[3] and *for* are the connective clause-markers used in this pattern. *Because* is probably the most frequent.

b.

RESULT	REASON
Prof. Allen enjoys working with foreign students	because he learns a lot from them.
Mrs. Allen helps him entertain his students	as she enjoys their company too.
Mrs. Baker takes care of the details	since her husband is very forgetful.
Mrs. Baker takes care of the details	for her husband is very forgetful.

[3] *Since* used in this way does not refer to time (cf. XI, 7).

Reason (dependent) + result (independent)

a. *Because, as,* and *since* are used in this pattern. *Since* is probably the most frequent. *For* is never used in a reason clause at the beginning of a sentence.

b. **Pronouns** usually occur in the second clause, the noun referents being placed in the first clause regardless of whether it is dependent or independent. Compare these sentences with the ones in § 4.

c.

REASON	RESULT
Because Prof. Allen learns a lot from his students,	he enjoys working with them.
As Mrs. Allen enjoys the company of her husband's students,	she helps entertain them.
Since Professor Baker is very forgetful,	his wife takes care of the details.

 ***Because of* + noun** is another way of expressing reason. It may be stated before or after the result.

> Prof. Allen spends time with his students because of the pleasure it gives him.
> Because of Prof. Baker's forgetfulness, Mrs. Baker takes care of the details.

7 **Reason (independent) + result (dependent): informal**

a. *So* introduces a dependent result clause. This is a colloquial pattern, very widely used, but not accepted in formal writing.

b.

REASON	RESULT
George became interested in sociology	so he changed his program.
Mrs. Allen wants to help her husband	so she arranges social evenings.

8 **Reason (independent) + result (independent): formal**

a. *Thus, therefore, consequently, as a result* are the formal ways of telling that what follows is the result of what precedes. They express the same meaning as *so* in the pattern above, but they are grammatically different.

b. These words do not connect clauses. They introduce complete sentences. Thus, when using one of these transition words, we must be careful of punctuation. A reason is stated in one sentence, and the result is stated in the following sentence.

REASON	RESULT
Mrs. Allen wants to help her husband.	Thus, she arranges social evenings.
Professor Baker is a little tired of teaching.	Consequently, he is looking forward to his retirement.

c. *And* or a semicolon (;) may join the two sentences, making one compound sentence (see II, 11).

REASON	AND ;	RESULT
Some of the patterns are complex, and therefore, we have left them until last.		
We haven't practiced cause–result expressions before; consequently, we must practice them now.		

9 *So (adj./adv.) that* expresses result as a function of the degree of a characteristic. Neither clause may be used alone. *That* is sometimes omitted.

REASON	SO . . . THAT	RESULT
Bruce Baker is so forgetful		that his wife has to take care of the details.
Betty is so interested in everything		that she's having trouble choosing a career.
We have studied so diligently		that we know all the patterns in this book.

10 **Such/so (modifiers + noun) *that*** is a variant of pattern 9. Neither clause is independent. *That* is sometimes omitted.

REASON	SUCH/SO . . . (N.) . . . THAT		RESULT
Prof. Baker has been teaching	such a long time	that	he is a little tired.
Westview is	such a beautiful place	that	Bill likes to go there.
George had	so little money	that	he had to get a job.
There are	so many patterns	that	it takes a long time to learn them.

11 ***The reason (why*** [4] ***/that/——) . . . is that*** [5] is another way to introduce reason.

One reason why Bill goes home so often	is that his father died last year.
Another reason he goes home	is that he likes Westview.
The reason that we haven't taken up why-questions	is that the answers are so complex.

 12 ***So that*** introduces a purpose clause containing a modal, usually *can, could, will,* or *would.* The usual order is after the result clause, though occasionally it precedes.

a.

RESULT (independent)	PURPOSE (dependent)
Mrs. Baker is making the arrangements	so that there won't be any trouble.
Prof. Allen tries to learn new things	so that he can improve his teaching.

b. In conversation, *so that* is often reduced to *so.* This is quite a different pattern from the one described in § 7, however. Note the difference in the relationship between the clauses.

---

[4] Some people object to the use of *why* here. They argue that it is redundant after *reason.* You will hear *why.* It is probably better to use *that* or no clause marker.
[5] You will undoubtedly hear someone say, ". . . the reason is because. . . ." This locution is very much frowned upon by English teachers and some other educated people, also on the grounds of redundancy. It's better to avoid it.

13 **Purpose** is also sometimes expressed by an infinitive, with or without the words *in order* (see XVI, 7c).

RESULT	PURPOSE
Miss Liu came here	to learn to be a librarian.
Bill goes home	to see his mother.
A teacher needs to keep learning in order to improve his teaching.	

14 **For + noun** also states a purpose.

RESULT	PURPOSE
Miss Liu is studying	for a degree in library science.
Mrs. Baker went to a travel agent	for her tickets.

15 **What . . . for** is a separable colloquial expression which has the same meaning as *why*. Note the following examples.

What did Mrs. Baker go to the travel agent for?
What does Professor Allen spend so much time with his students for?

Answers to *what . . . for* questions are the same as answers to questions beginning with *why*.

16 **Concession** statements accompany clauses concerning unexpected results.

c. *Although* and *even though* introduce dependent clauses. They may precede or follow the result clause.

> Although we have almost completed our review, we haven't taken up *why* yet.
> Mrs. Allen arranges social evenings even though she has a lot of work at the library.

b. *In spite of* is followed by a noun, an *ing*-form, or a clause introduced by *the fact that.*

> In spite of Miss Liu's present problems, she will probably do quite well.
> Mrs. Allen arranges social evenings in spite of being quite busy at the library.
> George's father is proud of his son in spite of the fact that he doesn't understand what George is studying.

c. *But . . . anyway*

> George's father doesn't know what a sociologist does, but he is proud of his son anyway.

17 **Besides** means *in addition to.* It should not be confused with *beside,* which means *by the side of* (XV, 7a).

> Jack is still trying to find something he is interested in besides having a good time.

18 **However** indicates contrast with a statement just made (see *but,* II, 11b). It is not a sentence connector, however. It may occur in any one of a number of different points in a sentence.

> Bill hopes to live in Westview after he graduates.
> (However,) he must (, however,) stay in College Town (, however,) for a few more years (, however).

19 Punctuation

Prof. Allen enjoys working with students because he learns a lot from them.

Because Prof. Allen learns a lot from students ⊙ he enjoys working with them.

a. In a cause–result sentence, when the main clause comes first, there is no internal comma (sentence 1 above and § 4b). When the dependent clause comes first, it is usually followed by a comma (sentence 2 above and § 5c).

b. When writing, remember that transition words (§ 8) are not sentence connectors like *and, but,* and *or.* Sentences preceding these words must end with periods (full stops), not commas.

c. The word *however* is separated from the rest of the sentence by commas (§ 18).

20 Exercises

a. The instructor will pronounce a sentence fragment.

Student 1: Construct a *why*-question.
Student 2: Make an oral response.
Student 3: Make a summary statement.

Questions may be affirmative or negative, and vary in subject and tense.
Responses will begin with *because, so* (§ 12b), *to,* or *in order to* (§ 2).

Instructor: wear a tie
Student 1: Why are you wearing a tie today, Bob?
Student 2: Because I have an appointment with the dean.
Student 3: Bob is wearing a tie because he has an appointment with the dean.

1. wear glasses
2. wear blue jeans
3. look in a mirror
4. carry an umbrella
5. always count your change
6. set your alarm clock
7. study before exams
8. write letters
9. smoke
10. watch TV
11. drive so fast
12. shake hands
13. retire
14. give public lectures
15. live in Westview

b. Change *because* to *because of* in the following sentences. Make all other necessary changes (§ 6).

Instructor: The plane didn't fly because there was a storm.
Student: The plane didn't fly because of the storm.

1. Jack didn't go downtown on Monday because it was raining.
2. He didn't go downtown on Tuesday because he didn't feel well.
3. He didn't go downtown on Wednesday because he missed the bus.
4. He didn't go downtown on Thursday because he didn't have any money.
5. He didn't go downtown on Friday because I advised him not to.

Jane did go downtown. She tried on a dress.

6. She didn't buy it because it was a strange color.
7. She didn't buy it because it was too long.
8. She didn't buy it because it wasn't a good style.
9. She didn't buy it because it had buttons on it.
10. She didn't buy it because the price was too high.

11. We don't feel like working in summer because it's too hot.
12. We don't feel like working in winter because it's too cold.
13. We don't feel like working on holidays because we have visitors.
14. We don't feel like working at night because there are parties going on.
15. We don't feel like working now because our assignments are difficult.

c. Complete the following by adding a result clause to each. Remember that this is a colloquial pattern (§ 7).

> Instructor: We arrived late for the lecture so . . .
> Student: We arrived late for the lecture so we sat in the back.

1. Jack didn't know what the chemistry assignment was so . . .
2. He couldn't do one of the problems so . . .
3. His pencil broke so . . .
4. He was hungry so . . .
5. It was late so . . .

6. Jane wanted to go downtown in a hurry so . . .
7. She wanted to buy a new dress so . . .
8. She didn't like the dresses she saw so . . .
9. She saw a hat that she liked so . . .
10. She saw a pair of shoes that she liked, too, but they were too expensive so . . .

11. Bus fare is cheaper than taxi fare so . . .
12. Taxis are faster than buses so . . .
13. Miss Liu lives very near the library so . . .
14. George lives a long way from the school buildings so . . .
15. There are no classes tomorrow so . . .

d. Use the following expressions in sentences. Omit *that* if you wish (§ 9).

> Instructor: so tall (that)
> Student: Our basketball center is so tall that he has to bend down to get through the door.

1.	so rich that	6.	so interesting that	11.	so expensive that
2.	so poor that	7.	so boring that	12.	so much trouble that
3.	so happy that	8.	so easy that	13.	so many times that
4.	so sad that	9.	so hard that	14.	so much money that
5.	so busy that	10.	so cheap that	15.	so many people that

e. Use the following expressions in sentences (§ 10).

> Instructor: such a frightening dream
> Student: I had such a frightening dream that I woke up.

1. such a long lecture
2. such an unusual exercise
3. such long assignments
4. such a hard problem
5. such a difficult course
6. such a pleasant day
7. such a comfortable car
8. such a delicious lunch
9. such beautiful flowers
10. such a good time
11. such dark clouds
12. such a bad storm
13. such helpful people
14. such good insurance
15. such a worthy cause

f. Tell one reason why you want to do something. Use the pattern illustrated in § 11.

> One reason I want to go to California is that I'd like to see Disneyland.

g. Change *for* to *to* in the following sentences. Make all other necessary changes (§§ 13 and 14).

> Instructor: Sue went to the drugstore for some medicine.
> Student: Sue went to the drugstore to get some medicine.

1. We came here for the engineering course.
2. We study hard for good grades.
3. We need good grades for scholarships.
4. We need scholarships for tuition.
5. We read for information.
6. We talk for pleasure.
7. We play cards for amusement.
8. We take walks for enjoyment.
9. We drink coffee for stimulation.
10. We take showers for refreshment.
11. We listen to the radio for news.
12. We watch TV for sports.
13. We play records for dancing.
14. We eat fruit for our health.
15. We work for a living.

h. Change *to* to *for* in the following sentences. Make all other necessary changes (§§ 13 and 14).

> Instructor: Bill went to the barber to get his hair cut.
> Student: Bill went to the barber for a haircut.

1. Joe went to the bank to get some money.
2. He went to a store to buy a new shirt.
3. He went to a restaurant to eat dinner.
4. He went to the library to get a book.
5. He went to bed to get some rest.

6. He asked his doctor to prescribe some medicine for his hay fever.
7. He asked his jeweler to show him a band for his wrist watch.
8. He asked his dentist to send him a bill.
9. He asked the waiter to bring him some coffee.
10. He asked his friend to let him have a cigarette.

11. His landlady asked him to give her two references.
12. His landlady asked him to pay her the rent.
13. His landlady asked him to give her two weeks' notice when he was going to move.
14. He asked his landlady to give him a key.
15. He asked his landlady to give him a clean towel.

i. Tell about something you do regularly and explain your purpose in doing it (§ 12).

I save some money every month so that I will have some for my vacation.

j. Complete the following, using the patterns illustrated in § 16.

1. We always complete our assignments although . . .
2. Even though we don't get much sleep . . .
3. We always rest on Sunday even though . . .
4. Although we are away from home on holidays . . .
5. Although we aren't always successful . . .

6. It was snowing very hard one morning, but Betty went to class in spite of . . .
7. It was late when she reached school, but she went to class in spite of . . .
8. The lecture was half over, but she tried to understand it in spite of . . .
9. She took some notes in spite of the fact that . . .
10. She's going to have to ask the professor about the lecture in spite of . . .

11. Bill's mother doesn't expect him to call her every week, but . . .
12. Jane knows that she shouldn't spend so much time shopping, but . . .
13. George doesn't always understand what his assignments mean, but . . .
14. Miss Liu doesn't like American food, but . . .
15. Betty knows that Jane isn't a good student, but . . .

21 Assignments

a. Change the following colloquial sentences to acceptable formal written statements, being very careful to observe the conventions of punctuation. Use all of the different transition words in § 8.

1. Some lessons are more difficult than others so it takes longer to master them.
2. We practice oral English several hours a week so we soon learn to understand spoken English.
3. Some of the model paragraphs are records of conversations so they include some colloquial expressions.

4. This course is designed for students who have studied English for a long time so there are many patterns in each lesson.

5. Mispunctuating what we write is very confusing to readers so we should try to avoid it.

b. Substitute *since* for *because* in the following sentences and change the order of the clauses (§ 5). Make all other word order changes which are necessary to make clearly stated, grammatical sentences. Watch punctuation (§ 19a).

1. Learning to write English is easier for Latin Americans than it is for Chinese students because the Latin Americans use the same alphabet as English speakers do.

2. A reading knowledge of English is not sufficient for students because they have to understand what their professors say.

3. Colloquial expressions should not be used in themes because they are not appropriate.

4. We should be very careful when we write because we don't want to be misunderstood.

5. Ph.D. candidates must take advanced courses in writing because they have to write theses.

c. Rewrite the sentences below, changing *but* to *however*. Make the necessary changes in punctuation.

1. English spelling is irregular but it is not entirely without pattern.

2. When someone speaks to us we see him, but when we read we do not see the writer.

3. Learning to read a foreign language is not very difficult, but learning to write one is.

4. Punctuation should indicate the rhythm and intonation of a language, but it doesn't always do so.

5. Leaving out important marks of punctuation is confusing to a reader, but putting in punctuation which is not appropriate is even more confusing.

REVIEW XX

The paragraphs below sound strange because they are written in simple sentences. Rewrite them in better prose by combining the sentences into compound and complex ones. Each paragraph can be written in seven sentences, as indicated.

a. (1) Robert Smith is a bachelor. He owns a department store. He operates it. It is small. It is in Westview. He inherited it from his uncle. (2) People live in Westview. Most of them buy their clothes in his store. He carries a large selection. His prices are reasonable. His salespeople are courteous and helpful. (3) Mr. Smith is very busy during the week. He manages his store then. On Saturday nights he likes to relax. He may go bowling. He may go to a movie. He may visit a friend. (4) On Sundays he has a big breakfast. He reads the newspaper. He especially reads the advertisements. He wants to see something. Other businessmen are advertising. (5) It is afternoon. He goes for a walk in some hills. They are around Westview. (6) He returns home. He showers. He changes his clothes. He goes to the Westview Hotel. He has a glass of wine. He has a good dinner. He is with his friends. (7) Dining at the Westview Hotel is very expensive. He can afford it. He makes a good profit from his department store. He is a bachelor.

b. (1) Steve lives in Texas. He decided to visit his cousin. His cousin lives in Colorado. His car wasn't in very good shape. He didn't have the price of a plane ticket. He went by bus. (2) The trip was long. It took eighteen hours. Steve didn't mind. He enjoys looking at scenery. He sat next to a fellow. The fellow was young. His name was Sam. Sam had just returned from Africa. He had been teaching mathematics. It was in a school. The school was tiny. It was in a village. (3) Sam told Steve stories. They were about Africa. They were interesting. Steve almost forgot something. He had to get off the bus. (4) The bus driver was ready to pull out. Steve got off. He looked for his luggage. It wasn't on the platform. (5) Perhaps it had been put on the wrong bus. Perhaps the driver had neglected to remove it from the luggage compartment. Perhaps he had removed it and put it back in again. No one had claimed it. (6) Steve found the station master. He reported the missing suitcase. He called up his cousin. His cousin came. He picked Steve up. (7) Steve's suitcase didn't show up at first. It did several days later. Steve had a good vacation. His cousin is just his size. His cousin lent him clothes. He needed them.

c. (1) Scrabble is a word game. It is played with tiles. The tiles have letters on them. (2) The players must place the tiles together. They must place them on a board. The letters must spell a word. (3) The first player may spell any word at all. The second player must use one or more of the letters already on the board to make his word. (4) The third player has more letters to play on. He has fewer free spaces. (5) Sometimes someone misspells a word. He loses his turn. (6) The words used in this game are quite short. The game soon becomes difficult. It is not permitted to have any non-words on the board. (7) Some people know a lot of uncommon short words. They usually win at Scrabble.

APPENDIX

■ THE SOUNDS AND SPELLINGS OF ENGLISH: A GUIDE TO INTELLIGENT GUESSING

Anyone who has studied English at all knows that the spelling is very irregular. When you see a new word, you can't be sure how it is pronounced; when you hear a new word, you can't be sure of the spelling. When you need to know the spelling of a word you are advised to look it up in a dictionary, but frequently you cannot find it in a dictionary precisely because you don't know how it is spelled.

The lists below are meant to help you find words in dictionaries. The symbols in brackets are those used by the International Phonetic Association (IPA) to represent the sounds of English. Many other equally satisfactory systems of symbols are currently in use; you may have had to learn one of them already. Most dictionaries, though, do not use phonetic symbols, but diacritics, and each dictionary has its own system. Thus it is not recommended that you attempt to learn to use the symbols, but simply that you refer to the lists as a guide to intelligent guessing.

Consonant sounds

Symbols	Spellings
[p]	pen, apt, cup
[b]	boy, robbed, cab
[t]	two, bottle, cat
[d]	dog, order, had
[k]	come, kick, anchor, chorus
[g]	go, dragged, wig, ghost, guide, guess
[f]	face, calf, phase, cough
[v]	very, average, above, of
[θ]	thin, tooth
[ð]	then, other, breathe
[s]	see, ceiling, psychic
[z]	zoo, jazz, was
[ʃ]	she, sure, chauffeur, cash
[ʒ]	measure, garage
[h]	he, who
[tʃ]	cheese, question, capture, which, witch
[dʒ]	judge, gem, giant
[m]	man, thumb, calm, damn
[n]	no, know, gnaw, reign, pneumatic

[ŋ]	thi*ng*, thi*n*k
[l]	*l*ike, a*ll*ow, mi*ll*, mi*l*e
[w]	*w*on, *o*ne, q*u*ick, *wh*y
[hʍ]	*wh*y, *wh*ere (some dialects)
[j]	*y*ou, *u*se, on*i*on
[r]	*r*ight, *w*rite, *rh*yme

Vowel Sounds

Unlike the consonants, which are quite stable, the vowels are pronounced differently in the different parts of the world where English is spoken as a first or second language. The pronunciations indicated here represent the type of speech which is commonly referred to as General American. It does not attempt to reflect geographical differences.

Symbols	Spellings
[i]	*ea*t, m*ee*t, ch*ie*f, k*ey*, c*ei*ling, mach*i*ne
[ɪ]	s*i*t, ph*y*sics
[e]*	*a*te, pl*ay*, gr*ey*, gr*ea*t
[ɛ]	g*e*t, *e*very, h*ea*d, s*ai*d
[æ]	h*a*d, c*a*sh, pl*ai*d
[a]	n*o*t, c*a*lm, b*o*mb, f*a*ther, h*ea*rt
[ɔ]	s*aw*, t*au*t, t*au*ght, th*ou*ght, t*a*lk, cl*o*th
[o]*	s*o*, s*ow*, s*ew*, s*oa*p, t*oe*
[ʊ]	p*u*t, p*u*sh, w*oo*d, w*ou*ld, p*u*ll, w*oo*l
[u]	b*oo*t, s*ui*t, s*ue*, y*ou*, e*we*, y*ew*
[ʌ]	s*o*me (when stressed), s*o*n, s*u*n, bl*oo*d, c*ou*ntry
[ɝ]	h*er*, h*er*d, h*ear*d, b*ir*d, w*or*d, f*ur*, w*ere*
[ə]	*a*bove, b*e*tween, d*i*rect, c*o*mmit, *u*pon
	Vowels in unstressed syllables sound almost alike regardless of how they are spelled. This sound may be spelled with any of the vowel letters.

Diphthongs

[ai]	*I*, *i*ce, h*i*gh, h*ei*ght, d*ie*, b*y*, b*uy*, b*ye*, rh*y*me
[au]	*ou*t, *ow*l, c*ow*, b*ou*gh
[ɔi]	b*oy*, b*oi*l
[iu]	b*eau*ty, f*u*se, f*ew*, v*iew*

* [e] and [o] are considered diphthongs in many phonetic systems.

SUMMARY OF USES OF PUNCTUATION

The sole purpose of punctuation is to help the reader understand what the writer means. Thus, there is a certain amount of freedom in the use of various marks, particularly the comma. The uses noted in this text and summarized below are generally adhered to, though not everyone would agree with them. For a more complete treatment, see any reference guide or desk dictionary.

a. The Apostrophe (')
Use an apostrophe

1. to mark omissions in contracted forms (I, 17b)
2. in the word *o'clock* (II, 19b)
3. to indicate possession, origin, measure (VI, 10c)

b. The Colon (:)
Use a colon

1. to introduce a list (V, 22a)
2. after the names of speakers, when writing dialogue (V, 22a)

c. The Comma (,)
Use a comma

1. after *yes* or *no* in a response (I, 17d)
2. before the connective in a long compound sentence (II, 19d)
3. to separate items in addresses (IV, 14d)
4. to separate equivalent sentence parts in a series (IV, 14d)
5. to separate a speaker's words from the introductory statement (IV, 14d)
6. to group large numbers into thousands (IV, 14d)
7. to set off the addressee in direct address (VI, 13c)
8. to separate an introductory clause from the rest of the sentence (VII, 13; XIX, 13; XX, 19a)
9. after a mild exclamation (X, 13a)
10. before and after an appositive (X, 13b)
11. to separate a tag question from the rest of the sentence (XIII, 16)
12. before and after a non-restrictive adjective clause (XVI, 9b3 and 11b)

d. The Hyphen (-)
Use a hyphen

1. in certain fixed expressions: person-to-person, station-to-station (IV, 14c)
2. in compound numerals (IV, 14c)
3. at the end of a line when dividing a word (VI, 13b)

e. The Period (.)
Use a period

1. at the end of every statement (I, 17c)
2. after most abbreviations (I, 17c)
3. in the expressions a.m. and p.m. (IV, 14b)
4. to indicate cents and other decimals (IV, 11)

f. The Question Mark (?)
Use a question mark

1. at the end of a direct question (I, 17e)
2. after a tag question (XIII, 16)

g. Quotation Marks (". . .")
Use quotation marks

1. to enclose the actual words of a speaker (IV, 14e)
2. around foreign words used in English sentences

h. The Semicolon (;)
Use a semicolon

1. in a compound sentence without a connective (II, 19c)
2. between phrases in a series when they contain commas

i. Capital Letters
Style in the use of capital letters is rapidly changing in the printed media. The following are some traditional rules which your teachers will probably expect you to follow, even though many publishers do not. Use a capital initial for

1. the first word of every sentence (I, 17a)
2. titles (I, 17a)
3. proper nouns: names of people, places, courses (I, 17a; II, 19a)
4. adjectives derived from names of nations (I, 17a)
5. the days of the week (II, 19a; IV, 14a)
6. holidays (II, 19a)
7. the months of the year (IV, 14a)
8. streets, cities, states, countries, continents (IV, 14a)
9. the first quoted word of a speaker (IV, 14a)